The Official
American Numismatic Association
Grading Standards
for United States Coins
FIFTH EDITION

AmericanNumismatic
A S S O C I A T I O N

Compiled, Arranged and Edited by

KEN BRESSETT

and

A. KOSOFF

Introduction by

Q. DAVID BOWERS

Principal Contributors to
This Edition
Leonard Albrecht, Michael Fahey, Leonard Shafer

Copyright © 1987, 1991, 1996
American Numismatic Association
818 No. Cascade Avenue
Colorado Springs, Colorado 80903-3279

No. 9097-3   ISBN: 0-307-09097-3   Printed in U.S.A.

CONTENTS

Preface to the First (1977) Edition
by A. Kosoff

The American Numismatic Association has undertaken a program to produce one of the most ambitious and significant books ever compiled—a book containing official grading standards for every United States coin.

Coin grading has been important to collectors probably since coins were first minted in Lydia some 2700 years ago. In 1973, Virginia Culver, then President of the American Numismatic Association, recognized the problem and asked me to try to solve it. Our goal was to standardize grading by defining significant degrees of wear and establishing guidelines so that the various grades may be easily identified.

Now, after four years of effort on the part of many, there is an easy-to-use and officially approved set of standards which everyone can apply to the grading of United States coins. Now the confusion in grading caused by multiple systems and biased private opinions should be eliminated or at least considerably lessened.

Special attention is called to the Introduction in which the many varying factors concerning proper coin grading are described in detail. Many questions about coins and grading techniques are answered in this section so ably prepared by my good friend and colleague, Q. David Bowers, who also prepared the Glossary of Terms.

Many experts cooperated to clarify the standards and descriptions. The needs of everyone have been considered; beginners, advanced collectors and dealers will all find the text to be understandable and useful. I am grateful to Myron M. Kliman for coordinating the early volume of correspondence required to create this team of experts. I want to thank the following for their assistance on the preparation of the text and help in many other ways:

J. H. Cline, David W. Davis, Lawrence Goldberg, David Hall, James Halperin, Max Humbert, Steve Ivy, Keith N. Kelman, Myron M. Kliman, John Love, Fred Malone, A. George Mallis, Ray Merena, Ray Reinoehl, Joel Rettew, Benjamin Stack, Leroy Van Allen, Malcolm Varner and Tom Wass.

Special mention for their extraordinary efforts as members of this team must be made of Kamal Ahwash, Del Bland, Walter H. Breen, Michael Brownlee, Jon Hansen, Denis Loring and Anthony Swiatek.

Suggestions, special help and encouragement has been given by the following to whom we are grateful:

Eva Adams, David W. Akers, Stanley Apfelbaum, Dr. Richard Bagg, James E. Charlton, Alan D. Craig, Grover C. Criswell, Joe Flynn, Jr., John J. Ford, Jr., David L. Ganz, Ron Gillio, John Hamrick, Cloyde P. Howard, Jesse Iskowitz, James G. Johnson, Paul Koppenhaver, Kurt Krueger, Wayne Lawrence, Julian Leidman, Fred Malone, Steve Markoff, Ed Milas, Paul Munson, Jess Peters, John J. Pittman, James B. Pryor, Edward C. Rochette, Joseph Rose, Dr. Sol Taylor, Warren Tucker, Thomas G. Wood and Charles M. Wormser.

All previously used methods of grading were analyzed and studied for points of merit. The new ANA system has clarified each grade definition and has established a minimum number of uniform and easily understandable descriptive terms.

Standard grades are further identified through the use of a numerical scale from 1 to 70. This scale was originally devised by Dr. William H. Sheldon for his book *Early American Cents* (later retitled as *Penny Whimsy*) and has now been adapted for use with the entire United States series, thus providing uniform grading terminology.

Both for the text and the format, criticism from Q. David Bowers and Harvey Stack proved to be very valuable toward the evaluation of the final product. F. Morton Reed and Glenn Smedley spent much time in reviewing the work and made valuable suggestions.

Special thanks must be given to the staff members of the Whitman Coin Products Division of Western Publishing Company, Inc. under the direction of Ken Bressett. Basic (line drawing) illustrations were prepared by artist Arthur Mueller, and the degrees and points of wear were simulated by Richard Thompsen, Ed Metzger, Dolores Toll and Jenny Tomaszek.

While I have been given much of the credit for this production, I must acknowledge that it was the tremendous help given by Ken Bressett during the last six months that made it all come to fruition. Bressett, assisted by Neil Shafer, is responsible for the format. He supervised the art work. He simplified the language for all of the copper, nickel and silver series. He and I edited each other's work as we zeroed in on our targets. Many have told me that without me this work would not have been accomplished.

Without Ken Bressett this would not have been the significant, understandable and useful work that it is. So strongly do I feel about his contribution to this effort that I insisted that his name join mine as compilers, arrangers and editors.

Virgil Hancock, President of the ANA 1975-1977, reappointed me as ANA's Grading Chairman and gave me his complete support for which I am grateful. I also want to express my appreciation to ANA's succeeding President, Grover C. Criswell, for also reappointing me so that I could finish the job, and to the members of the ANA Board of Governors for their votes of confidence.

Finally my thanks to my secretary, Clair Lulla, for her untiring typing and re-typing, to my daughter, Sonnie Kliman, for her assistance in organizing the original material and to my wife, Molly, for her patience in putting up with my spreading out the paper work all over the place.

ABE KOSOFF—1977

Preface to the Fourth (1991) Edition
by Q. David Bowers

Veteran dealer Abe Kosoff, who wrote the preface for the first edition, passed away in 1983, but not before living to see the ANA grading system adopted by collectors, dealers, and investors throughout the world.

The Fourth Edition of this book replaces all earlier editions and contains many changes from the earlier texts, including an expanded system of numbers (particularly evident in intermediate grades from MS-60 to MS-70 and Proof-60 to Proof-70), changing philosophies in certain areas, and utilization of suggestions made by many who have read and used the book.

Among those making specific contributions to the Fourth Edition were Leonard Albrecht, Kenneth E. Bressett (editor of the fourth edition), Tom DeLorey, Michael Fahey (an editor of photographs), Bill Fivaz (who has shared his knowledge used in ANA grading seminars), David L. Ganz, David Hall, James Halperin, George Hatie, Robert Hoge, Robert J. Leuver, J.P.Martin, Raymond N.Merena, William S. Panitch, Donn Pearlman, John J. Pittman, Leonard Shaffer (an editor of photographs), Harvey G. Stack, Anthony Swiatek, James Taylor (coordinator of the book), Scott Travers and Nancy Wilson, each of whom submitted written critiques and recommendations for changes. Leonard Albrecht, furnished many valuable ideas. Additional help was provided by members of the current ANA Board of Governors and the staff at ANA Headquarters.

For a long time, until July 31, 1990, the ANA operated the American Numismatic Association Certification Service (ANACS), also known as the ANA Grading Service. On August 1, 1990 this operation was sold to Amos Press and no longer is an official arm of the ANA.

While ANACS was the first third-party grading service to achieve great popularity and recognition, over the years many other services have emerged, some to exist briefly and others to remain in business to this day. In 1986 David Hall launched the Professional Coin Grading Service, which pioneered the concept of sonically sealing coins in clear plastic holders containing an assigned numerical grade as well as a registration number. Other grading services soon offered encapsulated coins, popularly referred to as "slabs." As of autumn 1990 among the grading services offering encapsulated coins were ANACS (offering the "Cache" slab), Hallmark Grading Service, Numismatic Certification Institute (NCI), Numismatic Guaranty Corporation of America (NGC), Photo Certified Coin Institute, and Professional Coin Grading Service (PCGS). These services all utilize the ANA-Sheldon numerical system.

In 1990 computer grading came of age, and early in the year PCGS unveiled a laser-controlled computer which assigned numerical grades to Mint State silver dollars. ANACS and Compu-Grade announced they were also developing computer grading.

Despite the popularization of the computer age and, beginning in 1990, even grading by the use of lasers and computers, the grade of coins remains a matter of opinion, and the same coins resubmitted to the same grading service may be (and frequently have been) graded differently upon resubmission. Although the opinions rendered by third-party commercial services are valuable, it is important to remember these things:

(1) Grading is a matter of opinion, and coins graded at one point in time can be graded higher or lower at a later point in time.

[4]

(2) While grading is important to the value of a coin, other considerations are also important.

(3) In the past grading standards have evolved, and there have been numerous changes. This may occur in the future as well.

(4) In order to buy and sell coins to your best advantage, it is important to familiarize yourself with the basic precepts of grading and, ultimately, to learn how to do your own grading. This book is a good start.

Q. David Bowers
April 22, 1991

Preface To The Fourth Edition
by Kenneth L. Hallenbeck

This fourth edition of the *Official ANA Grading Standards for United States Coins* has been significantly improved. The finest minds in numismatics have contributed to its development, and construction of this, the fourth edition. A special "thank you" goes to Ken Bressett as editor of this and all previous editions, and to Q. David Bowers, Leonard Albrecht, Michael Fahey, Leonard Shafer and James Taylor for their efforts and input.

A main constant in life is change and improvement, and so it is here. Many minor and a few major refinements have been made in this edition in order to update the text to accurately reflect current collecting modes and conditions. Collectors, dealers and investors will all benefit from this edition which continues well beyond what has been published in the past. Much effort has been expended to produce the most accurate and useful guide yet. The ANA is pleased to make this numismatic work available in accordance with its educational charter by the Congress of the United States.

Kenneth L. Hallenbeck
President
American Numismatic Association
April 22, 1991

Preface To The Fifth (1996) Edition
by Ken Bressett

Each revised edition of this book brings to it a new flavor and new techniques for more accurate interpretation of the standards set forth in previous printings. Grading has continued to evolve each year, and will probably do so well into the future. The new sections, new information and new practices described in this edition reflect current trends away from the strict technical grading of the past, and towards what is today called "market grading."

While the two systems are relatively equal, the new "market grading" takes into account factors of eye appeal that have a direct bearing on each coin's commercial value. This is especially significant in the case of Mint State coins which must be graded on the basis of aesthetic appearance rather than wear or loss of details.

A new section has been added to this edition to show in full color some of the differences in uncirculated coins that have a bearing on the eye appeal, and thus the grade and value of these coins. Throughout the text nothing has been changed to alter the definitions of grade standards. What has been added is designed to clarify the descriptions and make the grading process as simple and accurate as possible.

Ken Bressett, President
American Numismatic Association
October 22, 1996

HOW TO USE THIS BOOK

This book consists of three main parts: 1. The introduction which has been written by Q. David Bowers, and gives information and insight into the principals of grading. 2. Basic Grading Techniques which has been written by Michael Fahey, and gives a description of how coins should be graded for maximum accuracy. The third part of this book describes the grading standards for various United States coins in each series. In the final chapter are special notes for the grading of Commemorative coins that have been provided by Anthony Swiatek.

Information given in each of these sections is vital to the grading of a coin and must be used in connection with the balance of the text.

PHOTO CREDITS

Contributors of time and coins for photography:

Michael Adams	J.P. Martin
Vijon Avar	Lynn Ann Matteo
Steve Bugden	Clifford Mishler
Ray Burns	Michael Olnick
Lee Crane	William Paul
Eric Croader	John Saunders
James Guinesso	Leonard Saunders
John Gulde	Jerome S. Sajbel
Henry Heller	Marvin Shear
Robert W. Hoge	Anthony Swiatek
Art Jorgensen	Scott Travers
Johnathan Kern	D. Clark White
Tom Kotche	Serge Zaidman
Eric Kreuter	

Members of the Professional Numismatists Guild who contributed coins, time and expertise:

Martin E. Anderson	Paul Koppenhaver
Walt Ankerman	Bruce Kutcher
Jack Beymer	Julian Leidman
Donald Brigandi	Ed Leventhal
Jerry Cohen	Samuel Lopresto
Kent Froseth	James Payette
Henry Garrett	Richard Ponterio
Jeff Garrett	Norman Pullen
Dennis Gillio	Joel Rettew
Ronald Gillio	Richard Schwery
Ira Goldberg	John Smies
Kenneth Goldman	David C. Staggs III
Donald Hauser	Leonard Standley
David Hendrickson	Gary Sturtridge
Leon Hendrickson	F.S. Werner
Harry E. Jones	Harlan White
Jack Klemes	

INTRODUCTION

Background. Since the days of antiquity people have been collecting coins. To build their collections and exhibits, coin collectors enjoy buying, selling, and exchanging desirable pieces.

Grade, the condition or state of wear of a coin, is one of the main determining factors of a coin's value. Until relatively recent decades grading was by "instinct." Based on his own knowledge and personal observations, one seller would have his own system, and another seller with another set of observations, experiences, and opinions, would have a different one. There was little standardization.

In recent times coin values have increased sharply. In many instances coins that were worth $100 twenty years ago are worth $2,000 or more now. A very small difference in grade can mean a very large difference in price. The exact grade of a coin is more important now than ever before.

In 1958 Martin R. Brown and John W. Dunn published "A Guide to the Grading of United States Coins," the first widely-accepted standardized guide to grading. In 1970 James F. Ruddy published "Photograde," a photographic guide to the same subject. Both of these reference books, each of which primarily emphasized circulated grades of coins, were in time designated as official grading guides by the American Numismatic Association.

In the first decade of the present century, the ANA Board of Governors had appointed a committee to establish uniform grading standards, but no conclusions were reached.

In 1913 an ANA member, C.E. Bunnell, wrote to the editor of *The Numismatist,* stating: "It is very important to members of the A.N.A. or the Board of Governors to take some kind of stand with reference to issuing some kind of statement classifying coins that all dealers that catalogue and sell coins . . . must use the same classification . . . ."

Discussion continued on the subject for many years, but it was not until the 1970s that definite steps were taken by the ANA Board of Governors to create a grading book. Abe Kosoff, who was a well-known dealer, founder of the Professional Numismatists Guild, and was highly respected in numismatics, was selected to head the project.

In 1978 the *ANA Official Grading Standards for United States Coins* book was publsihed, representing a consensus of numismatists who had made suggestions to Abe Kosoff and to Kenneth E. Bressett, editor of the work.

In the late 1970s and early 1980s, after the publication of the first edition of *ANA Official Grading Standards for United States Coins,* the continued escalation of coin values brought about even finer grading distinctions than before. For example, the Mint State or Uncirculated grade was originally divided into three classifications: Uncirculated (typical) or, in the numerical scale MS-60; Choice Uncirculated or MS-65, and Perfect Uncirculated or MS-70. Gradually, use in the market modified this, and MS-63 became known as Choice Uncirculated, and the Gem Uncirculated designation was reserved for MS-65.

Over a period of time, intermediate grades were added, to the point at which we now have MS-60, MS-61, MS-62, etc. in one-point increments continuously to MS-70. During the mid-1980s grading interpretations tightened considerably and became more strict. *The Coin Dealer Newsletter* and other periodicals carried much editorial comment on the changes. In the meantime, the ANA Board of Governors recognized the changing grading interpretations, and in January 1986 the Board announced that in some instances coins which had been officially certified by the ANA Grading Service as MS-65 earlier were now in lower grade classifications. On February 19, 1986, this resolution was adopted by the Board:

"Grading is an art and not an exact science. More precisely, grading is a matter of opinion. Differences of opinion may occur among graders as to a particular coin, and any grader could conceivably change his interpretation of the grading standards over the years.

"When the *ANA Official Grading Standards for United States Coins* was published in 1978, it represented a new grading system previously untried. . . . The grading standards as enumerated in the book were and are not precise, with the descriptions lending themselves to different interpretations. The marketplace composed of collectors and dealers has tightened its interpretation in recent years and ANACS [the ANA Grading Service] has reflected those changes. Accordingly, the ANA Grading Service, endeavoring to keep in step with current market interpretations (rather than create

[7]

interpretations of its own), has in recent times graded coins more conservatively than in the past, in many instances.

"Hence, it may be the situation that a coin which was graded MS-65 by the Grading Service in 1981 or 1982, for example, may, if regraded in 1985 or 1986, merit the current interpretation of MS-63 or less. Similarly, dealers and others in the commercial sector have found that coins graded MS-65 several years ago may merit MS-64 or lower interpretations today."

Dealers, collectors, museums, auction houses, and all others had to adjust the grades of their coins accordingly. Many coins which were correctly graded as MS-65 in the early 1980s were regraded to MS-63 or less, in order to be in step with 1986 interpretations.

Because of these changes, in many instances coins which grade today in the 1990s in the ranges from MS-60 to MS-63 are fully equal in quality to what the numismatic fraternity designated as MS-65 before 1986. For this reason, printed prices of certain Mint State graded coins published before 1986 are not directly comparable to those published since 1986.

The present book endeavors to give guidelines concerning these and many other distinctions. It also gives important information concerning surface characteristics, methods of striking, different gradations of wear, and much other information which will assist the user in grading any United States coin minted from 1793 to the present.

We have endeavored to make this book easy to read and interesting while at the same time preserving logic, accuracy, and consistency. As United States coins, particularly early issues, are subject to many variations of die preparation and striking, we urge the user of the book to read the front part as an adjunct to the later text.

This grading book is sponsored by the American Numismatic Association. It is recommended that it be used as the standard reference in transactions between all buyers and sellers. The system used in this book should be referred to as the "Official ANA Grading System."

Coins are listed in order of ascending denomination from half cents to gold pieces. Within each denomination, design types are listed in chronological order. To grade a coin, compare it with the illustration and brief description which most closely matches it. Then read the adjacent text. If a coin does not quite fit the text description, then try the next higher or next lower grade. In all instances, the information in this book should be used in conjunction with advice from grading experts and with experience gained from the actual observation of many coins. It is difficult to make sound grading determinations, especially in higher numerical levels, without a great deal of practical experience.

NOTE CONCERNING MARKET VALUES: In addition to numerical grade, the market value of a coin is determined by several other factors, including sharpness or weakness of strike, quality of brilliance or toning, centering, planchet quality, aesthetic appeal, and the laws of supply and demand. It is also important to remember that a coin graded MS-65 by one individual or grading service may be graded higher or lower at a later date by that individual or grading service or by another grading authority. Readers are cautioned to investigate carefully before paying a large amount of money for a coin which carries a high market price because of a relatively small increment in grade above the next one or two levels, and not to hesitate to seek one or more additional opinions.

THE PRESENT BOOK IS INTENDED AS A GENERAL INFORMATION GUIDE AND UNIFORM INDUSTRY STANDARD FOR GRADING COINS, NOT AS THE FINAL WORD IN A COMMERCIAL TRANSACTION OR DISPUTE.

WHY IS GRADING IMPORTANT?

Why are there differences of opinion in the field of grading coins? There are numerous reasons, but the most common are as follows:

Grading coins can never be completely scientific in all areas. One may weigh a coin and also obtain its specific gravity by mechanical devices, and the results will be factual if accurate equipment was used carefully. While the surface marks on a coin can be counted by a laser-computer device, to date there has been no way to consistently translate these findings into grades which are universally accepted as a determinant of market values.

In grading coins, considerations such as clarity of the strike, surface of the planchet, the presence of heavy toning (which may obscure certain surface characteristics), the design, and other factors each lend an influence. A panel containing a dozen of the foremost numismatic hobby leaders justifiably could have some *slight* differences of opinion on the precise grade of some coins (with *occasional* major differences on others).

However, it is not *slight* differences which concern us here; it is serious or major differences. Unfortunately, it is not easy to define what major differences are. The problem is that grading is a matter of opinion, and experts may differ.

I cite several examples:

(1) I have in my office a silver dollar sent to a leading grading service on three different occasions, and it came back with three different grades.

(2) Barry J. Cutler, formerly of the Federal Trade Commission, told a symposium at the ANA convention in Seattle, August 1990, that he had conducted a blind test of grading accuracy. Although professional graders had claimed beforehand that they were so accurate that they could consistently tell the difference between a coin graded MS-63 and one graded "MS-63 plus" (or very slightly better than MS-63; plus marks are not part of the ANA grading system), in the test conducted by Mr. Cutler, expert opinions given for the same specimen of a Saint-Gaudens $20 gold piece ranged from AU-58 to MS-64.

(3) In 1990 I sent an Uncirculated 1893-S Morgan dollar, one of the most highly prized varieties in the series, to a leading grading service where it was graded as MS 63. I then sent it to another leading service, where it was graded MS-65. At the time the market difference between the MS-63 and MS-65 grade was approximately $100,000!

(4) Several years ago Kevin Foley, editor of *The Centinel*, official journal of the Central States Numismatic Society, sent 10 different coins to four different professional grading services. In not a single instance could all four services agree on even a single coin, and in one instance, that of a 1919 Standing Liberty quarter, professional opinions ranged from AU-55 to MS-65.

Notwithstanding what has just been stated, most grading experts can agree within a point or two in the Uncirculated range. However, as just demonstrated, the differences of opinion can sometimes be considerable. Then arises this question: How can overgrading be determined?

In the past it has been suggested that a difference of two points, three points, or some other difference in the Mint State category indicated overgrading, but the situation is not that simple. Unquestionably, no one wants to buy a coin described as MS-65, and then have an unbiased third-party certification service call it MS-63 or some other lower grade. Conversely, just about everyone would agree that it would be a pleasurable situation if a coin were to be bought as MS-63, sent to a certification service, and be returned as MS-65.

What, then, constitutes overgrading? What constitutes grading accuracy? How can one approach the situation? There are no answers that will satisfy everyone. My answers, coupled with practical suggestions, are these:

1. When you buy a coin, especially one of high value, have the grading checked by a knowledgeable friend, a third-party service, or some other individual or entity. If your consultant believes that the coin is overgraded, don't buy it. (The coin still may be correctly graded, but in such an instance you would not have a feeling of comfort in owning it.)

2. If a person or firm consistently sells coins which in the opinions of grading experts are overgraded, this would seem to indicate that overgrading is being deliberately practiced, or that the seller was ignorant of acceptable prevailing grading practices. It must be realized, however, that even the most knowledgeable graders often disagree with each other. It is a trend or consistent overgrading practice which is at issue here.

3. Be aware that prices often vary widely for higher-grade coins, and, as an example, a coin can be listed as worth $1,000 in MS-64 grade, $2,500 in MS-65 grade, and $5,000 at the MS-66 level. Also be aware that what one person calls MS-66 another may call MS-65 or some other grade. Be careful when paying a large amount of money for a very small difference in technical grade. The problem admits of no easy resolution.

4. Leonard Albrecht, former executive director of the ANACS third-party grading service, has suggested the following statement, which seems to be reasonable: "If a person or company consistently overgrades a wide number of coins relative to accepted standards, we are probably dealing with a case of overgrading. As clearly shown in too many cases, a small or occasional difference in grading opinion should not be considered as evidence of overgrading; however, the pattern of consistent or continual overgrading in opposition to accepted numismatic standards probably indicates an overgrading problem."

Kenneth E. Bressett adds the following comment: "I have seen many coin investment portfolios in which the common coins were all graded accurately, but in which the expensive pieces were all overgraded. That gives the seller a high batting average for accurate grading, but an unethical profit edge on the costly coins."

Attorney David L. Ganz has pointed out the subjectivity of determining what does or does not constitute overgrading:

"In 1977, the U.S. Postal Service brought claim against Riverside Coin Company (Docket # 5/130) in which the court noted (paragraph 8) that 'there is at the present time no one, official standard for grading coins binding on both collectors and dealers.'

In his conclusion of law, the Administrative Law Judge stated: 'There are various, similar guides for the grading of United States coins, some of them widely accepted, but there is no single, official standard for grading accepted by, and binding on all dealers and collectors of such coins. The grading of coins is a matter of judgment. Five experienced graders may grade the coins five different grades.' "

Attorney Ganz continues:

"Years later, in the case of *United States vs. Kail* (804 F 2d 441 8th Cir., 1986), the Court of Appeals for the 8th Circuit stated:

'Kail asserts . . . there were honest differences of opinion and judgment as to the grade and value of the coins, therefore furnishing no basis for a finding that the defendant had committed fraud. . . . The evidence established the existence of official grading standards promulgated by the American Numismatic Association which, while not having the force of law, were recognized by the government's experts as having wide acceptance in the industry. . . . Therefore, Kail's assertion that there is an absence of standards in the industry must be in doubt from this record. . . . ' "

In actuality, in lower grades, the financial consequences of a 10-point difference, such as between VF-20 and VF-30, might be relatively unimportant, but in higher levels the difference between AU-55 and MS-65, also 10 points, might be devastating. I suggest that each situation be handled on its own merits, for it is difficult to form precise guidelines in a field which, although it has numbers that imply precision, is still subject to wide variations in expert opinions, especially in the Mint State category.

In general, if a coin in AU (About Uncirculated) grade is called Uncirculated, it is overgraded. If a coin in Very Fine grade is called Extremely Fine, it is overgraded. If a coin in MS-60 grade is called MS-63 or some higher grade it is overgraded.

What induces overgrading? Here are some of the factors:

Buyers Seeking Bargains. The desire to get a bargain is part of human nature. If a given Uncirculated coin actively traded at $1,000 is offered at $700, it will attract a lot of bargain seekers. These same buyers would reject an offering such as: "I am offering this stock which trades on the New York Stock Exchange for $1,000 for just $700 cash," or "I am offering $1,000 bills for $700 each."

In coins, as in any other walk of life, you get what you pay for. If a coin which has a standard value of $1,000 is offered for $700 there may be nothing wrong, but chances are good that the piece is overgraded.

False Assumptions. Buyers often assume falsely that any advertisement or listing which appears in a numismatic publication, daily newspaper, or electronic exchange has been approved by that publication or exchange. Actually, publishers and exchange operators cannot be expected to examine coins and approve of all listings offered. A person who has no numismatic knowledge or expertise whatsoever can have letterheads and business cards printed and, assuming he has good financial and character references (but not necessarily numismatic expertise), run large and flashy advertisements. Months or years later it is often too late for the deceived buyer to get his money back. In recent years some buyers have been lured into buying encapsulated coins but have not recognized that commercial grading services can indeed differ in their professional opinions. Coins can be overgraded within "slabs" as well as outside of them.

THE SOLUTION TO THIS IS TO LEARN HOW TO GRADE COINS AND THINK FOR YOURSELF. Examine the credentials of the seller. Is the seller truly an expert in the coin field? How do you know? What do collectors with more experience think of this seller? To what professional organizations does the dealer belong? It is usually foolish to rush in and spend your hard earned money with a coin seller who has no professional credentials and whose only attraction is that seller is offering "bargains." Think for yourself!

The Profit Motive. Sellers seeking an unfair markup may overgrade. For purposes of illustration, let us assume that a given variety of coin is worth the following prices in these grades: AU $75, and Uncirculated $150. A legitimate dealer in the course of business would buy, for example, an AU coin at $50 or $60 and sell it retail for $75, thus making a profit of $15 to $25. However, there are sellers who are not satisfied with the normal way of doing business. They take shortcuts. They pay $50 or $60 for the same AU coin which is worth $75 retail, but rather than calling it AU they call it "Uncirculated" and sell it for $150. So, instead of making $15 to $25 they may make $90 to $100! The abuses can be much larger among various grades in the Mint State level.

Inexperience. Inexperience or error on the part of the seller may lead to incorrect grading—both overgrading and undergrading.

The fact that grading coins is no simple matter is reflected by a comment submitted by Bill Fivaz, who has conducted grading seminars for the ANA:

"Ken Bresset [editor of *A Guide Book of U.S. Coins* and at one time head of ANACS] has a phrase that I often quote, and it seems very apropos: 'Grading is really very simple. All you need is four things: (1) A good magnifying glass, (2) A good light, (3) A good memory, and (4) 20 years of experience.' In order to grade effectively, one must look at a *lot* of coins, especially when you are trying to determine if the particular piece is the 'normal' way you usually find that date or if it is above the average."

LIGHTING AND MAGNIFICATION

The same coin can have a different appearance depending upon the lighting conditions and also the amount of magnification used to examine it. For purposes of standardization, we recommend that a magnifying glass of at least three (3x) to seven power (7x) be used. At ANA seminar courses on grading conducted by Bill Fivaz, the Bausch & Lomb Hastings Triplet 7X has been found to be ideal. This is sufficient to reveal all the differences and peculiarities necessary to grade the coin accurately. At the same time it is not too much magnification. Under extensive magnification—10 power or more—even the finest coin may show many marks and imperfections in an exaggerated fashion. You may wish to keep a stronger magnifying glass on hand, however for examination of minute die details.

It is also desirable to use a magnifying glass of sufficient width so that a fairly large amount of the coin's surface can be studied at one time.

Recommended for grading is a 100 watt incandescent light bulb approximately three feet from the coin (or a 50 watt bulb at an appropriately lesser distance, or other equivalents). Incandescent light furnishes a pinpoint light source and enables surface characteristics to be studied in more detail. "Tensor" type lamps using halogen bulbs, popular at coin conventions, furnish a high intensity pinpoint light source and are highly recommended for grading, although some numismatists find that they are uncomfortable to use.

Warning: Fluorescent light, which spreads illumination from a diffused origin, is apt to conceal minute differences and camoflage certain defects, and should not be used. Distant light sources, such as overhead lighting in a room or auditorium, are unreliable and can give a coin the appearance of being in a grade higher than it actually is. In all instances, grading should be accomplished in an area free from light from other sources than the grading lamp.

To grade a coin, hold it between your fingertips (over a soft surface to prevent damage in the event of dropping) at an angle so that light from the bulb reflects from the coin's surface into your eye. Turn or rotate the coin so that different characteristics can be observed in detail from *all* angles. You will want to examine the edge also.

Lamp wattages and magnifying intensities are less critical with circulated grades. They are very important, however, for Uncirculated and Proof coins where judgment is dependent upon relatively small differences in surface appearance.

CHARACTERISTICS OF A COIN'S SURFACE

There are three factors which establish the characteristics of a coin's surface. Marks or imperfections on the surface of a coin can occur because of: (1) characteristics of the die used to strike the coin, (2) irregularities and characteristics of the planchet on which the coin was struck, and (3) damage, marks, wear, etc. acquired by the coin after it was struck.

(1) Marks in the Die. United States coins of the eighteenth and early nineteenth centuries were struck from handmade dies. The engraver took a steel die blank, punched or engraved the central figure, punched stars around the border, punched in letters, and finally engraved or punched the date. Beginning in 1836, when steam powered presses were first used at the Philadelphia Mint, die making became more mechanical. The hub or master die contained not only the central design but letters and stars as well. The only thing left for the engraver was retouching areas of weakness and also punching in the date. In our own time even the date has become part of the master die.

Occasionally during the preparation of a die, especially in the early years, some damage would occur. For example, on one variety of 1804 half cent an unexplained accident produced a thornlike projection jutting out from the chin of Liberty, creating the "Spiked Chin" variety. Sometimes the careless use of a punch or tool would result in a scratch or chip in the die. As such marks were in the die surface, on coins struck from these dies the same marks appear raised.

Once the die began production it was used, especially in the earlier years, until it literally fell apart. This use often resulted in several situations which affected a coin's appearance.

Die breaks, especially on eighteenth and nineteenth century coins, are quite common. Due to excessive strain or continued use a die would often develop one or more cracks or breaks. When a die with cracks was used to strike coins, metal from the planchet would squeeze up into the die crack producing a raised irregular ridge on the surface of the coin. Die breaks usually do not affect the value of a coin one way or the other, unless they caused weakness or die buckling.

Sometimes an error would be made during the coining process when no planchet would be fed into the press when the dies came together. Then the obverse and reverse dies would strike each other with great pressure and force, producing what are called "clash marks," or impressions of parts of the reverse design on the obverse or vice versa. These are often noticeable in the fields of certain coins, particularly on issues from the first half of the nineteenth century. The presence or absence of clash marks usually does not affect the coin's value.

At times a die would be used until it became quite worn. To render the die fit for additional coinage it would be resurfaced. This was done by polishing the surface of the die and, if necessary, strengthening certain features. Sometimes the polishing of the die's surface would entirely remove shallow details. This resulted in certain varieties which are familiar to collectors today, including the 1795 half cent without pole to cap (the pole was removed by polishing the die) and the 1845-O half dollar without drapery from Liberty's elbow (the drapery was in low relief and was ground away during the resurfacing of the die). The so-called 1922 "Plain" Lincoln cent and the 1937-D three legged five-cent coin are examples of coins struck from dies which became worn or resurfaced so that parts of the design were lost.

Sometimes a die would be carelessly stored and would acquire rust or corrosion on the surface. These pits in the die surface would then result in raised bumps on any coin struck from these dies. One variety of 1833 quarter dollar shows extreme rust marks in the field.

Generally, marks in the die, clash marks, die breaks, rust spots, and the like need not be described when grading a coin unless such characteristics are *extremely unusual* for the variety. For example, when describing a 1795 half cent without a pole, a coin struck from a fairly weak and resurfaced die, it would be satisfactory to state simply the variety and grade without further comment. However, if one were describing a later coin which normally comes from sharp dies (a 1938-D half dollar, to cite one of hundreds of examples), and if it were struck from worn or defective dies, it would be appropriate to say, "1938-D half dollar struck from defective dies"—and then describe the defect.

(2) Planchet Characteristics. Another way that marks or characteristics on a coin's surface can arise is from the quality of the original coining blank (planchet) used to make the piece. During the planchet preparation process, prepared metal alloy is rolled into long flat strips. Coinage blanks or planchets are then punched from these strips. If a planchet is without any serious defects or marks, a perfect coin results—assuming that the dies operate properly. However, occasionally the planchet is not perfect. Some of the imperfections are:

Adjustment Marks. During the late 18th and early 19th centuries, planchets struck from silver and gold at the Philadelphia Mint were individually weighed. This was essential because of legal requirements that each coin be of proper weight. Realizing that weight cannot be added to a planchet once it is made, it was often the practice to make the planchet slightly heavier than required. The planchet would then be weighed and any excess metal would be removed by drawing a file horizontally across the face of the planchet. This would result in deep grooves or what collectors know today as "adjustment marks."

Adjustment marks are different from scratches inasmuch as they occurred before the coin was struck. Usually adjustment marks consist of a series of parallel lines. Also, as adjustment marks were produced before the coin was struck, the adjustment marks will follow all characteristics of a coin's design. For example, an adjustment mark may begin on a flat surface of a coin, extend through a letter and through the spaces of a letter, and continue through the other side. On the other hand, a scratch (acquired after striking) will tend to skip the protected areas of a coin's surface as the instrument causing the scratch could not reach these areas. Adjustment marks are perfectly normal on early coins. When they are of sufficient size to be seen without magnification they should be mentioned in addition to a coin's grade if it is Uncirculated. Thus, a Mint State 65 coin with noticeable adjustment marks could be described as: "MS-65 with adjustment marks around the reverse border," "MS-65 with noticeable adjustment marks at the center of the obverse," or something similar. It is not necessary to mention normal adjustment marks in grades less than Uncirculated unless the marks are excessive or disfiguring. Some graders feel that if a coin has significant adjustment marks, it should be graded no higher than MS-64. In any event, an MS-65 coin with adjustment marks may be valued at substantially less than an MS-65 coin without them.

Sometimes during the preparation of a planchet strip, there would be improper bonding of the metal. The result is that flaking or chipping of the metal occurs, leaving irregular crevices, recessed areas, and other evidences. These planchet defects, which occur in all periods of coinage, should be specifically mentioned in describing such a coin. While the presence of normal adjustment marks does not alter a coin's condition, both these and planchet defects tend to decrease a coin's value to some degree.

In some instances a planchet is thin on one edge and thick on the other. When such a piece is fed into the coining press the design will not strike up fully on the thin section. Usually the rim or design along one edge will then be defective. Such irregularities should be fully described. A similar effect can occur if the dies are not parallel to each other (see below).

Coins struck on defective planchets or in a defective manner are usually called "misstruck coins" and are a special field of collecting in themselves. Generally, noticeable defects will lower the value of an expensive coin. However, on a modern coin of low value, an imperfect planchet or an imperfect strike may increase the value.

(3) Marks Acquired After a Coin Is Struck. The preceding text described how marks or characteristics in the dies and planchets can affect a coin's appearance. The following concerns marks which occur after a coin is minted.

In nearly all instances, coins struck for regular circulation purposes, often called "business strikes" by numismatists, were minted as follows: After the planchets are prepared they were put into a large bin or hopper. They were then fed into a coining press which struck one or more coins (certain types of modern presses have multiple dies) and were then ejected into a metal box. From there the coins went into a large storage bin. As each bin became full it was taken to another area of the mint where it was unloaded into a counting machine. The coins were then run at high speed through a mechanical counter. Then they were put into cloth bags and stored. No attempt was made to preserve the coins carefully for future collectors or to prevent them from coming into contact with each other. The goal was to produce coins at the highest possible speed for the channels of commerce, not for collectors.

Bag Marks (Contact Marks). The term "bag mark" (actually a contact mark) refers to a nick, small cut, or other similar contact mark on a coin's surface. These occur during the minting process as well as when the coins come into contact with each other in mint bags or, later, in the Treasury Department or, still later, while being stored in bank vaults. It is usual for Uncirculated coins to have some bag or contact marks, even among those sold in modern sets by the Treasury Department to collectors.

The larger and heavier the coin, the more bag marks it may have. Among older coins the characteristics of the striking mint and its location play a part also. For example, double eagles struck at Carson City, Nevada, a remote location, nearly always have very heavy bag marks. This is because of the rigors of transportation from the Carson City Mint as well as the fairly primitive conditions (compared with Philadelphia) there at the time.

Heavier coins such as half dollars, silver dollars, or large gold coins will have more and deeper bag marks than will light coins such as silver three cent pieces, half dimes, or dimes.

A coin can have bag marks but still be Uncirculated (never having seen actual hand-to-hand use in commerce). The presence or absence of bag marks is an important guide to the various grades of Mint State from MS-60 (usually with numerous bag marks) to MS-70 (theoretical perfection, with no marks at all).

Bag marks are permissible on coins other than MS-70 and do not have to be mentioned unless they are of an exceptional or serious nature. The very differentiation of grading (MS-60 as opposed to MS-65, for example) takes bag marks into account.

Scratches. Scratches are grooves or marks on a coin's surface which result from careless handling. Scratches, if serious and prominent on a coin, should always be described.

Edge Bumps, Nicks or Dents. When a coin, particularly a heavy one, is dropped it may acquire an edge bump. This is caused by the rim being bruised. In Extremely Fine or better grade, significant edge bumps must be described. In lower grades they should be described if serious or prominent.

Repairs. It was common practice years ago to use coins for jewelry. As a result, coins were often holed near the outer edge. Valuable coins which have been holed are sometimes carefully plugged and repaired. Also, it was often the practice to affix loops or mounting brackets on the edge of a coin so it could be used as jewelry. Such repairs must always be mentioned in detail. Examples would be: "holed and plugged," or "jewelry loop removed from edge."

STRIKING AND DIE WEAKNESSES

Sometimes one or more areas of a coin will appear weak while at the same time other characteristics do not indicate that the coin has received comparable wear. Such weaknesses are attributable to two causes: Imperfect striking, or a weak or worn die.

Generally speaking, coins struck from worn dies show weaknesses in areas of low relief on the coins and display irregularities in the fields, and pieces that are weakly struck from sharp dies show weaknesses in the high relief areas of the coin. This distinction is so technical that many experts are often not able to determine whether a given weakness was the result of the die, the striking, or a combination of both.

Die Weakness. Die weakness originates from several causes. After extensive use, certain features of a coin, particularly those in lower relief, tend to become worn. Often when a die became very worn it was reground and then reengraved. Certain features were strengthened.

In other instances, some areas of the die were weak to begin with. For example, certain varieties of half cents dated 1793 and 1802 have the words **HALF CENT** very light, because when the die was prepared these two words were lightly impressed. At times, portions of the central design were lightly impressed into the die resulting in weaknesses in the coins struck, usually on the areas in lower relief. Further, improperly hardened dies had a tendency to sink in certain areas, thus causing a weakness in the design.

Striking Weakness. Most weaknesses on modern coins are a result of striking. Striking weakness takes many different forms. Several times throughout United States coinage history, a design was prepared which had areas of high relief on the obverse and on the reverse in opposing areas of the coin. When an area of high relief on the obverse on a coin appeared directly opposite an area of high relief on the reverse, striking pressure was often inadequate, or not enough metal was available in the planchet to be pushed up fully into both recesses. The result was a weakness in the design on the coin.

For example, in 1854 the design of the United States gold dollar was changed, and the head of Liberty had its highest parts opposite the date numerals on the reverse. The mint experienced great difficulty in having both the high parts of the obverse and the date strike up sharply; the result was that most specimens of this design showed the two center numerals of the date quite weakly. The mint realized this design error and corrected it in 1856.

When the Peace dollar was first struck in 1921, a high relief motif was used. It was impossible to fully strike up the highest parts of the obverse (Liberty's hair strands) as well as the eagle on the reverse, with the result that 1921 Peace dollars are nearly always shallowly struck. In 1922 the mint revised the design to a lower relief.

On many types of United States silver coins of the 1807-1836 period, the raised band containing the motto **E PLURIBUS UNUM** on the reverse is lightly struck in portions; this is because it appeared on the coin opposite the bust of Liberty and not enough metal, or striking pressure, was available to bring up fully both the raised motto ribbon on the reverse and the corresponding details on the obverse.

If the dies were spaced too widely apart, or if thin or uneven planchets were used, striking weakness occurred on the higher parts of the coin. Such a coin is often referred to as being "lightly struck" or "weakly struck."

When an Uncirculated coin shows exceptional weakness of the design either due to the die (unless all struck from that design are the same way) or due to the striking of the coin itself, the weakness should be specifically described after the grade number or description. For example, a coin could be described as: "MS-63, weakly struck." If the striking is extremely or extraordinarily weak then it should be described further in detail. An example would be a typical 1926-D buffalo nickel, nearly all of which are very weakly struck: "1926-D MS-63, but very weakly struck."

A coin which is MS-65 from a technical or numerical viewpoint but which is lightly struck can be described as MS-64, MS-63, or some lower grade, without mentioning the weakness; this is the practice of most third-party grading services at present. A weakly struck coin cannot be graded MS-65 or finer. To qualify as MS-65 a coin must have a fairly sharp strike (but not necessarily a completely full strike).

Sometimes the faces of early dies were not parallel to each other in the coining press. For example, when one die was made, either the obverse or the reverse, the die may have been ground off so that it was at a very slight slant. As a result, a coin struck from these dies would be very weakly impressed on the right side or the left (or the top or the bottom). There are numerous examples of this, including the 1794 large cent known as the "Shielded Hair" variety (sharp at the left side, weak at the right), the 1817 large cent with 15 obverse stars (sharp at left, weak at right), and all 1794 silver dollars (weak at left, sharp at right).

Very Important Note: When a coin is weakly struck or from unevenly aligned dies it is usually weak only in selected areas. Thus, the stars may be sharp on the right side of the coin and weak on the left side. Or, lettering may be sharp on the top of the coin and weak at the bottom. Or, the eagle may be very weakly struck on the reverse but the head of Liberty may be very sharp on the obverse. It is important to take variations of striking into consideration and to check carefully *all key features* for wear. It is not likely that the stars would wear just on the left side of the coin and not the right. One may assume that a coin with these characteristics was struck this way. This is a point which very often comes up in grading discussions, and it requires special attention.

Throughout the detailed sections on grading in this book, we mention areas in which striking may be characteristically weak. Examples are certain branch mint coins of the 1920s. Specifically, nearly all 1926-D nickels and quarters are very weakly struck. Certain New Orleans Mint Morgan dollars are weakly struck at the centers. Numerous other examples occur. However there are apt to be isolated varieties which are not specifically mentioned in the text. When this occurs, be sure to check all areas of the coin to determine whether a weakness is the result of striking or of wear. Under current grading standards, coins which exhibit significant weakness of strike cannot be graded MS-65 (or Proof-65) or higher. To qualify as MS-65 a coin must have a fairly sharp strike (but not necessarily a completely full strike).

Bill Fivaz, who has conducted seminars on the subject of grading for the ANA, offers this commentary:

"Regarding a coin not qualifying for an MS-65 grade if it is weakly struck, this is like comparing apples (the technical grade) and oranges (the market grade). Technically, if a coin leaves the dies exhibiting a weak strike but has enough lustre and absence of contact marks to qualify as an MS-65, it *is* a (technical) MS-65. The market, on the other hand, will not accept this negative feature. Because the coin will trade at a lesser dollar value, it is downgraded from the technical grade to the appropriate market grade corresponding to that price level. My feeling is that the ANA standards should agree with the market philosophy, and strike should be a factor in the grading formula.

"Learning the typically weakly struck issues in any given series is essential as this is also taken into consideration to a certain degree when grading in the marketplace."

This philosophy differs from that used earlier in grading. Today the grade of a coin, particularly in the Mint State levels, represents a grade oriented toward achieving a market price. "If a coin is worth an MS-64 price because it is lightly struck, then it should be graded MS-64," even though it is technically an MS-65.

NATURAL COLORATION OF COINS

Knowledge of the natural color which coinage metals acquire over a period of years is useful to the collector. To an extent, a coin's value is determined by the attractiveness of its coloration. Also, certain types of unnatural color might indicate that a coin has been cleaned, artificially toned, or otherwise treated to make the coin appear to be in a higher grade than it actually is, or to hide flaws.

The basic coinage metals used in the United States prior to 1965 are alloys of copper, nickel, silver, and gold. Copper tends to tone the most rapidly. Gold is the least chemically active and will tone only slightly and then only over a long period of years.

Copper. Copper is among the most chemically active of all coinage metals. Half cents and large cents of 1793-1857 were made of nearly pure copper. Later "copper" coins are actually bronze.

When a copper coin is first struck, it emerges from the dies with a brilliant red-orange surface, similar to a newly minted modern Lincoln cent. There were some exceptions in the early years among half cents and large cents. Copper was obtained from many different sources, traces of impurities varied from shipment to shipment, and some newly minted coins had a subdued brilliance, sometimes with a brownish or grayish cast.

Once a freshly minted copper coin enters the atmosphere it immediately begins to oxidize. Over a period of years, especially if exposed to actively circulating air or if placed in contact with sulfur-content materials (such as most paper or cardboard), the coin will acquire a glossy brown surface. In between the brilliant and glossy brown stages it will be part red and part brown.

A medium-quality Uncirculated coin with full original mint brilliance, frequently slightly subdued in coloration, is typically described as MS-63 Red (the color should be capitalized to show that it is a part of the grading terminology). One with a combination of original red surface and natural brown toning is described as MS-63 Red and Brown, and one with brown surfaces is noted as being MS-63 Brown. In all instances, expanded adjectival descriptions are desirable and add to the visual picture a buyer or seller can obtain of the piece in question; for example: "1817 cent. MS-65 Red and Brown, with glossy, lustrous surfaces. A small area of discoloration is seen near the 6th star. At the left side of the wreath on the reverse several leaves are weakly struck." Such a word picture is, in the writer's opinion, more desirable than just MS-65 Red and Brown. Of course, economy may dictate that an inexpensive coin may not merit a lengthy description in print, but expensive and/or rare coins do.

Note: There is divided opinion as to whether a coin has to be Red in order to merit the MS-65 grade. Most commercial grading services allow Red and Brown and Brown coins to be classified as MS-65 if all other criteria are met, while some collectors and dealers suggest that an MS-65 copper or bronze coin must have full original Red mint color.

Brilliant Proof (with mirrorlike fields) copper and bronze coins are red-orange when first struck. Over a period of time they, like Uncirculated pieces of the same metal, tend to tone brown. Often attractive iridescent hues will develop in the intermediate stages. A Proof copper coin can be described as Brilliant Proof (if the surfaces are still "bright"), Red and Brown Proof, or Brown Proof, accompanied by the appropriate numerical grade. A typical description follows: "Proof-65, Red and Brown." Rare and expensive pieces may merit additional adjectives.

Matte Proofs were made at the Philadelphia Mint in the Lincoln cent series from 1909 to 1916. When first introduced, these were stored in yellow tissue paper which tended to tone them quickly to shades varying from deep reddish-brown to dark brown with iridescent tones. This surface coloration is normal today for a Matte Proof bronze coin and should be expected. Most "bright" Matte Proofs seen today are that way because they have been cleaned or dipped.

Early copper and bronze coins with full original mint brilliance are more valuable than Red and Brown Uncirculated or Brown Uncirculated pieces. The more original mint brilliance present, the more valuable a coin will be. The same is true for Proofs.

Circulated copper coins are never fully brilliant, but are usually toned varying shades of brown. Certain early large cents and half cents often tone black because of the presence of impurities in the original metal.

Nickel. Uncirculated nickel (actually an alloy of copper and nickel) coins when first minted are silver-gray in appearance, not as bright as silver but still with much brilliance. Over a period of time nickel coins tend to tone a hazy gray, gray, or golden coloration, sometimes with bluish overtones. Proof nickel coins will tone in the same manner.

The presence or absence of attractive toning does not affect an Uncirculated or Proof nickel coin's value for some buyers. However, most knowledgeable collectors will actually prefer and will sometimes pay a premium for very attractive light toning. Very dull, heavily toned, or spotted coins are considered less valuable. Circulated nickel coins have a gray appearance.

Silver. When first minted, silver coins have a bright silvery-white surface. Over a period of time silver, a chemically active metal, tends to tone deep brown or black.

Uncirculated and Proof silver pieces often exhibit very beautiful multi-colored iridescent hues after a few years. The presence or absence of *attractive* toning does not affect a silver coin's value one way or the other for some buyers. Beginners sometimes think that "brilliant is best." However, experienced buyers will often prefer attractively toned coins. Circulated silver coins will often have a gray appearance, sometimes with deep gray or black areas.

Silver coins can be described using numbers, as MS-60, MS-63, or whatever. For additional information, adjectives can be used but are not capitalized in numismatic usage. Examples: "1882-CC dollar. MS-65. Light iridescent toning on the obverse; brilliant reverse." "1794 half dollar. VF-30. Light gray surfaces."

Gold. When first struck gold coins are a bright yellow-orange color. As gold coins are not pure gold but are alloyed with copper and traces of other substances, they do tend to tone over a period of time. Over a period of decades a gold coin will normally acquire a deep orange coloration, sometimes with light brown or orange-brown toning "stains" or streaks in certain areas (resulting from improperly mixed copper traces in the alloy). Light toning generally does not affect the value of a gold coin.

Very old gold coins, particularly those in circulated grades, will sometimes show a red oxidation. Gold coins which have been recovered from treasure wrecks after centuries at the sea bottom will sometimes have a minutely porous surface because of the corrosive action of sea water on the metals (primarily copper and/or silver) with which gold coins are alloyed. Such pieces sell for less than specimens which have not been so affected. Care must be taken to distinguish these from cast copies which often possess a similar surface.

Gold coins are usually described by using numbers. Adjectives are rarely added, for most coins are brilliant. Examples: "1903 $2.50 gold. MS-60." "1915-S Panama-Pacific gold dollar. EF-45."

CLEANING COINS

Experienced numismatists will usually say that a coin is best left alone and not cleaned. However, most beginning collectors have the idea that "brilliant is best" and somehow feel that cleaning a coin will "improve" it. As the penchant for cleaning seems to be universal, and also because there are some instances in which cleaning can actually be beneficial, some important aspects are presented here.

All types of cleaning, "good" and "bad," result in the coin's surface being changed, even if only slightly. Even the most careful "dipping" of a coin will, if repeated time and time again, result in the coin acquiring a dullish and microscopically etched surface. It is probably true to state that no matter what one's intentions are, for every single coin actually improved in some way by cleaning, a hundred or more have been reduced in value. Generally, experienced numismatists agree that a coin should not be cleaned unless there are ugly spots of oxidation, pitting which might worsen in time, or unsightly streaking or discoloration. Even then, a coin should only be cleaned by a professional.

PROCESSING, POLISHING,
AND OTHER MISTREATMENT OF COINS

There have been many attempts made to give a coin the appearance of being in a higher grade than it actually is. Numismatists refer to such treatments as "processing." Being different from cleaning (which can be "good" or "bad"), processing is never beneficial.

Types of processing include polishing and abrasion which removes metal from a coin's surface, etching and acid treatment, and "whizzing." The latter usually refers to abrading the surface of a coin with a stiff wire brush, often in a circular motion, to produce a series of minute tiny parallel scratches which to the unaided eye or under low magnification often appear to be like mint lustre. Under high magnification (in this instance a very strong magnifying glass should be used) the surface of a whizzed coin will show countless tiny scratches as well as a metal build-up on the edges of letters and numerals. Also, the artificial "mint lustre" will usually be in a uniform pattern across the coin's surfaces, whereas on an Uncirculated coin with true mint lustre the sheen of the lustre will be different on the higher parts than on the field. Some whizzed coins can be extremely deceptive. Comparing a whizzed coin with an untreated coin is the best way to gain experience in this regard. If in doubt, consult an expert.

The reader is advised that the American Numismatic Association's bylaws make a member subject to disciplinary action if he or she advertises or offers for sale or trade any coin that has been whizzed and the coin is represented to be of a better condition than it was previously.

[17]

Often one or more methods of treating a coin are combined. Sometimes a coin will be cleaned or polished and then by means of heat, fumes, or other treatment artificial toning will be applied. There are many variations.

When a coin has been polished, whizzed, artificially retoned, or in any other way changed from its original natural appearance and surface, it must be so stated in a description. For example, a coin which was EF-40 but whizzed to give it the artificial appearance of Uncirculated should be described as "EF-40, whizzed." An AU-55 coin which has been recolored should be described as "AU-55, recolored." The simple "dipping" (without abrasion) of an already Uncirculated or Proof coin to brighten the surface does not have to be mentioned unless such dipping alters the appearance from when the coin was first struck (for example, in the instance of a copper or bronze coin in which dipping always produces an unnatural color completely unlike the coin when it was first struck).

HANDLING AND STORAGE OF COINS

As a coin collector you are commissioned by posterity to handle each coin in your possession carefully and to preserve it in the condition in which it was received.

When examining a coin you should hold it by its edges and over a cloth pad or other soft surface. In this way if it accidentally falls no harm will be done. A coin should never be touched on either of its faces, obverse or reverse, for the oil and acid in one's skin will eventually leave fingerprints—if not soon, then years later. Also, one should avoid holding a coin near one's mouth while talking as small drops of moisture may land on the coin's surface and later cause what are commonly referred to as "flyspecks"—tiny pinpoints of black oxidation.

Coins should be stored in a dry location free from harmful fumes. The presence of sulfur in the atmosphere, a situation caused by certain types of coal combustion and also by industrial processes, sometimes will impart to silver coins in particular a yellowish or blackish toning. Dampness will result in oxidation or, in extreme instances, surface corrosion. Dampness can be best solved by moving coins to a drier location. If this is not possible, then a packet of silica gel (available in drugstores or photographic supply stores) put in with the coins, and replaced regularly, will serve to absorb moisture and may alleviate the problem. Also, the storage of coins in airtight containers will help.

The more a coin is exposed to freely circulating air, the more tendency it has to change color or to tone. Storage of coins in protective envelopes and hard plastic holders will usually (but not always) help prevent this. Holders containing polyvinyl chloride (PVC) should be avoided for other than temporary storage. Do not buy any coin storage containers without ascertaining their chemical composition.

PROOF COINS

The term "Proof" (always capitalized in numismatic usage) refers to a manufacturing process which results in a special surface or finish on coins made for collectors. Most familiar are modern brilliant Proofs. These coins are struck at the mint by a special process. Carefully prepared dies, sharp in all features, are made. Then the flat surfaces of the dies are given a high mirrorlike polish. Specially prepared planchets are fed into low-speed coining presses. Each Proof coin is slowly and carefully struck more than once to accentuate details. When striking is completed the coin is taken from the dies with care and not allowed to come into contact with other pieces. The result is a coin with mirrorlike surface. The piece is then grouped together with other denominations in a set and offered for sale to collectors.

From 1817 through 1857 inclusive, Proof coins were made only on special occasions and not for general sale to collectors. They were made available to visiting foreign dignitaries, government officials, and those with connections at the mint. Earlier (pre-1817) United States coins may have prooflike surfaces and many Proof characteristics (1796 silver coins are a good example), but they were not specifically or intentionally struck as Proofs. These are sometimes designated as "specimen strikings."

Beginning in 1858, Proofs were sold to collectors openly. In that year 80 silver Proof sets (containing silver coins from the three-cent piece through the silver dollar), plus additional pieces of the silver dollar denomination, were produced as well as perhaps 200 (the exact number is not known) copper nickel cents and a limited number of Proof gold coins.

The traditional mirrorlike or "brilliant" type of Proof finish was used on all United States Proof coins of the nineteenth century. During the twentieth century, cents through the 1909 Indian, nickels through the 1912 Liberty, regular issue silver coins

[18]

through 1915, and gold coins through 1907 were of the brilliant mirrorlike type. When modern Proof coinage was resumed in 1936 and continued through 1942, then 1950-1964, and 1968 to date, the brilliant mirrorlike finish was used. While these types of Proofs are referred to as "brilliant Proofs," actual specimens may have toned over the years. The mirrorlike surface is still evident, however.

From 1908 through 1915, Matte Proofs and Sandblast Proofs (the latter created by directing fine sand particles at high pressure toward the coin's surface) were made of certain gold coins (exceptions are 1909-1910 Proofs with Roman finish). While characteristics vary from issue to issue, generally all of these pieces have extreme sharpness of design detail and sharp, squared-off rims. The surfaces are without lustre and have a dullish matte surface. Sandblast Proofs were made of certain commemorative coins also, such as the 1928 Hawaiian issue.

Roman finish Proof gold coins were made in 1909 and 1910. These pieces are sharply struck, have squared-off edges, and have a satin-like surface finish, not too much different from an Uncirculated coin (which causes confusion among collectors today, and which at the time of issue was quite unpopular as collectors resented having to pay a premium for a coin without a distinctly different appearance).

Matte Proofs were made of Lincoln cents 1909-1916 and buffalo nickels 1913-1916. (Some say that 1917 Matte Proofs were also made.) Such coins have extremely sharp design detail, squared-off rims, "brilliant" (mirrorlike) edges, but a matte or satin-like (or even full satin, not with flashy mint lustre) surface. In some instances Matte Proof dies may have been used to make regular circulation strikes once the requisite number of Matte Proofs were made for collectors. So, it is important that a Matte Proof, to be considered authentic, have squared-off rims and mirrorlike perfect edges in addition to the proper surface characteristics.

Additional Points Concerning Proofs: Certain regular issue or business strike coins have nearly full prooflike (unlike Proof, the word *prooflike* is not capitalized) surfaces. These were produced in several ways. Usually regular issue dies (intended to make coins for circulation) were polished to remove surface marks or defects for extended use. Coins struck from these dies were produced at high speed, and the full Proof surface is not always evident. Also, the pieces are struck on ordinary planchets. Usually such pieces, sometimes called "first strikes" or "prooflike Uncirculated," have patches of Uncirculated mint frost. A characteristic in this regard is the shield on the reverse (on coins with this design feature). The stripes within the shield on Proofs are fully brilliant, but on prooflike non-Proofs the stripes usually are not mirrorlike. Also, the striking may be weak in areas and the rims might not be sharp.

The mirrorlike surfaces of a brilliant Proof coin are much more susceptible to damage than are the surfaces of an Uncirculated coin. For this reason Proof coins which have been cleaned almost always show a series of fine hairlines or minute striations. Also, careless handling results in certain Proofs acquiring marks, nicks, and scratches more readily than business strikes.

Some Proofs, particularly nineteenth century issues, have "lintmarks." When a Proof die was wiped with an oily rag, sometimes threads, bits of hair, lint, and so on would remain. When a coin was struck from such a die, an incuse or recessed impression of the debris would appear on the piece. Lintmarks visible to the unaided eye should be specifically mentioned in a description.

Proofs are divided into classifications from Proof-60 (a Proof with handling marks, but without wear) continuously through Proof-70 (a coin with no hairlines, handling marks, or other defects; in other words, a flawless coin. Such a coin may be brilliant or may have natural toning.

Impaired Proofs; Other Comments. If a Proof has been excessively cleaned, has many marks, scratches, dents or other defects, it is described as an impaired Proof. If the coin has seen actual wear then it will be graded one of the lesser grades such as Proof-55, Proof-45, or whatever. It is not logical to describe a slightly worn Proof as "AU" (Almost Uncirculated) for it never was "Uncirculated" to begin with—in the sense that Uncirculated describes a top grade normal production strike. So, the term "impaired Proof" is appropriate. It is best to describe fully such a coin, examples being: "Proof with extensive hairlines and scuffing," or "Proof-50 with numerous nicks and scratches in the field," or "Proof-55, with light wear on the higher surfaces."

UNCIRCULATED COINS

The term "Uncirculated" interchangeable with "Mint State," refers to a coin which has never seen general circulation. Such a piece has no wear of any kind. A coin as bright as the time it was minted or with very light natural toning can be described as "brilliant Uncirculated." A coin which has natural toning can be described as "toned Uncirculated." Except in the instance of copper coins, the presence or absence of light toning does not negatively affect an Uncirculated coin's grade. Among silver and nickel coins, attractive natural toning often results in the coin bringing a premium.

The quality of lustre or "mint bloom" on an Uncirculated coin is an essential element in correctly grading the piece, and has a significant bearing on its value. Lustre may in time become dull, frosty, spotted or discolored. Unattractive lustre will normally result in a lower assigned grade and/or value.

With the exception of certain Special Mint Sets made in recent years for collectors, Uncirculated or normal production strike coins were produced on high speed presses, stored in bags together with other coins, run through counting machines, and in other ways handled without regard to numismatic posterity. As a result, it is the rule and not the exception for an Uncirculated coin to have bag marks and evidence of coin-to-coin contact, although the piece might not have been actual commercial circulation. The number of such marks will depend upon the coin's size. Differences in criteria in this regard are given in the individual sections under grading descriptions for different denominations and types.

Uncirculated coins range from MS-60 (a coin with no evidence of actual wear but with numerous bag marks and contact marks and/or poor or impaired lustre) to MS-70 (a flawless coin). Intervening grades are MS-61, MS-62, MS-63, etc.

STRIKING AND MINTING PECULIARITIES
OF UNCIRCULATED COINS

Certain early United States gold and silver coins have mint-caused planchet or adjustment marks (a series of parallel striations). If these are unusually prominent they should be described adjectivally in addition to the numerical or regular descriptive grade. For example: "MS-60 with adjustment marks," or "MS-65 with adjustment marks," or, for a worn coin, "VF-20 with very light adjustment marks," or something similar.

If an Uncirculated coin exhibits weakness due to striking or die wear or unusual (for the variety) die wear, this must be adjectivally mentioned in addition to the grade. Examples are: "MS-60, lightly struck," or "EF-45, lightly struck." And "MS-63, lightly struck."

Currently, the prevailing standards dictate that for a coin to be graded MS-65 (or Proof-65) or higher it must be an above average strike. This is a departure from earlier standards which stated that sharpness of strike was one consideration determining a coin's value, and technical or numerical grade was another; and that a coin could be MS-65 and be weakly struck. Today, a weakly struck coin must be graded below MS-65 or Proof-65. For example, an 1892-O Morgan dollar which by all other factors merits the MS-65 designation, but which is weakly struck, should be graded MS-64, MS-63, or some lower grade, depending upon the negative "market value" of the weakness. This point has not been completely defined in the literature and is not completely consistent in practice at the present time.

David Hall, founder of the Professional Coin Grading Service, stated the following in a communication dated November 10, 1990:

"It is my view that the numismatic marketplace currently accepts the following minimum standards for strike: MS-64: must be a decent strike; MS-65: must be a sharp strike, does not have to be a full strike; MS-66: same as MS-65; MS-67 or better: must be fully struck."

Bill Fivaz, who has conducted grading seminars for the ANA, stated the following in a communication dated November 7, 1990:

"No, a coin needn't be (absolutely) fully struck in order to be graded MS-65." He further noted that knowledge of individual coins and their peculiarities of striking was necessary in order to determine what the market considered acceptable for the MS-65 level.

CIRCULATED COINS

Once a coin enters general circulation in the channels of commerce it begins to show signs of wear. As time goes on the coin becomes more and more worn until, after a period of many decades, only a few features may be left.

Dr. William H. Sheldon devised a numerical scale to indicate degrees of wear. According to this scale, a coin in condition 1 or "Basal State" is barely recognizable. At the opposite end, a coin touched by even the slightest trace of wear (below MS-60) cannot be called Uncirculated.

Q. David Bowers

OFFICIAL ANA GRADING TERMINOLOGY

While numbers from 1 through 59 are continuous, it has been found practical to designate specific intermediate numbers to define grades. Hence, this text uses the following descriptions and their numerical equivalents, as approved by the ANA Board of Governors.

UNCIRCULATED GRADES

The following general descriptions for the 11 Mint State grades are intended for application to the entire United States range of coins. As such, these descriptions are not specific in nature. Refer to the individual coin types listed in each respective section for a more precise explanation.

In all instances, a grader needs experience in any given type of U.S. coin to be able to accurately and consistently apply the 11 point system within the Mint State category.

Note: The ANA has not established equivalent official adjectival grades for the listings within the MS-60 to MS-70 range. Commercially, MS-70 coins are often called Perfect Uncirculated, MS-65 coins Gem Uncirculated, and MS-63 coins Choice Uncirculated. In the past, these and other adjectives have been used to designate various grades of condition.

MS-70. The perfect coin. Has very attractive sharp strike and original luster of the highest quality for the date and mint. No contact marks are visible under magnification. There are absolutely no hairlines, scuff marks or defects. Attractive and outstanding eye appeal. Copper coins must be bright with full original color and luster.

MS-69. Must have very attractive sharp strike and full original luster for the date and mint, with no more than two small non-detracting contact marks or flaws. No hairlines or scuff marks can be seen. Has exceptional eye appeal. Copper coins must be bright with full original color and luster.

MS-68. Attractive sharp strike and full original luster for the date and mint, with no more than four light scattered contact marks or flaws. No hairlines or scuff marks show. Exceptional eye appeal. Copper coins must have lustrous original color.

MS-67. Has full original luster and sharp strike for date and mint. May have three or four very small contact marks and one more noticeable but not detracting mark. On comparable coins, one or two small single hairlines may show under magnification, or one or two partially hidden scuff marks or flaws may be present. Eye appeal is exceptional. Copper coins have lustrous original color.

MS-66. Must have above average quality of strike and full original mint luster, with no more than two or three minor but noticeable contact marks. A few very light hairlines may show under magnification, or there may be one or two light scuff marks showing on frosted surfaces or in the field. The eye appeal must be above average and very pleasing for the date and mint. Copper coins display full original or lightly toned color as designated. (See page 16).

MS-65. Shows an attractive high quality of luster and strike for the date and mint. A few small scattered contact marks, or two larger marks may be present, and one or two small patches of hairlines may show under magnification. Noticeable light scuff marks may show on the high points of the design. Overall quality is above average and overall eye appeal is very pleasing. Copper coins have full luster with original or darkened color as designated. (See page 16).

MS-64. Has at least average luster and strike for the type. Several small contact marks in groups, as well as one or two moderately heavy marks may be present. One or two small patches of hairlines may show under low magnification. Noticeable light scuff marks or defects might be seen within the design or in the field. Attractive overall quality with a pleasing eye appeal. Copper coins may be slightly dull. Color should be designated. (See page 16).

MS-63. Mint luster may be slightly impaired. Numerous small contact marks, and a few scattered heavy marks may be seen. Small hairlines are visible without magnification. Several detracting scuff marks or defects may be present throughout the design or in the fields. The general quality is about average, but overall the coin is rather attractive. Copper pieces may be darkened or dull. Color should be designated.

MS-62. An impaired or dull luster may be evident. Clusters of small marks may be present throughout with a few large marks or nicks in prime focal areas. Hairlines may be very noticeable. Large unattractive scuff marks might be seen on major features. The strike, rim and planchet quality may be noticeably below average. Overall eye appeal is generally acceptable. Copper coins will show a diminished color and tone.

MS-61. Mint luster may be diminished or noticeably impaired, and the surface has clusters of large and small contact marks throughout. Hairlines could be very noticeable. Scuff marks may show as unattractive patches on large areas or major features. Small rim nicks, striking or planchet defects may show, and the quality may be noticeably poor. Eye appeal is somewhat unattractive. Copper pieces will be generally dull, dark and possibly spotted.

MS-60. Unattractive, dull or washed out mint luster may mark this coin. There may be many large detracting contact marks, or damage spots, but absolutely no trace of wear. There could be a heavy concentration of hairlines, or unattractive large areas of scuff marks. Rim nicks may be present, and eye appeal is very poor. Copper coins may be dark, dull and spotted.

	CONTACT MARKS	HAIRLINES	LUSTER	EYE APPEAL
MS-70	None show under magnification	None show under magnification	Very attractive Fully original	Outstanding
MS-69	1 or 2 miniscule none in prime focal areas	None visible	Very attractive Fully original	Exceptional
MS-68	3 or 4 miniscule none in prime focal areas	None visible	Attractive Fully original	Exceptional
MS-67	3 or 4 miniscule 1 or 2 may be in prime focal areas	None visible without magnification	Above average Fully original	Exceptional
MS-66	Several small; a few may be in prime focal areas	None visible without magnification	Above average Fully original	Above average
MS-65	Light and scattered without major distracting marks in prime focal areas	May have a few scattered	Fully original	Very pleasing
MS-64	May have light scattered marks; a few may be in prime focal areas	May have a few scattered or small patch in secondary areas	Average Full original	Pleasing
MS-63	May have distracting marks in prime focal areas	May have a few scattered or small patch	May be original or slightly impaired	Rather attractive
MS-62	May have distracting marks in prime focal and/or secondary areas	May have a few scattered to noticeable patch	May be original or impaired	Generally acceptable
MS-61	May have a few heavy (or numerous light) marks in prime focal and/or secondary areas	May have noticeable patch or continuous hairlining over surfaces	May be original or impaired	Unattractive
MS-60	May have heavy marks in all areas	May have noticeable patch or continuous hairlining throughout	May be original or impaired	Poor

CIRCULATED GRADES

Very Choice About Uncirculated-58. Abbreviation: AU-58. The barest trace of wear may be seen on one or more of the high points of the design. No major detracting contact marks will be present and the coin will have attractive eye appeal and nearly full lustre, often with the appearance of a higher grade.

Choice About Uncirculated-55. Abbreviation: AU-55. Only small traces of wear are visible on the highest points of the coin. As is the case with the other grades described here, specific information is listed in the following text under the various types, for wear often occurs in different spots on different designs.

About Uncirculated-50. Abbreviation: AU-50. With traces of wear on nearly all of the highest areas. At least half of the original mint lustre is present.

Choice Extremely Fine-45. Abbreviation: EF-45. With light overall wear on the coin's highest points. All design details are very sharp. Mint lustre is usually seen only in protected areas of the coin's surface such as between the star point and in the letter spaces.

Extremely Fine-40. Abbreviation: EF-40. With only slight wear but more extensive than the preceding, still with excellent overall sharpness. Traces of mint lustre may still show.

Choice Very Fine-30. Abbreviation: VF-30. With light even wear on the surface; design details on the highest points lightly worn, but with all lettering and major features sharp.

Very Fine-20. Abbreviation: VF-20. As the preceding but with moderate wear on the higher parts.

Fine-12. Abbreviation: F-12. Moderate to considerable even wear. Entire design is bold. All lettering, including the word LIBERTY (on coins with this feature on the shield or headband), visible, but with some weaknesses.

Very Good-8. Abbreviation: VG-8. Well worn. Major designs visible, but with faintness in areas. Head of Liberty, wreath, and other major features visible in outline form without center detail.

Good-4. Abbreviation: G-4. Heavily worn. Major designs visible, but with faintness in areas. Head of Liberty, wreath, and other major features, as applicable, visible in out line form without center detail.) To qualify for the intermediate grade of G-6, a coin must have full rims.)

About Good-3. Abbreviation: AG-3. Very heavily worn with portions of the lettering, date, and legends being worn smooth. The date barely readable.

Note: The exact descriptions of circulated grades vary widely from one coin issue to another, so the preceding commentary is only of a very general nature. It is essential to refer to the specific text when grading any coin.

Note concerning nomenclature: The correct adjectival term is Extremely, not Extra, in connection with such categories as EF-40 and EF-45, and the correct abbreviation, for example, is EF-40, not XF-40. Similarly, the "A" in AU refers to About, not Almost.

While the preceding guidelines will undoubtedly prove useful to the reader, it is highly recommended that the viewing of actual coins in the marketplace will enable you to better determine grading practices affecting the series which interest you most. For example, the collector of Morgan silver dollars would do well to examine coins graded by a variety of services and sellers in order to determine in general what is considered to be MS-63, MS-64, MS-65, and higher grades.

SPLIT AND INTERMEDIATE GRADES

It is often the case that because of the peculiarities of striking or a coin's design, one side of the coin will grade differently from the other. When this is the case, a diagonal mark is used to separate the two. For example, a coin with an AU-50 obverse and an EF-45 reverse can be described as AU-50/EF-45. A coin with an MS-63 obverse and an MS-65 reverse can be described as MS-63/65.

A split grade is a simple and effective way of further describing a coin's surface and imparting additional information concerning its preservation. In most instances, the "market grade" of a coin is the lower of the two grades of its sides. Using the above two examples, if it were necessary to assign just a single number to each of these coins, as many of the third-party grading services do, then these coins would be designated as EF-45 in the first example and MS-63 in the second. Some have suggested that the grades be averaged, and that a coin technically grading MS-63/65 be assigned the number MS-64 (especially if it has nice eye appeal), but few do this.

On this subject, Leonard Albrecht comments as follows:

"Translating a split grade into a single overall 'market grade' can be difficult as there is no mathematical formula that can be employed for all coins. With most U.S. coins the obverse is the most important side, and thus the obverse grade carries the most weight. For example, coins with split grades of MS-63/64, MS-63/65, and even MS-63/66 are usually assigned a single grade of MS-63.

Most of the problems associated with split grades arise when the two sides are *widely* different from each other, or when the dominant (obverse) side grades higher than the reverse. Examples would be split grades of MS-60/67 (obverse and reverse grades *widely* different), MS-65/63, and MS-64/60 (obverse grades significantly higher than the reverse). Fortunately, these examples are seldom encountered, but they do produce grading quandaries, even among experts.

Depending on the person doing the grading and the overall eye appeal of the coins, one might reasonably expect the following: a single grade for the MS-60/67 of MS-60 or MS-61; for the MS-65/63 most likely a single grade of MS-64; and for the MS-64/60 a possible range of MS-60 through MS-63, with MS-62 being most likely."

Note: Published references do not always agree on which side is the obverse and which is the reverse. In the field of U.S. commemorative half dollars, for example, there are differences of opinion, even within mint and government records.

The ANA standard numerical scale is divided into the following grades: 3, 4, 8, 12, 20, 30, 40, 45, 50, 55, 58, 60, 61, 62, 63, 64, 65, 66, 67, 68, 69 and 70.

In addition to these official ANA numbers, graders sometimes use the following additional numbers for clarification: 25, 35, and 53. The designation "PQ," for Premium Quality, is sometimes applied in the marketplace to designate a coin with exceptional quality as to strike, planchet quality, centering, and aesthetic appeal, but no formal standards have ever been formulated in this regard. It should be noted that a coin of excellent aesthetic appeal to one viewer might not have the same appeal to another; beauty is in the eye of the beholder, as the old saying goes.

Most advanced collectors and dealers find that the gradations from AG-3 through AU-58 are sufficient to describe nearly every coin showing wear. The use of additional intermediate grade levels such as EF-42, EF-43, and so on is not encouraged. Grading is not that precise, and using such finely split intermediate grades is imparting a degree of accuracy which probably will not be able to be verified by other numismatists. However, in recent years a number of sellers and grading services have indeed assigned such intermediate numbers to coins.

An exception to intermediate grades can be found amount Mint State coins grading from MS-60 through MS-70. Among Mint State coins the hobby has adopted an 11-point scale embodying all numbers in the MS-60 to MS-70 range. Readers are cautioned that differences of opinion often occur, and what one person calls MS-65 another might designate as MS-64, and that even wider variations are not uncommon. Grading is not so precise that individual numerical differences can be consistently and correctly assigned, even by experts. The human eye is dependent upon lighting and extraneous factors such as emotions, time of day, and even the state of the market. For this reason, a person using an assigned grading number should use care in utilizing such a number as a means of grading or pricing a coin.

The ANA grading system considers it to be good numismatic practice to adhere to the standard MS-60 through MS-70 numbers. The use of further intermediate grades such as MS-64+, "High end MS-63," etc. is discouraged. Experienced numismatists can generally agree on whether a given coin is MS-60, MS-63, or MS-65. However, not even the most advanced numismatists can necessarily agree on a consistent basis whether a coin is MS-62 or MS-63, or MS-64 or MS-65, etc.; the distinction is simply too minute to permit consistent accuracy, although there are some who may disagree with this statement.

Important note: While other grading systems are in use, and while no requirement is made that any collector, dealer, or other numismatist must use the ANA grading system, it is required that when a statement is made that coins are graded according to the ANA system, then the ANA system in its correct and strict form must be followed) without unauthorized hyphenated grades, plus or minus signs, or other adjectives not found in the ANA grading system).

INFORMATION ABOUT COINS AND VALUES

For additional information concerning the history and technical aspects of all United States coins we recommend that readers consult such sources as *A Guide Book of United States Coins* (the Red Book), by R. S. Yeoman. This book is published annually by Western Publishing Company, Inc., Racine, Wisconsin, and contains technical data on coins as well as current valuations.

Other sources of price information include the "Trends" section of *Coin World*, the "Market Report" column in *Numismatic News, The Coin Dealer Newsletter*, dealer price lists, and reports of coins sold at auction.

In all instances it must be remembered that coins which show significant defects, adjustment marks, cleaning, or other problems may be valued at prices substantially less than equivalent coins without these problems.

The market changes, often rapidly, and published sources may not be current. It is important to check latest market conditions carefully before buying or selling coins.

GLOSSARY

The following list contains terms that are most frequently used or that have a special meaning to coin collectors other than their ordinary definitions.

Abrasions—Light rubbing or scuffing from friction. Not the same as hairlines or bag marks.

Adjustment Marks—Small striations or file marks found on early United States coins. Caused during planchet preparation (before striking) by drawing a file across the coins to remove excess metal so as to reduce the planchet to its proper weight. The result is a series of parallel grooves.

Alloy—A combination of two or more metals.

Alteration—The tampering with a feature of a coin's surface such as the date, mint mark, etc. to give it the appearance of being another date, mint mark, or variety. An illegal practice.

Altered Date—A false date on a coin—a date altered to make a coin appear to be one of a rarer or more valuable issue.

Bag Mark—A surface mark, usually in the form of a nick, acquired by a coin when it came in contact with others in a mint bag. Bag marks are most common on large and heavy silver and gold coins.

Blemishes—Minor nicks, marks, flaws or spots of discoloration that mar the surface of a coin.

Brockage—A misstruck coin, generally one showing the normal design on one side and an incuse mirror image of this design on the other side.

Bronze—An alloy of copper, zinc, and tin.

Bullion—Uncoined gold or silver in the form of bars, ingots or plate.

Business Strike—A coin intended for circulation in the channels of commerce (as opposed to a proof coin specifically struck for collectors).

Choice—An adjective used to describe an especially select specimen of a given grade. Thus, Choice EF-45 represents an especially select Extremely Fine coin (normal or typical Extremely Fine being EF-40).

Clad Coinage—Issues of United States dimes, quarters, halves, and dollars made since 1965. Each coin has a center core, and a layer of copper-nickel or silver on both sides.

Clash Marks—Impressions of the reverse design on the obverse of a coin or the obverse design on the reverse of a coin due to die damage caused when the striking dies impacted each other with great force and without an intervening planchet.

Cleaning—Refers to removing dirt or otherwise altering the appearance of a coin through the use of chemical or abrasive materials that damage or scratch the surface in a detectable fashion. Cleaning is different than whizzing or mechanical alteration of the surface.

A gentle cleaning in water or solvent that leaves no marks or residue is usually not considered harmful. Cleaning by either mechanical or chemical means that are detectable will generally result in lowering the grade and value of a coin.

Commemorative—A coin issued to mark a special event or to honor an outstanding person.

Counterstamp—A design, group of letters, or other mark stamped on a coin for special identification or advertising purposes. Counterstamped coins are graded the way regular (uncounterstamped) coins are, but the nature and condition of the counterstamp must also be described.

Designer—The artist who creates a coin's design. The engraver is the person who cuts a design into a coinage die.

Details—Small features and fine lines in a coin design. Particularly those seen in hair, leaves, wreaths and feathers.

Die—A piece of metal engraved with a design for use in stamping coins.

Die Defect—An imperfection in a coin caused by a defective die.

Die Variety—A variation of a design attributed to a particular die. For example, among

United States cents of 1793 over a dozen different dies were used, all hand-cut, and each a different die variety.

Dipping—Refers to removing tarnish, surface dirt or changing the coloration of a coin by applying chemicals, or otherwise artificially treating it with liquids.

Disme—One tenth of a dollar. The early spelling of the word "dime."

Double Eagle—A United States $20.00 gold coin.

Eagle—A United States $10.00 gold coin. Name also applied to gold bullion coins.

Electrotype—A counterfeit coin made by the electroplating process.

Exergue—That portion of a coin beneath the main design generally separated by an exergual line.

Field—That portion of a coin's surface not used for a design or inscription.

Fillet Head—The head of Liberty on United States coins with hair tied with a band, generally on the forehead.

Fineness—Purity of gold or silver, normally expressed in terms of one thousand parts.

First Strike—An unofficial term referring to a coin struck shortly after a new die is put into use. Such coins often have prooflike surfaces and resemble proofs in certain (but not all) characteristics. Resurfaced previously-used dies sometimes also have these characteristics.

Flan—A blank piece of metal in the size and shape of a coin. Also called a planchet.

Flyspecks—Minute oxidation spots often seen on the surfaces of coins, particularly higher grade copper and nickel coins, caused by exposure to small drops of moisture.

Grade—The condition or amount of wear that a coin has received. Generally, the less wear a coin has received, the more valuable it is. In this reference, coins are graded on the ANA numerical system from About Good-3 to Perfect Uncirculated-70.

Hairlines—A series of minute lines or scratches, usually visible in the field of a coin, caused by cleaning or polishing.

Half Eagle—A United States $5.00 gold coin.

High Points—Areas of highest relief in a coin design. The first small parts to show evidence of wear or abrasion, and also the last areas to strike up fully.

Impaired Proof—A proof which has been damaged either by careless handling or circulation.

Incuse—The design of a coin which has been impressed below the coin's surface. When the design is raised above the coin's surface it is said to be in *relief.*

Inscription—The legend or lettering on a coin.

Legend—The principal inscription on a coin.

Lettered Edge—The narrow edge of a coin bearing an inscription, found on some foreign and older United States coins.

Lintmarks—Small incuse or incised marks on the surface of a Proof or Uncirculated coin caused by stray hairs, threads, and the like adhering to the die after it was wiped with an oily rag.

Luster—The glossy mint bloom on the surface of an Uncirculated coin. Although normally brilliant, with time luster may become dull, frosty, spotted or discolored.

Matte Proof—A special type of proof finish used at the Philadelphia Mint prior to World War I. This method was first employed by the Paris Mint and was later adopted for a limited time during the 1908-1916 years for certain (but not all) issues by the Philadelphia Mint. The surface is prepared by a special process which gives it a grainy appearance. See further information in text.

Micro—Very small or microscopic.

Milled Edge—A raised rim around the outer surface of a coin. Not to be confused with the reeded or serrated narrow edge of the coin.

Mint Error—A misstruck or defective coin produced by a mint.

Mint Luster—The "frost" on the surface of a Mint State or nearly Mint State coin. Caused by a series of microscopic lines formed during the striking process.

Mint Mark—A symbol, usually a small letter, used to indicate at which mint a coin was struck.

Modification—A minor alteration in the basic design of a coin.

Motto—A word or phrase used on a coin.

Mule—A coin struck from dies not originally intended to be used together.

Nick—A small mark on a coin caused by another coin bumping against it or by contact with a rough or sharp object.

Numismatist—A student or collector of coins, medals or related items.

Obverse—The front or face side of a coin, generally the side with the date and the principal design.

Overdate—The date made by superimposing one or more different numbers on a previously dated die.

Overgrading—Giving a coin a higher grading description than it merits.

Overstrike—An impression made with different dies on a previously struck coin.

Oxidation—The formation of oxides or tarnish on the surface of a coin from exposure to air, dampness, industrial fumes, or other elements.

Patina—A green or brown surface film found on ancient copper and bronze coins caused by oxidation over a long period of time.

Pattern—An experimental or trial coin, generally of a new design, denomination or metal.

Planchet—The blank piece of metal on which a coin design is stamped.

Processing—A term describing the mistreatment of a coin by wire brushing, acid dipping, or otherwise abrading or eroding the surface in an effort to make it appear in a higher grade than it actually is. Processed coins must be specifically described as such.

Proof—Coins struck for collectors and using specially polished or otherwise prepared dies. (See individual descriptions.)

Prooflike—Describes an Uncirculated coin with a mirrorlike reflective surface but lacking the full characteristics of a proof.

Quarter Eagle—A United States two and a half dollar gold coin.

Reeded Edge—The edge of a coin with grooved lines that run vertically around its perimeter. The edge found on all current United States coins other than cents and nickels.

Relief—Any part of a coin's design that is raised above the coin's surface is said to be in relief. The opposite of relief is *incuse*.

Restrike—A coin struck from a genuine die at a date later than the original issue.

Reverse—The side of a coin carrying the design of lesser importance. Opposite of the obverse side.

Ribs or Ribbing—The fine vein lines on the surface of a leaf.

Rim—The raised portion of a coin encircling the obverse and reverse which protects the designs of the coin from wear.

Roman Finish Proof—A special finish on proof coins minted at Philadelphia 1909-1910. (See text.)

Sandblast Proof—Special type of proof coin produced at the Philadelphia Mint for certain issues circa 1908-1915. Made by blowing fine particles of sand against the coin's surface. Similar in appearance to a matte proof (see Matte Proof).

Scratch—A deep line or groove in a coin caused by contact with a sharp or rough object.

Series—One coin of each year issued from each mint of a specific design and denomination, e.g., Buffalo Nickels 1913-1938.

Striations—Thin, light raised lines on the surface of a coin, caused by excessive polishing of the die.

Striking—Refers to the process by which a coin is minted. Also refers to the sharpness of design details. A sharp strike or strong strike is one with all of the details struck very sharply; a weak strike has the details lightly impressed at the time of coining.

Toning—Natural patination or discoloration of a coin's surface caused by the atmosphere over a long period of time. Toning is often very attractive, and many collectors prefer coins with this feature.

Truncation—The sharply cut off bottom edge of a bust.

Type—A coin's basic distinguishing design.

Unique—An item of which one specimen only is known to exist.

Variety—A minor change from the basic type design of a coin.

Weak Strike—A coin with certain of its details (in the areas of high relief) not fully formed because of the hardness of alloy, insufficient striking pressure or improper die spacing.

Wear—The abrasion of metal from a coin's surface caused by normal handling and circulation.

Whizzing—The alteration of a coin's appearance by use of a rotating bristled (wire or other material) brush to move or remove metal from the surface. This process generally gives a coin the artificial appearance of being in a higher grade than it actually is. Areas of a whizzed coin usually show a series of minute scratches or surface disruptions simulating artificial luster, and the buildup of metal ridges on raised letters or other design features.

GRADING ABBREVIATIONS

Corresponding numbers may be used with any of these descriptions.

MS-60 to 70	Uncirculated or Mint State	Unc. or MS	Unc.-60 to 70
AU-58	Very Choice About Uncirculated	V. Ch. Abt. Unc.	V. Ch. AU
AU-55	Choice About Uncirculated	Ch. Abt. Unc.	Ch. AU
AU-50	About Uncirculated	Abt. Unc.	AU
EF-45	Choice Extremely Fine	Ch. Ex. Fine	Ch. EF
EF-40	Extremely Fine	Ex. Fine	EF
VF-30	Choice Very Fine	Ch. V. Fine	Ch. VF
VF-20	Very Fine	V. Fine	VF
F-12	Fine	Fine	F
VG-8	Very Good	V. Good	VG
G-4	Good	Good	G
AG-3	About Good	Abt. Good	AG

USE OF THE OFFICIAL ANA GRADING SYSTEM

The descriptions of coin grades given in this book are intended for use in determining the relative condition of coins in various states of preservation. The terms and standards are based on the commonly accepted practices of experienced dealers and collectors. Use of these standards is recommended by the American Numismatic Association to avoid misunderstandings during transactions, cataloging and advertising.

The method of grading described in this book should be referred to as the Official ANA Grading System. When grading by these standards, care should be taken to adhere to the standard wording, abbreviations and numbers used in this text.

When a coin first begins to show signs of handling, abrasion, or light wear, only the highest parts of the design are affected. Evidence that such a coin is not Uncirculated can be seen by carefully examining the high spots for signs of a slight change in color, surface texture, or sharpness of fine details.

In early stages of wear the highest points of design become slightly rounded or flattened, and the very fine details begin to merge together in small spots.

After a coin has been in circulation for a short time, the entire design and surface will show light wear. Many of the high parts will lose their sharpness, and most of the original mint luster will begin to wear away except in recessed areas.

Further circulation will reduce the sharpness and relief of the entire design. High points then begin to merge with the next lower parts of the design.

After the protective rim is worn away the entire surface becomes flat, and most of the details blend together or become partially merged with the surface.

It should be understood that because of the nature of the minting process, some coins will be found which do not conform exactly with the standard definitions of wear as given in this text or as shown in the illustrations. Specific points of wear may vary slightly. Information given in the notes at the end of some sections does not cover all exceptions, but is a guide to the most frequently encountered varieties.

Also, the amount of mint luster (for the highest several grades) is intended more as a visual guide rather than a fixed quantity. The percentage of visible mint luster described in the text is the *minimum* allowable amount, and a higher percentage can usually be expected. Luster is not always brilliant and may be evident although sometimes dull or discolored.

A *Choice* coin in any condition is one with an attractive, above average surface relatively free from nicks or bag marks. A *Typical* coin may have more noticeable minor surface blemishes.

In all cases, a coin in lower condition must be assumed to include all the wear features of the next higher grade in addition to its own distinguishing points of wear.

Remarks concerning the visibility of certain features refer to the *maximum* allowable amount of wear for those features.

BASIC GRADING TECHNIQUES
By Michael Fahey

Everyone interested in coins should learn how to grade coins properly. This knowledge will become an invaluable asset, and is well worth the required time and effort. Grading terms are simply a shorthand version of a complete description of the coin. For instance, an 1880-S dollar can be described as MS-63, rather than: "no trace of wear; full original mint luster; lightly toned surfaces; a number of light bag marks on the fields and devices, including two noticeable marks on Liberty's cheek; hairline free surfaces; and good eye appeal."

With a minimal amount of effort, any individual can learn the circulated grades. Every circulated grade is based upon the amount of wear and remaining details, so the grades between AG-3 and AU-55 do not cause too much difficulty. However, the Mint State grades are determined by a more complex procedure. The following factors are utilized to arrive at a particular Mint State grade: luster, color, detracting marks, mishandling and eye appeal. Below is a brief description of each factor.

LUSTER - Luster is simply the way light reflects from the microscopic flow lines of a coin. These lines are created on the surface of a coin during the striking process. The interaction between the planchet and the face of the die produces thousands of tiny raised lines on the coin. These flow lines radiate outward from the center of the coin. Variances in planchet quality and preparation, die quality and preparation, and striking pressure can change the patterns and depth of flow lines, which causes the number of different lusters on U.S. coins. These range from the intense flash of a cameo prooflike coin to a subdued, satiny luster.

Average luster implies that the coin has not been overdipped, cleaned, polished or whizzed (mechanically wire-brushed), and that the luster is essentially the same as when the coin was struck. Dull or heavy toning that impairs the reflectivity of a coin's surfaces reduces the noticeability of luster to below average. Above average to exceptional luster typifies the type of coin that stands out from all others. Knowledge of specific characteristics for individual issues is required to recognize exceptional luster, which varies from issue to issue.

COLOR - Color is a combination of the natural hue of the struck metal and toning or patina. On copper coins, color often determines value for MS-65 and higher classifications; "original mint red" is most highly desired. For nickel, silver and gold coins, especially fresh, original color would be above average, as would attractive iridescent toning. Anything dull or artificial would be below average. Luster and color are closely related for most coins because exceptional color will enhance average luster, while poor color will visibly detract from good luster.

DETRACTING MARKS - This classification encompasses everything that happens to a coin during normal handling, from the moment it is struck to the point when it is removed from the bag and wrapped for use by a bank. This includes contact marks, nicks, scratches and surface abrasions. Manufacturing defects do not usually alter the grade of a coin, but may affect the value and should be mentioned in any description.

CLEANING-MISHANDLING - This refers to numismatic abuse, such as hairlines or damage from abrasive cleaning, polishing or acid, spotting and staining from improper storage, tooled surfaces, repairs, slide marks and scratches from holders, and "cabinet friction".

EYE APPEAL - Basically a combination of all the previous factors, eye appeal refers to the visual attractiveness of a coin.

Since each of these factors is subjective in nature, vague limits must be set on each as it relates to a specific grade. A novice grader should start by grading all coins using the same basic standards. Once a beginner feels comfortable with these, the individual traits and characteristics of specific coins can then be incorporated. The ultimate grader would be familiar with the various lusters, striking problems and states of preservation of every coin ever struck. Most grading experts are specialists in one particular series of coins, and only attain their expertise after years of study.

The following basic standards are commonly used to determine Mint State grades:

Mint State 67: exceptional luster and color; virtually no detracting marks; no signs of mishandling; exceptional eye appeal.

Mint State 65: average to above average luster and color; light marks; no signs of mishandling; good eye appeal.

Mint State 63: below average to above average luster and color; some noticeable marks; minor mishandling; below average to average eye appeal.

Mint State 60: below average to average luster and color; numerous noticeable marks; obvious mishandling; below average eye appeal.

These guidelines are very basic and will not neatly classify every Mint State coin, so they must be interpreted to fit the specific example. Additionally, there is no mathematical formula that can be used to evaluate a given coin. No matter how exceptional the luster and color may be on a coin, if it is covered with contact marks it will grade no higher than MS-60. In the same way, if a coin is absolutely mark-free but the luster has been seriously impaired by repeated dippings, it may only grade MS-60.

Having set the basic parameters, it is now necessary to define each grading factor in detail.

Luster is perhaps the single most important grading factor for Mint State coins. When assigning a grade to a Mint State coin, the first thing to check is the fullness and originality of the luster. The ability to recognize natural versus impaired luster should be the most important goal for any grader. Without this knowledge, grading accuracy will never be attained.

Unfortunately, learning about luster is also the most difficult task a novice grader faces. Thousands of Mint State coins must be carefully inspected just to begin to acquire a "feel" for the various types of lusters one will encounter. One of the best ways to start is by attending a major coin show and spending several days looking at coins. A knowledgeable dealer can be a great help, if for nothing else than identifying your mistakes. Remember that all coin dealers are in business and will be much more willing to help if you are a customer.

Another method is to experiment with low value Mint State material from original rolls. A copper enthusiast could pick up a Mint State roll of 1958 Lincoln cents quite inexpensively, and even a roll of Mint State 1964 quarters or halves is not prohibitive in cost. A handful of coins from these rolls can then be dipped, cleaned, thumbed, and carried loose in a pocket for a week or so. By comparing the abused coins to untouched coins that have been set aside, the novice will become better acquainted with natural, unimpaired luster.

The best way to inspect a coin for luster is to slowly rotate the piece at several angles under an incandescent light, checking for breaks in the "cartwheel effect". This effect will appear as a band of light across the face of the coin, changing as the coin is rotated. With a little practice this band of light can be made to spin around the coin like the spokes of a wheel. It is best to start with a larger coin, such as a half dollar or dollar, if you are inexperienced with the "cartwheel effect".

A coin with impaired luster will often exhibit a shiny or glossy luster which is usually very uniform on both fields and devices. Heavily impaired pieces will show dull gray or brown areas in the fields. A coin with full original luster typically exhibits good contrast between the fields and devices, and the luster will show no dull areas or breaks.

Luster directly relates to the various Mint State classifications. For a coin to qualify as an MS-65 or higher grade, it *must* have full, original, unimpaired luster. A Mint State 63 example is allowed to have slight luster impairments. Any coin that has serious luster impairments, where there are obvious disruptions in the original surfaces of the coin, can grade no higher than Mint State 60. Typically a coin like this has been repeatedly dipped in a chemical solution, abrasively cleaned, or damaged in a similar fashion.

Color is an especially subjective factor with Mint State coins. High grade copper coins are most highly sought after when they possess "original mint red" color. Unfortunately, original color on U.S. copper coinage varies widely from issue to issue. Olive-red, brick-red, deep orange, bronze, reddish-gold and reddish-steel hues all exist on original Mint State copper coins. An individual interested in Mint State U.S. copper coinage has a great deal to learn. As with luster, original color is extremely difficult to precisely reproduce photographically. One must learn these areas from the coins themselves.

The main difficulty with copper-nickel and silver coins is determining natural from artificial toning. If the toning on a copper-nickel or silver coin is natural and original, its attractiveness is strictly up to the individual. Exceptions to this rule would be heavy, dark toning that obscures the luster of a coin, heavy spotting or streaking, or any other type of toning that impairs the reflectivity of the coin's surfaces.

When a Mint State coin has been artificially toned, it is usually for a specific reason. The toning could be covering hairlines, excessive contact marks, or impaired luster. Some artificially toned coins have been irreparably damaged by the toning process. Familiarity with all variations of natural toning is the best defense against artificial color. Grading expertise relies more heavily on experience than anything else. However, a novice should not despair over this fact—everyone must begin somewhere.

Color does not directly affect the grade of a Mint State coin. Artificial toning that has damaged the surfaces of the coin will downgrade the piece, but this is due to the damage, not the toning. Color more directly relates to the eye appeal of a given coin, and its desirability by collectors.

Assuming that a Mint State coin possesses full original luster and has not suffered from abusive mishandling, detracting marks are the primary consideration when assigning a grade. Detracting marks are also referred to as contact marks, bag marks, scuffs, nicks, scratches and abrasions. Basically, all these terms refer to the damage a coin receives during manufacturing and shipping. When one pictures the various steps U.S. coins endure during their journey from the mint press to a bank, it is very surprising that any Mint State 65 coins have survived.

After a coin is struck, it falls down a chute and lands in a large hopper, after which hundreds of additional coins fall on top of it. When this hopper is full, the coins are taken to a weighing and inspection room. After inspection they are weighed, counted and dumped into large canvas bags. These bags are shipped to their eventual destination, where they are again counted and wrapped in rolls. During all of these steps little or no effort is made to preserve the quality of the coins. Typically a Mint State coin will exhibit a large number of small nicks and abrasions as a direct result of all the handling it has received.

MS-63   UNCIRCULATED

Detracting marks cannot be easily measured, counted, or otherwise mechanically assessed to arrive at an accurate grade. Too many variables are involved. This is the main reason for the general vagueness of the grading descriptions regarding marks. Additionally, what would be a heavy mark on a Barber dime might be an insignificant blemish on a Peace dollar. The size and weight as well as mint handling and storage of each specific coin must be taken into consideration.

The best way to assess detracting marks is by defining general ranges for the various Mint State grades. Again, keep in mind that these descriptions are for coins that possess full original mint luster, have no traces of wear, and have no signs of collector mishandling. The worst possible coin is covered with heavy contact marks, to the point where the devices are disfigured from the damage. The best possible coin has absolutely perfect surfaces, without even the most microscopic blemishes. These two coins lie at opposite ends of the grading scale, and every other Mint State coin falls in between.

This is where the word descriptions come into play. The majority of all Mint State U.S. coins will grade MS-60. This grade has been referred to as typical for this exact reason. A Mint State 60 coin can have a large number of tiny nicks, a handful of heavy marks, or one giant scratch. In each case the detracting marks on the surface of the coin are immediately noticeable. A person inspecting a Mint State 60 coin cannot help but notice that the coin has been damaged in some way.

The next most frequently encountered grade is Mint State 63. A Mint State 63 coin can have a moderate number of light marks, or one or two heavy marks. Overall the surfaces will be fairly clean and attractive. A "heavy mark" is the type of mark that is immediately visible after a brief inspection. Such a mark usually moves metal away from the source of the mark.

To qualify for the grade Mint State 65, the coin should exhibit only light marks. Both fields and devices should be clean and attractive to the eye. Those areas of the coin that first draw your attention, for example, the cheek on a Morgan dollar or the words "ONE CENT" on an Indian cent, should not exhibit any distracting marks.

Very few U.S. coins qualify for the grade Mint State 67. For all practical purposes business strike coins do not exist in absolutely perfect condition, and MS-67 usually is the highest attainable grade. A Mint State 67 coin can have nothing more than a light scattering of tiny marks. In most cases these marks are hidden in the devices of the coin. At first glance a Mint State 67 coin appears to be perfect, and only after close inspection does one locate the minor blemishes.

Collector mishandling encompasses a wide range of problems. It results in as much damage to numismatic pieces as any other form of abuse. Over the years coins have been cleaned with abrasives, dipped in various acids, treated with chemicals, stored in unstable holders, "thumbed", polished, and "whizzed", usually in a misguided attempt to improve them. Learning to detect these numismatic abuses is not difficult, especially if one is familiar with original versus impaired luster and surfaces.

Abrasively-cleaned coins always exhibit light scratches on the coin's surface which can be detected by angling and rotating the coin under an incandescent light source. These light scratches are typically referred to as hairlines. Heavy patches of hairlines disrupt the luster of a coin, especially if they are located in the fields. Care must be taken not to confuse hairlines with die polish lines, which are tiny *raised* lines on the surface of the coin. Die polish lines are transferred from the face of the die onto the coin during the striking process, and do not affect the grade of a coin unless they are severe enough to affect the coin's eye appeal.

Damage from holders is an accidental rather than intentional form of abuse that is becoming more widespread. Many coins receive hairline scratches and slide marks from the plastic slides used in display albums. Similar damage can occur if coins are stored in oversized hard plastic holders. However, PVC contamination presents the most serious threat. Soft vinyl flips containing polyvinyl chloride have a plasticizer that can break down under certain conditions and deposit an oily-looking film on the surface of the coin. Initially, this film will form green spots or streaks, but after a period of time the film will begin to eat into the surface of the coin, producing a lightly-pitted appearance. Copper and copper-nickel coins seem to be the most susceptible to PVC contamination.

Cleaned, dipped, treated, and polished coins can usually be detected by surface hairlines and luster disruptions. If detecting any of these problems is difficult, a little experimentation with some low value pieces can be very helpful.

Whizzing is not the epidemic that it once was, but it is still a major problem. A whizzed coin has been mechanically wire-brushed, usually to simulate original mint luster on a circulated coin or to conceal alterations, tooling or repairs. The luster of a whizzed coin is very unnatural, often giving off an intense, almost electric glow. Under magnification the surfaces will appear to be lightly pitted or microscopically porous, or marks from the wire brush may appear as curved, parallel lines.

The most important diagnostic is the build-up of metal on the coin's raised devices. As the wire brush moves across the surface of the coin, a microscopic layer of metal is liquified by the heat produced by friction. The metal is pushed along in front of the brush until a raised device is encountered, upon which a ridge of metal is deposited.

Thumbing is a relatively new method of disguising defects on a coin and "improving" its appearance. Generally, Mint State Morgan dollars with light marks on the cheek are prime targets for thumbing. The unscrupulous practitioner gently rubs or smears the cheek area of the coin with his thumb. The surface oils on the thumb, combined with the slight friction applied, will dull the light surface marks and create an unnatural frost over the area. This process can also be employed with a powder or chemical that frosts or clouds the surfaces of the coin.

Coin mishandling affects the grade of a Mint State coin the same way as detracting marks. Generally a coin with noticeable mishandling will grade Mint State 60. If the damage is minor, a coin can still qualify for the Mint State 63 classification. However, to make Mint State 65 the mishandling would have to be so insignificant, it would be practically invisible. Coins that have been mishandled are best described as "problem pieces" and are valued much lower than coins without such marks.

The last grading factor to be discussed is eye appeal, which is unquestionably the most subjective area in grading. No two individuals will ever agree precisely on what makes one coin more attractive and pleasing to the eye than another. A general definition of eye appeal is "the immediate impression a coin makes upon the viewer when it is casually inspected for the first time". Coins with good eye appeal will stand out in a group of coins that are in similar condition. A coin with exceptional eye appeal will immediately capture virtually everyone's attention. Such a coin will have one or more of the following characteristics:

- especially attractive original toning
- noticeable cameo contrast between the fields and the devices, whether prooflike or not
- "knock-out" luster for the issue
- a fresh, original look (as if the coin was minted just last week)

The overall eye appeal of a coin often has an influence on the grade, and almost always has a direct bearing on its commercial value. This is the most subjective factor in coin appreciation, and the reason why some coins with the same numerical grade are priced differently, or why some coins in a lower grade of, say AU-58, may be considered more valuable than a similar piece in a higher uncirculated grade of say, MS-62.

Few coins ever correspond exactly to the criteria given in book standards, or contain all of the blemishes described for each designation. The overall eye appeal, while subjective, is a consideration of both superior and inferior qualities from all catagories, and may raise or lower the value of a borderline coin. In no case can a coin be graded higher than shown for the lowest applicable description in any single category, but it may be valued higher on the basis of superior qualities.

Coins exhibiting any of the following detracting features are usually priced at or below the level indicated, and are evaluated on the basis of severity of the blemish.

Adjustment marks	–	66 and lower
Planchet defects	–	65 and lower
Striking defects	–	64 and lower
Unattractive toning	–	64 and lower
Carbon streaks	–	64 and lower
Fingermarks	–	63 and lower
PVC (Vinyl) damage	–	63 and lower
Black spots	–	63 and lower
Artificial treatment	–	63 and lower
Slide marks (rub)	–	63 and lower
Overdipping (washed out)	–	62 and lower
Cleaning marks	–	62 and lower
Corrosion spots	–	62 and lower
Wear	–	58 and lower
Whizzing	–	50 and lower

HALF CENTS—1793

MINT STATE   *Absolutely no trace of wear.*

MS-70   UNCIRCULATED
A flawless coin exactly as it was minted, with no trace of wear or injury. Must have full mint luster and natural color. Any unusual die or planchet traits must be described.

MS-67   UNCIRCULATED
Virtually flawless but with very minor imperfections.

MS-65   UNCIRCULATED
No trace of wear; nearly as perfect as MS-67 except for some small blemish. Has full mint luster but may be unevenly toned or lightly fingermarked. A few barely noticeable nicks or marks may be present.

MS-63   UNCIRCULATED
A mint state coin with attractive mint luster, but noticeable detracting contact marks or minor blemishes.

MS-60   UNCIRCULATED
A strictly Uncirculated coin with no trace of wear, but with blemishes more obvious than for MS-63. May lack full mint luster; color is usually an even light brown.

ABOUT UNCIRCULATED   *Small trace of wear visible on highest points.*

AU-58   *Very Choice*

Has Some signs of abrasion: hair above forehead, ear; edge of ribbon on wreath, leaves above H in HALF.

AU-55   *Choice*
OBVERSE: Hair shows trace of wear on forehead and to right of the ear.
REVERSE: Leaves above H in HALF show trace of wear.
    Considerable mint luster still present.

AU-50   *Typical*
OBVERSE: Traces of wear at forehead, ear, and on the highest point of the shoulder.
REVERSE: Leaves above H show slight wear on the edges and ribs.
    Surface is still somewhat lustrous.

EXTREMELY FINE *Very light wear on only the highest points.*

EF-45 *Choice*
OBVERSE: Hair well detailed. Wear shows at forehead, to right of ear, and on parts of the shoulder.
REVERSE: Slight wear on most of the leaves and on the bow knot.

EF-40 *Typical*
OBVERSE: Wear extends from forehead to right of ear, and along the high ridge of the shoulder.
REVERSE: Slight wear on most of the leaves and high parts of the bow.

VERY FINE *Light to moderate even wear. All major features are sharp.*

VF-30 *Choice*
OBVERSE: Hair ribbon is distinct. Hair is worn from forehead to ear but shows some details. Slight flatness on shoulder.
REVERSE: Leaves worn nearly flat but still show one-quarter detail. Knot of bow worn but visible.

VF-20 *Typical*
OBVERSE: Parts of hair worn from top of head to upper neck but some details show. Balance of hair and ribbon distinct. Shoulder is quite flat.
REVERSE: Leaves are worn flat and show very few details. Knot of bow is well worn.

FINE *Moderate to heavy even wear. Entire design clear and bold.*

F-12 OBVERSE: Two-thirds of hair worn from top of head to bottom of neck, but will still show one-half detail. Flowing ends of hair are separated. Hair ribbon and shoulder worn almost smooth. Legend and date worn but clear.
REVERSE: Leaves and bow heavily worn but edges still show. Legend is worn but clear.

VERY GOOD *Well worn. Design clear but flat and lacking details.*

VG-8 OBVERSE: Only the hair ends show detail. Shoulder and ribbon worn smooth. The eye shows clearly. Legend and date are readable.

REVERSE: Only the outline of the leaves and bow show. Legend is complete but some letters may be very weak.

GOOD *Heavily worn. Design and legend visible but faint in spots.*

G-4 OBVERSE: The hair and cap show no detail. Parts of the eye show, but hair ribbon and shoulder are worn smooth. Legend weak but visible.

REVERSE: Half of the letters in the legend are visible.

ABOUT GOOD *Outlined design. Parts of date and legend worn smooth.*

AG-3 OBVERSE: Head is outlined with all details worn away. Legend and date very weak but readable.

REVERSE: Entire design is partially worn away. Only a few of the letters in the legend are readable.

Note: These coins usually show the denomination HALF CENT weakly struck. Well struck specimens are very scarce. No MS-70 example of most pre-20th century coins are known to exist.

HALF CENTS—1794–1797

MINT STATE   *Absolutely no trace of wear.*

MS-70   UNCIRCULATED
A flawless coin exactly as it was minted, with no trace of wear or injury. Must have full mint luster and natural color. Any unusual die or planchet traits must be described.

MS-67   UNCIRCULATED
Virtually flawless but with very minor imperfections.

MS-65   UNCIRCULATED
No trace of wear; nearly as perfect as MS-67 except for some small blemish. Has full mint luster but may be unevenly toned or lightly fingermarked. A few barely noticeable nicks or marks may be present.

MS-63   UNCIRCULATED
A mint state coin with attractive mint luster, but noticeable detracting contact marks or minor blemishes.

MS-60   UNCIRCULATED
A strictly Uncirculated coin with no trace of wear, but with blemishes more obvious than for MS-63. May lack full mint luster; color is usually an even light brown.

ABOUT UNCIRCULATED   *Small trace of wear visible on highest points.*

AU-58   *Very Choice*

Has some signs of abrasion: hair at forehead, ear; edge of ribbon on wreath, leaves above and beside H in HALF.

AU-55   *Choice*
OBVERSE: Hair shows trace of wear at forehead.
REVERSE: Leaves above and beside H in HALF, bow knot and loose ends of ribbon, show trace of wear.
Considerable mint luster still present.

AU-50   *Typical*
OBVERSE: Traces of wear at forehead, above the ear, and on the highest point of the shoulder.

REVERSE: Leaves above and beside H show slight wear on the edges and ribs. Bow knot and ribbon ends show slight wear.

Surface is still somewhat lustrous.

EXTREMELY FINE   *Very light wear on only the highest points.*

EF-45   *Choice*
OBVERSE: Hair well detailed. Wear shows at forehead, above the ear, and on highest part of the shoulder.
REVERSE: Slight wear shows on most of the leaves and on the bow and ribbon ends.

EF-40   *Typical*
OBVERSE: Wear extends from forehead to ear, and along the high ridge of the shoulder.
REVERSE: Slight wear evident on most of the leaves and high parts of the bow. Upper part of ribbon nearly flat.

VERY FINE   *Light to moderate even wear. All major features are sharp.*

VF-30   *Choice*
OBVERSE: Many hair lines still distinct. Hair is worn nearly flat from forehead to ear but shows some details. There is slight flatness on shoulder.
REVERSE: Leaves worn nearly flat but still show one-quarter detail. Knot of bow worn but visible.

VF-20   *Typical*
OBVERSE: Parts of hair worn from top of head to upper neck but some details show. Balance of hair distinct. Shoulder is quite flat.
REVERSE: Leaves are worn flat and show very few details. Knot of bow is well worn.

FINE   *Moderate to heavy even wear. Entire design clear and bold.*

F-12   OBVERSE: Two-thirds of hair worn from top of head to bottom of neck, but will still show some detail. Flowing ends of hair are separated. Shoulder worn almost smooth. Legend and date worn but clear.

REVERSE: Leaves and bow heavily worn but edges still show. Legend is worn but clear.

VERY GOOD   *Well worn. Design clear but flat and lacking details.*

VG-8   OBVERSE: Only the hair ends show detail. Shoulder is worn smooth. The eye shows clearly. Legend and date are readable.

REVERSE: Only the outline of leaves and bow show. Legend is complete but some letters may be very weak.

GOOD   *Heavily worn. Design and legend visible but faint in spots.*

G-4   OBVERSE: The hair and cap show no detail. Parts of the eye show, but shoulder is worn smooth. Legend weak but visible.

REVERSE: Half of the letters in legend are visible.

HALF CENTS—1794–1797

ABOUT GOOD   *Outlined design. Parts of date and legend worn smooth.*

AG-3   OBVERSE: Head is outlined with all details worn away. Legend and date partially worn away but readable.

REVERSE: Entire design is partially worn away. Only a few letters in the legend are readable.

Note: Coins of this design were often made from worn or broken dies, and on poor quality planchets. Well struck specimens are scarce. The characteristic traits listed here to assist in grading must not be confused with actual wear.

1794 Gilbert 1   High relief head always appears worn at central obverse. Weaker on reverse than on obverse.

1794 G-2   High relief head always appears worn at central obverse.

1794 G-3   High relief head always appears worn at central obverse. Weaker on reverse than on obverse.

1794 G-5   Parts of hair are weakly struck.

1794 G-6   Parts of hair are weakly struck.

1794 G-7   Parts of hair are weakly struck.

1794 G-8   Parts of hair are weakly struck.

1794 G-9   (Pointed 9)   Normally dark.

1795 G-3   Weak at AME.

1795 G-4   Weak on upper central reverse because of die break.

1795 G-6   Often defective, showing cracks, lamination, porosity.

1795 G-8   Weak at AME.

1797 G-1   Sometimes overstruck on another coin; otherwise often porous and unevenly struck. Sometimes on small planchet.

1797 G-2   Weaker on reverse than on obverse and sometimes on small planchet.

REFERENCES

Gilbert, Ebenezer, *United States Half Cents.* New York, 1916.

Cohen, Roger, S., Jr., *American Half Cents—The "Little Half Sisters."* 1982.

Breen, Walter, *Walter Breen's Encyclopedia of United States Half Cents 1793–1857.* South Gate, Calif., 1983.

HALF CENTS—1800–1808

A modified reverse design was introduced during 1802 and used through 1808.

MINT STATE *Absolutely no trace of wear.*

MS-70 UNCIRCULATED
A flawless coin exactly as it was minted, with no trace of wear or injury. Must have full mint luster and natural color. Any unusual die or planchet traits must be described.

MS-67 UNCIRCULATED
Virtually flawless but with very minor imperfections.

MS-65 UNCIRCULATED
No trace of wear; nearly as perfect as MS-67 except for some small blemish. Has full mint luster but may be unevenly toned or lightly fingermarked. A few barely noticeable nicks or marks may be present.

MS-63 UNCIRCULATED
A mint state coin with attractive mint luster, but noticeable detracting contact marks or minor blemishes.

MS-60 UNCIRCULATED
A strictly Uncirculated coin with no trace of wear, but with blemishes more obvious than for MS-63. May lack full mint luster; color is usually an even light brown.

ABOUT UNCIRCULATED *Small trace of wear visible on highest points.*

AU-58 *Very Choice*
Has some signs of abrasion: hair at forehead, ear; edge of ribbon on wreath, leaves above and beside HALF.

AU-55 *Choice*
OBVERSE: There is a trace of wear on hair at forehead and to left of the ear.
REVERSE: Leaves, bow knot and ribbon show trace of wear.
Considerable mint luster still present.

HALF CENTS—1800-1808

AU-50 *Typical*

OBVERSE: Traces of wear show on hair at forehead, the ear, and on the highest points of the shoulder.

REVERSE: Leaves, bow knot and ribbon show slight wear on the edges and ribs.

Surface is still somewhat lustrous.

EXTREMELY FINE *Very light wear on only the highest points.*

EF-45 *Choice*

OBVERSE: Hair well detailed. Wear shows on hair at forehead, to left of ear, and above the shoulder.

REVERSE: Slight wear on most of the leaves and on the bow knot and ribbon.

EF-40 *Typical*

OBVERSE: Wear extends on hair from forehead to left of ear, at back of head, and along the high ridge near the shoulder.

REVERSE: Slight wear evident on most of the leaves and high points of bow and ribbon.

VERY FINE *Light to moderate even wear. All major features are sharp.*

VF-30 *Choice*

OBVERSE: Hair is worn from forehead to drapery but shows some details. There is slight flatness on shoulder.

REVERSE: Leaves worn nearly flat but still show some detail. Knot of bow worn but sharp.

VF-20 *Typical*

OBVERSE: Parts of hair worn from top of head to drapery but some details show. Balance of hair left of eye distinct. Folds in drapery show wear.

REVERSE: Leaves are worn flat and show very few details. Bow is well worn but bold.

FINE   *Moderate to heavy even wear. Entire design clear and bold.*

F-12   OBVERSE: Hair worn from top of head to drapery, but will still show some detail. Hair above forehead worn almost smooth. Legend and date worn but clear. Some details remain in drapery.

REVERSE: Leaves and bow heavily worn but edges still show. Leaves below CENT still have some visible details. Legend is worn but clear.

VERY GOOD   *Well worn. Design clear but flat and lacking details.*

VG-8   OBVERSE: Only the hair ends show detail. Shoulder and drapery worn smooth. The eye shows clearly. Legend and date are readable.

REVERSE: Only the outline of leaves and bow show. Legend is complete but some letters may be weak.

GOOD   *Heavily worn. Design and legend visible but faint in spots.*

G-4   OBVERSE: The hair shows no detail. Parts of eye show, but drapery and shoulder are worn smooth. Legend weak but readable.

REVERSE: Leaves complete but well worn. Bow knot and ribbon well outlined. Tops of some letters worn flat.

ABOUT GOOD   *Outlined design. Parts of date and legend worn smooth.*

AG-3   OBVERSE: Head is outlined with all details worn away. Legend and date very weak but mostly visible.

REVERSE: Entire design is partially worn away. Only half of the letters in legend are readable.

Note: Coins of this design were often made from worn dies. Well struck specimens are extremely scarce. The characteristic traits listed here to assist in grading must not be confused with actual wear.

1802 is usually dark and defective.

1802, first reverse, is weakly struck on reverse.

1804, plain 4 stemless wreath, is often weak at the borders.

1805, small 5 with stems, is weak on the reverse opposite the obverse bulge.

1806, large 6, is often weak at top of reverse.

1807 is usually weak at borders with no obverse dentils showing. Hair is often weakly struck.

HALF CENTS—1809–1836

MINT STATE *Absolutely no trace of wear.*

MS-70 UNCIRCULATED
A flawless coin exactly as it was minted, with no trace of wear or injury. Must have full mint luster and natural color. Any unusual die or planchet traits must be described.

MS-67 UNCIRCULATED
Virtually flawless but with very minor imperfections.

MS-65 UNCIRCULATED
No trace of wear; nearly as perfect as MS-67 except for some small blemish. Has full mint luster but may be unevenly toned or lightly fingermarked. A few barely noticeable nicks or marks may be present.

MS-63 UNCIRCULATED
A mint state coin with attractive mint luster, but noticeable detracting contact marks or minor blemishes.

MS-60 UNCIRCULATED
A strictly Uncirculated coin with no trace of wear, but with blemishes more obvious than for MS-63. May lack full mint luster; color is usually an even light brown.

ABOUT UNCIRCULATED *Small trace of wear visible on highest points.*

AU-58 *Very Choice*

Has some signs of abrasion: hair adjacent to LIBERTY; edge of ribbon and bow, leaves above H and LF in HALF.

AU-55 *Choice*

OBVERSE: Hair shows trace of wear above and below center letters of LIBERTY.

REVERSE: Leaves above H in HALF, and the bow, show trace of wear. Considerable mint luster still present.

AU-50 *Typical*

OBVERSE: There are traces of wear in hair adjacent to LIBERTY, and on the highest point above the shoulder.

REVERSE: Slight wear shows on bow and edges of leaves near H and LF. Surface is still somewhat lustrous.

[46]

EXTREMELY FINE *Very light wear on only the highest points.*

EF-45 *Choice*

OBVERSE: Hair well detailed. Wear shows above and below LIBER, and on parts of the head above RTY. Stars are sharp.

REVERSE: Slight wear on high points of leaves and ribs above H. Bow and ribbon are slightly worn.

EF-40 *Typical*

OBVERSE: Wear shows above LIBER and to the right of eye below those letters. Some wear shows on curls at back of head.

REVERSE: Slight wear on most of the leaves and high parts of ribs above H, bow and ribbon ends.

VERY FINE *Light to moderate even wear. All major features are sharp.*

VF-30 *Choice*

OBVERSE: Hair ribbon is distinct. Hair is worn from back of head to temples but shows many details. Slight flatness shows in curls on shoulder. LIBER-TY is strong, stars have full detail.

REVERSE: Leaves worn nearly flat but still show some detail. Bow and ribbon ends worn but clear.

VF-20 *Typical*

OBVERSE: Parts of hair worn from top of head to shoulder but some details show. Balance of hair and ribbon distinct. Curls on shoulder are quite flat. LIBERTY is clear. Star details are weak.

REVERSE: Leaves are worn flat and show very few details. Bow is well worn.

FINE *Moderate to heavy even wear. Entire design clear and bold.*

F-12 OBVERSE: Hair worn from top of head to bottom of neck, but will still show some detail. Hair ribbon and LIBERTY worn but readable. Stars have no central detail.

REVERSE: Leaves and bow heavily worn but edges still show some detail. Legend is worn but clear.

VERY GOOD   *Well worn. Design clear but flat and lacking details.*

VG-8   OBVERSE: Hair ends and parts near eye show some detail. LIBERTY is readable. The eye and ear are visible. Rim, stars and date are clear.

REVERSE: Only the outline of leaves and bow show. Legend is complete but some letters may be very weak.

GOOD   *Heavily worn. Design and legend visible but faint in spots.*

G-4   OBVERSE: Hair shows no detail. Parts of LIBERTY show, but ear, eye and rim are worn smooth. Stars weak but visible.

REVERSE: Half of letters in the legend are visible. Wreath is worn smooth with bow and ribbon outlined.

ABOUT GOOD   *Outlined design. Parts of date and legend worn smooth.*

AG-3   OBVERSE: Head is outlined with all details worn away. Date very weak but readable. LIBERTY and stars only partially visible.

REVERSE: Entire design and rim is partially worn away. Only a few letters in the legend are readable.

Note: 1828, 12 stars, normally shows weak spots on parts of hair and leaves. Proof specimens often do not have the usual sharp square borders.

MINT STATE   *Absolutely no trace of wear.*

MS-70   UNCIRCULATED
A flawless coin exactly as it was minted, with no trace of wear or injury. Must have full mint luster and natural color. Any unusual die or planchet traits must be described.

MS-67   UNCIRCULATED
Virtually flawless but with very minor imperfections.

MS-65   UNCIRCULATED
No trace of wear; nearly as perfect as MS-67 except for some small blemish. Has full mint luster but may be unevenly toned or lightly fingermarked. A few barely noticeable nicks or marks may be present.

MS-63   UNCIRCULATED
A mint state coin with attractive mint luster, but noticeable detracting contact marks or minor blemishes.

MS-60   UNCIRCULATED
A strictly Uncirculated coin with no trace of wear, but with blemishes more obvious than for MS-63. May lack full mint luster; color is usually an even light brown.

ABOUT UNCIRCULATED   *Small trace of wear visible on highest points*

AU-58   *Very Choice*
Has some signs of abrasion: hair above ear; bow of ribbon on wreath, leaves beside HALF.

AU-55   *Choice*
OBVERSE: Hair shows trace of wear above and to the right of the ear.
REVERSE: Leaves beside HALF show trace of wear.
   Considerable mint luster still present.

AU-50   *Typical*
OBVERSE: Traces of wear near ear, and on high points of curls, neck and below bust.

REVERSE: Leaves beside H and F show slight wear on the edges and ribs. There is a trace of wear on bow.
   Surface is still somewhat lustrous.

EXTREMELY FINE *Very light wear on only the highest points.*

EF-45 *Choice*

OBVERSE: Hair well detailed. Wear shows above ear, on parts of the curls, neck and below bust.

REVERSE: Slight wear on most of the leaves and on bow.

EF-40 *Typical*

OBVERSE: Wear above and to right of ear, at tip of coronet, and along the high curls on the shoulder.

REVERSE: Slight wear shows on most of the leaves and high parts of bow.

VERY FINE *Light to moderate even wear. All major features are sharp.*

VF-30 *Choice*

OBVERSE: Hair to right of ear is weak. Curl below bust is worn, and tip of coronet shows wear.

REVERSE: Leaves worn nearly flat but still show some detail. High point of bow worn but visible.

VF-20 *Typical*

OBVERSE: Parts of hair worn from top of head to upper neck but some details show. Balance of hair and coronet distinct. Shoulder curls are quite flat.

REVERSE: Leaves are worn flat and show only partial details. Part of bow is well worn.

FINE *Moderate to heavy even wear. Entire design clear and bold.*

F-12 OBVERSE: Hair worn from top of head to bottom of neck, but will still show some detail. Coronet shows wear along upper edge. Beads on hair cord sharp and LIBERTY bold. Stars and date worn but sharp.

HALF CENTS—1840–1857

REVERSE: Leaves and bow heavily worn but edges and a few details still show. Legend is worn but bold.

VERY GOOD   *Well worn. Design clear but flat and lacking details.*

VG-8   OBVERSE: Hair shows detail only in spots, mostly around the bun. The coronet is outlined and hair cord shows clearly. LIBERTY is worn but complete.

REVERSE: Only a bold outline of the leaves and bow show. Legend is complete but some letters may be weak.

GOOD   *Heavily worn. Design and legend visible but faint in spots.*

G-4   OBVERSE: Hair and bun show very few details. Parts of LIBERTY, the coronet, and the eye show. Hair cord still has some visible beads.

REVERSE: Most letters in the legend are visible.

ABOUT GOOD   *Outlined design. Parts of date and legend worn smooth.*

AG-3   OBVERSE: Head is outlined with nearly all details worn away. Stars and date very weak but visible.

REVERSE: Entire design is partially worn away. Only half of letters in the legend are readable.

Note: Proof restrikes of these coins sometimes have a weakness in the center of the reverse because of die failure or improper striking.

REFERENCES

Gilbert, Ebenezer, *United States Half Cents.* New York, 1916.

Cohen, Roger, S. Jr., *American Half Cents-The "Little Half Sisters." 1982.*

Breen, Walter, *Walter Breen's Encyclopedia of United States Half Cents 1793–1857.* South Gate, Calif., 1983.

LARGE CENTS—1793 CHAIN

MINT STATE   *Absolutely no trace of wear.*

MS-70   UNCIRCULATED
A flawless coin exactly as it was minted, with no trace of wear or injury. Must have full mint luster and natural color. Any unusual die or planchet traits must be described.

MS-67   UNCIRCULATED
Virtually flawless but with very minor imperfections.

MS-65   UNCIRCULATED
No trace of wear; nearly as perfect as MS-67 except for some small blemish. Has full mint luster but may be unevenly toned or lightly fingermarked. A few barely noticeable nicks or marks may be present.

MS-63   UNCIRCULATED
A mint state coin with attractive mint luster, but noticeable detracting contact marks or minor blemishes.

MS-60   UNCIRCULATED
A strictly Uncirculated coin with no trace of wear, but with blemishes more obvious than for MS-63. May lack full mint luster; color is usually an even light brown.

ABOUT UNCIRCULATED   *Small trace of wear visible on highest points.*

AU-58   *Very Choice*

Has some signs of abrasion: high points of hair near face; high points of links in chain.

AU-55   *Choice*
OBVERSE: Hair shows trace of wear from jawline to forehead.
REVERSE: High points of links in chain show trace of wear.
   Considerable mint luster still present.

AU-50   *Typical*
OBVERSE: Traces of wear from jawline to forehead on the highest points.

REVERSE: Chain links show slight wear on the edges and high spots.
   Surface is still somewhat lustrous. Minor blemishes detract from quality of surface.

LARGE CENTS—1793 CHAIN

EXTREMELY FINE   *Very light wear on only the highest points.*

EF-45   *Choice*
OBVERSE: Hair well detailed. Wear shows at back of temple.
REVERSE: There is slight wear on most of the links.

EF-40   *Typical*
OBVERSE: Wear extends from forehead to below ear, and along the high ridge of the shoulder.
REVERSE: Slight wear shows on most of the links.
Minor blemishes detract from surface quality.

VERY FINE   *Light to moderate even wear. All major features are sharp.*

VF-30   *Choice*
OBVERSE: Hair details are distinct but worn from forehead to below ear. Slight flatness on shoulder. The ear is visible.
REVERSE: Chain and legend are worn but sharp.

VF-20   *Typical*
OBVERSE: Parts of hair worn from top of head to upper neck but most details show. Hair closest to head and neck is quite flat. The ear is visible.
REVERSE: Chain and legend are worn but bold.

FINE   *Moderate to heavy even wear. Entire design clear and bold.*

F-12   OBVERSE: Hair worn from top of head to below neck, but will still show about half of detail. Flowing ends of hair are separated. Ear worn almost smooth. Legend and date worn but clear.
REVERSE: Chain and lettering well worn but complete.

[53]

VERY GOOD   *Well worn. Design clear but flat and lacking details.*

VG-8   OBVERSE: Only the hair ends show detail. Ear worn smooth. The eye shows clearly. Legend and date are readable.

REVERSE: Chain is well worn but complete. Legend is complete but some letters may be very weak.

GOOD   *Heavily worn. Design and legend visible but faint in spots.*

G-4   OBVERSE: Hair shows no detail. Parts of the eye show, but ear is worn smooth. Legend and date weak but visible and may merge with the rim.

REVERSE: Chain and letters in legend and denomination are all visible.

ABOUT GOOD   *Outlined design. Parts of date and legend worn smooth.*

AG-3   OBVERSE: Head is barely outlined with all details worn away. Legend and date very weak and only partially readable.

REVERSE: Entire design is partially worn away. Only a few of the letters in legend are readable.

Note: On the variety with legend abbreviated AMERI., the date is usually weak and the reverse is bolder than the obverse.

MINT STATE   *Absolutely no trace of wear.*

MS-70   UNCIRCULATED
A flawless coin exactly as it was minted, with no trace of wear or injury. Must have full mint luster and natural color. Any unusual die or planchet traits must be described.

MS-67   UNCIRCULATED
Virtually flawless but with very minor imperfections.

MS-65   UNCIRCULATED
No trace of wear; nearly as perfect as MS-67 except for some small blemish. Has full mint luster but may be unevenly toned or lightly fingermarked. A few barely noticeable nicks or marks may be present.

MS-63   UNCIRCULATED
A mint state coin with attractive mint luster, but noticeable detracting contact marks or minor blemishes.

MS-60   UNCIRCULATED
A strictly Uncirculated coin with no trace of wear, but with blemishes more obvious than for MS-63. May lack full mint luster; color is usually an even light brown.

ABOUT UNCIRCULATED   *Small trace of wear visible on highest points.*

AU-58   *Very Choice*

Has some signs of abrasion: high points of hair at forehead and left of ear; high points of leaves in wreath.

AU-55   *Choice*
OBVERSE: Hair shows trace of wear at forehead just behind temple.
REVERSE: High points of leaves show trace of wear.
Considerable mint luster still present.

AU-50   *Typical*
OBVERSE: Traces of wear at forehead on the highest points.

REVERSE: Leaves show slight wear on the edges and high spots.
Surface is still somewhat lustrous. Minor blemishes detract from quality of surface.

EXTREMELY FINE *Very light wear on only the highest points.*

EF-45   *Choice*

> OBVERSE: Hair well detailed. Wear shows at temple, behind the ear, and at back of neck.
>
> REVERSE: Slight wear on most of the leaves.

EF-40   *Typical*

> OBVERSE: Wear extends from ear to below bust. The ear is clearly defined.
> REVERSE: Slight wear on most parts of the leaves.
>   Minor blemishes detract from surface quality.

VERY FINE *Light to moderate even wear. All major features are sharp.*

VF-30   *Choice*

> OBVERSE: Hair details are distinct, but worn from forehead to below neck. Approximately three-fourths of hair details will show. The ear is visible.
> REVERSE: Leaves are worn but sharp.

VF-20   *Typical*

> OBVERSE: Parts of hair worn from top of head to below neck; about two-thirds of details show. Hair closest to face is quite flat. The ear is visible.
> REVERSE: Leaves are worn but bold and separated. Beaded border is sharp.

FINE *Moderate to heavy even wear. Entire design clear and bold.*

F-12   OBVERSE: Hair worn from top of head to below neck, but will still show about half of the details at flowing ends. Ear worn almost smooth. Legend and date worn but bold.
> REVERSE: Leaves and border well worn but complete.

LARGE CENTS—1793 WREATH

VERY GOOD   *Well worn. Design clear but flat and lacking details.*

VG-8   OBVERSE: Only the back third of hair ends show detail. Ear worn smooth. Legend and date are clear.

REVERSE: Leaves are well worn but completely outlined. Legend is complete but some letters may be weak. Border partially visible.

GOOD   *Heavily worn. Design and legend visible but faint in spots.*

G-4   OBVERSE: Hair shows no detail. Parts of the eye show, but ear is worn smooth. Legend and date weak but visible and may merge with the rim.

REVERSE: Leaves and letters in the legend are all visible. Only a trace of the border remains.

ABOUT GOOD   *Outlined design. Parts of date and legend worn smooth.*

AG-3   OBVERSE: Head is barely outlined with all details worn away. Legend and date very weak and only partially readable.

REVERSE: Entire design is partially worn away. Only a few of the letters in the legend are readable.

Note: The Sheldon numbers 5 and 7 varieties of this type have weak dates. Defective planchets were often used to make Sheldon number 11.

REFERENCE

Sheldon, Wm. H., *Penny Whimsy (1793–1814)*. New York, 1958.

MINT STATE *Absolutely no trace of wear.*

MS-70 UNCIRCULATED
A flawless coin exactly as it was minted, with no trace of wear or injury. Must have full mint luster and natural color. Any unusual die or planchet traits must be described.

MS-67 UNCIRCULATED
Virtually flawless but with very minor imperfections.

MS-65 UNCIRCULATED
No trace of wear; nearly as perfect as MS-67 except for some small blemish. Has full mint luster but may be unevenly toned or lightly fingermarked. A few barely noticeable nicks or marks may be present.

MS-63 UNCIRCULATED
A mint state coin with attractive mint luster, but noticeable detracting contact marks or minor blemishes.

MS-60 UNCIRCULATED
A strictly Uncirculated coin with no trace of wear, but with blemishes more obvious than for MS-63. May lack full mint luster; color is usually an even light brown.

ABOUT UNCIRCULATED *Small trace of wear visible on highest points.*

AU-58 *Very Choice*

Has some signs of abrasion: high points of hair at forehead and above the ear; high points of leaves adjacent to O and C in denomination.

AU-55 *Choice*
OBVERSE: Trace of wear on hair above forehead, and on high points of the shoulder.
REVERSE: High points of leaves above O in ONE show trace of wear.

Considerable mint luster still present.

LARGE CENTS—LIBERTY CAP 1793-1796

AU-50 *Typical*

OBVERSE: Traces of wear evident at forehead and on highest points of the shoulder.

REVERSE: Leaves above O in ONE show slight wear on the edges and high spots.

Surface is still somewhat lustrous. Minor blemishes detract from quality of surface.

EXTREMELY FINE *Very light wear on only the highest points.*

EF-45 *Choice*

OBVERSE: Hair well detailed. Wear shows above forehead, over the ear, and on the shoulder.

REVERSE: There is slight wear on leaves, and almost all of ribbing shows.

EF-40 *Typical*

OBVERSE: Slight wear extends from forehead to ear. The shoulder is worn but clearly defined.

REVERSE: Slight wear on most of the leaves. Three-quarters of leaf ribbing shows.

Minor blemishes detract from surface quality.

VERY FINE *Light to moderate even wear. All major features are sharp.*

VF-30 *Choice*

OBVERSE: Many hair lines still distinct. Hair is worn nearly flat from forehead to ear but shows some details. Slight flatness on shoulder.

REVERSE: Leaves worn nearly flat but still show half of the ribbing. Knot of bow worn but visible.

VF-20 *Typical*

OBVERSE: Parts of hair worn from top of head to upper neck but some details show. Balance of hair distinct. Shoulder is quite flat.

REVERSE: Leaves are worn flat but one-quarter of ribbing shows. Knot of bow is well worn.

FINE *Moderate to heavy even wear. Entire design clear and bold.*

F-12   OBVERSE: Hair worn from top of head to bottom of neck, but back half still shows some detail. Flowing ends of hair are separated. Shoulder worn almost smooth. Legend and date worn but clear.

        REVERSE: Leaves and bow heavily worn but some ribbing still shows. Legend is worn but clear.

VERY GOOD   *Well worn. Design clear but flat and lacking details.*

VG-8   OBVERSE: Only the back third of hair ends show detail. Shoulder is worn smooth. The eye shows clearly. Legend and date are readable.

        REVERSE: Only the outline of the leaves and bow show. Legend is complete but some letters may be very weak.

GOOD   *Heavily worn. Design and legend visible but faint in spots.*

G-4   OBVERSE: Hair and cap show no detail. Parts of the eye show, but shoulder is worn smooth. Legend weak but visible.

        REVERSE: Letters in the legend are barely visible.

LARGE CENTS—LIBERTY CAP 1793–1796

ABOUT GOOD   *Outlined design. Parts of date and legend worn smooth.*

AG-3   OBVERSE: Head is outlined with all details worn away. Legend and date partially worn away but readable.

REVERSE: Entire design is partially worn away. Only a few letters in the legend are readable.

Note: Coins of this design were often made from worn or broken dies, and on poor quality planchets. The characteristic traits listed here to assist in grading must not be confused with actual wear.

1793 Sheldon 12 and 15 often have defective streaky planchets with reverse uneven at center.

1793 S-14	Usually has a weak date.
1794 S-17	Streaky defective planchet.
1794 S-22	Reverse is weak at the rim.
1794 S-24	Top of the hair is flat.
1794 S-32	Unevenly struck.
1794 S-38	Planchet is usually rough.
1794 S-42	Reverse is weak at upper right.
1794 S-50	Reverse is weak at the rim.
1794 S-54	Reverse is weak at the rim.
1794 S-57	Obverse is extremely weak.
1794 S-64	Reverse uneven in center.
1794 S-65	Top of the hair is flat. Obverse is off-center to upper right.
1795 S-77	Reverse uneven because of defective die.
1796 (all)	The obverses are usually stronger than the reverses.
1796 S-87	The 96 fades because of defective die.

REFERENCE

Sheldon, Wm. H., *Penny Whimsy (1793–1814)*. New York, 1958.

LARGE CENTS—DRAPED BUST 1796–1807

MINT STATE *Absolutely no trace of wear.*

MS-70 UNCIRCULATED
A flawless coin exactly as it was minted, with no trace of wear or injury. Must have full mint luster and natural color. Any unusual die or planchet traits must be described.

MS-67 UNCIRCULATED
Virtually flawless but with very minor imperfections.

MS-65 UNCIRCULATED
No trace of wear; nearly as perfect as MS-67 except for some small blemish. Has full mint luster but may be unevenly toned or lightly fingermarked. A few minute nicks or marks may be present.

MS-63 UNCIRCULATED
A mint state coin with attractive mint luster, but noticeable detracting contact marks or minor blemishes.

MS-60 UNCIRCULATED
A strictly Uncirculated coin with no trace of wear, but with blemishes more obvious than for MS-63. May lack full mint luster; color is usually an even light brown.

ABOUT UNCIRCULATED *Small trace of wear visible on highest points.*

AU-58 *Very Choice*

Has some signs of abrasion: high points of hair at forehead and above the ear; high points of leaves adjacent to S and second T in STATES.

AU-55 *Choice*
OBVERSE: Trace of wear evident on hair above forehead.
REVERSE: High points of leaves below S and second T in STATES show trace of wear.
Considerable mint luster still present.

LARGE CENTS—DRAPED BUST 1796–1807

AU-50 *Typical*

OBVERSE: Traces of wear show at forehead and on the highest points of drapery.

REVERSE: Leaves below S and second T in STATES show slight wear on edges and high spots.

   Surface is still somewhat lustrous. Minor blemishes detract from quality of surface.

EXTREMELY FINE *Very light wear on only the highest points.*

EF-45 *Choice*

OBVERSE: Hair well detailed. Wear shows above forehead, over the ear, and on the drapery.

REVERSE: There is slight wear on leaves, but almost all of ribbing shows.

EF-40 *Typical*

OBVERSE: Slight wear extends from forehead to ear. Drapery is worn in spots but clearly defined.

REVERSE: Slight wear on most of the leaves. Three-quarters of ribbing shows.

   Minor blemishes detract from surface quality.

VERY FINE *Light to moderate even wear. All major features are sharp.*

VF-30 *Choice*

OBVERSE: Many hair lines still distinct. Hair is worn nearly flat from forehead to eye line but shows some details. Slight flatness shows on bust and drapery at shoulder.

REVERSE: Leaves worn nearly flat but still show half of the ribbing. Knot of bow worn but sharp.

VF-20 *Typical*

OBVERSE: Parts of hair worn from top of head to upper ear but some details show. Balance of hair distinct. Bust and drapery at shoulder are quite flat.

REVERSE: One-third of the ribbing in leaves can be seen. Bow and knot worn but bold.

FINE *Moderate to heavy even wear. Entire design clear and bold.*

F-12 OBVERSE: Hair worn from top of head to bottom of neck, but overall still shows two-thirds of details. Parts of drapery folds are visible.

REVERSE: Leaves and bow well worn but some ribbing still shows. Legend is worn but very clear.

VERY GOOD *Well worn. Design clear but flat and lacking details.*

VG-8 OBVERSE: Only the back third of hair ends show detail. Drapery is worn nearly smooth. Parts of eye and curl on neck show. Legend and date are readable.

REVERSE: Only the outline of leaves and bow show. Legend is complete but some letters may be weak.

GOOD *Heavily worn. Design and legend visible but faint in spots.*

G-4 OBVERSE: Hair and ribbon show no detail. Drapery at shoulder is worn smooth. Legend weak but readable.

REVERSE: Letters in legend are barely visible. Ribbon ends merge with surface.

LARGE CENTS—DRAPED BUST 1796–1807

ABOUT GOOD   *Outlined design. Parts of date and legend worn smooth.*

AG-3   OBVERSE: Head is outlined with all details worn away. Legend and date partially worn away but visible.

REVERSE: Entire wreath is faint but visible. Only a few letters in the legend are readable.

Note: Coins of this design were often weakly struck, and made on poor quality planchets. The characteristic traits listed here to assist in grading must not be confused with actual wear.

1796 Sheldon 94, NC-3, S-100, and S-116 are always very weak on the reverse at the rim.
1796 S-94   Planchet is usually rough.
1796 S-102 and S-109   Weakness on the obverse at the rim.
1796 S-113, S-114, and S-115   Reverse is unevenly struck.
1796 S-118 and S-119   Center of bust is weakly struck.
1797 S-121   Central hair is flat.
1797 S-122, NC-2, and NC-3   Planchets are dark and rough.
1797 S-125   Heavy swelling at lower right obverse.
1797 S-132   Date is very weak.
1797 S-133   Entire bust is weak.
1797 S-134   Reverse is uneven and weak at left.
1797 S-136   Reverse is usually very blunt due to an injury.
1797 S-138 and S-140   Heavy swelling on reverse.
1798 S-144, S-145, and S-149   Center of bust is weakly struck.
1798 S-147   Reverse is weak at lower left.
1798 S-150 and S-151   Entire bust is very weakly struck.
1798 S-154 and S-156   Center of bust is weakly struck.
1798 S-177 and S-178   The obverse die is heavily rusted.
1798 S-185   The obverse is weak. The reverse is very sharp.
1799 S-188   Planchets are often dark and rough.
1800 S-191   Reverse is uneven because of die failure.
1800 S-201   Reverse is subject to unevenness because of defective die.
1800 S-203   The face and forelock are usually flatly struck.
1800 S-211   The central obverse is often weak.
1801 S-216   The obverse is very weakly struck.
1801 S-222   The reverse is weak at lower right.
1802 S-225   The reverse leaves are flat.
1802 S-238   Reverse is weak at the left.
1803 S-248   The reverse leaves are not sharp.
1807 S-271   Center of bust is weakly struck.

REFERENCE

Sheldon, Wm. H., *Penny Whimsy (1793–1814).* New York, 1958.

MINT STATE   *Absolutely no trace of wear.*

MS-70   UNCIRCULATED
A flawless coin exactly as it was minted, with no trace of wear or injury. Must have full mint luster and natural color. Any unusual die or planchet traits must be described.

MS-67   UNCIRCULATED
Virtually flawless but with very minor imperfections.

MS-65   UNCIRCULATED
No trace of wear; nearly as perfect as MS-67 except for some small blemish. Has full mint luster but may be unevenly toned or lightly fingermarked. A few barely noticeable nicks or marks may be present.

MS-63   UNCIRCULATED
A mint state coin with attractive mint luster, but noticeable detracting contact marks or minor blemishes.

MS-60   UNCIRCULATED
A strictly Uncirculated coin with no trace of wear, but with blemishes more obvious than for MS-63. May lack full mint luster; color is usually an even light brown.

ABOUT UNCIRCULATED   *Small trace of wear visible on highest points.*

AU-58   *Very Choice*

Has some signs of abrasion: high points of hair at forehead and above the eye; high points of leaves adjacent to O and T in denomination.

AU-55   *Choice*
OBVERSE: Trace of wear on hair above the eye under L.
REVERSE: High points of leaves above O in ONE and adjacent to T in CENT show trace of wear.
Considerable mint luster still present.

AU-50   *Typical*

OBVERSE: Traces of wear show at forehead and above the eye.

REVERSE: Leaves and ribbon show slight wear on the high spots.

Surface is still somewhat lustrous. Minor blemishes detract from quality of surface.

EXTREMELY FINE   *Very light wear on only the highest points.*

EF-45   *Choice*

OBVERSE: Hair well detailed. Wear shows above eye and on curls near the ear.

REVERSE: Slight wear on bow and leaves; almost all of ribbing shows.

EF-40   *Typical*

OBVERSE: Slight wear extends from forehead to below LI. The curls near the ear are worn but clearly defined.

REVERSE: Slight wear on bow and most of the leaves. Three-quarters of ribbing shows in leaves.

Minor blemishes detract from surface quality.

VERY FINE   *Light to moderate even wear. All major features are sharp.*

VF-30   *Choice*

OBVERSE: Hair around ear is worn but distinct. Eyebrow and hair above eye are worn but show many details. Slight flatness in curls on shoulder.

REVERSE: Leaves well worn but still show two-thirds ribbing. Bow and ribbon ends worn but clear.

VF-20   *Typical*

OBVERSE: Parts of hair worn from top of head to shoulder but all major details show. Star details are weak.

REVERSE: Leaves are worn but one-third of ribbing shows. Bow is well worn.

FINE   *Moderate to heavy even wear. Entire design clear and bold.*

F-12   OBVERSE: Hair worn from top of head to bottom of neck, but will still show about two-thirds detail. Stars have no central detail.

REVERSE: Bow and leaves heavily worn but edges still show some ribbing. Legend is worn but clear.

VERY GOOD   *Well worn. Design clear but flat and lacking details.*

VG-8   OBVERSE: Hair ends and curls are smooth but show some detail. LIBERTY is readable. The eye and ear are visible. Stars and date are clear.

REVERSE: Only the outline of the leaves and bow show. Legend is complete but some letters may be very weak.

GOOD   *Heavily worn. Design and legend visible but faint in spots.*

G-4   OBVERSE: Hair shows no detail. LIBERTY is readable but ear, eye and rim are worn smooth. Stars weak but visible.

REVERSE: Letters in legend are well worn but visible. Wreath is worn smooth with bow and ribbon outlined.

ABOUT GOOD *Outlined design. Parts of date and legend worn smooth.*

AG-3   OBVERSE: Head is outlined with all details worn away. Date very weak but readable. LIBERTY and stars only partially visible.

REVERSE: Entire design and rim are partially worn away. Only a few of the letters in the legend are readable.

Note: Coins of this design are usually found with poor detail, and with the tops of letters merged with the rim. Centering is frequently poor. The hair above LIBERTY is usually weakly struck.

   1808   Sheldon 279 has obverse blunted by die injury.

   1809   Sheldon 280 reverse is much sharper than the obverse.

REFERENCE

Sheldon, Wm. H., *Penny Whimsy (1793–1814)*. New York, 1958.

MINT STATE *Absolutely no trace of wear.*

MS-70 UNCIRCULATED
A flawless coin exactly as it was minted, with no trace of wear or injury. Must have full mint luster and natural color. Any unusual die or planchet traits must be described.

MS-67 UNCIRCULATED
Virtually flawless but with very minor imperfections.

MS-65 UNCIRCULATED
No trace of wear; nearly as perfect as MS-67 except for some small blemish. Has full mint luster but may be unevenly toned or lightly fingermarked. A few barely noticeable nicks or marks may be present.

MS-63 UNCIRCULATED
A mint state coin with attractive mint luster, but noticeable detracting contact marks or minor blemishes.

MS-60 UNCIRCULATED
A strictly Uncirculated coin with no trace of wear, but with blemishes more obvious than for MS-63. May lack full mint luster; color is usually an even light brown.

ABOUT UNCIRCULATED *Small trace of wear visible on highest points.*

AU-58 *Very Choice*

Has some signs of abrasion: hair adjacent to LIBERTY; edge of ribbon and bow, leaves above O and E in ONE.

AU-55 *Choice*
OBVERSE: Hair shows trace of wear above the eye.
REVERSE: Leaves above O in ONE, and the bow show trace of wear.
Considerable mint luster still present.

AU-50 *Typical*
OBVERSE: Traces of wear evident in hair above the eye, and on the curl in front of the ear.

REVERSE: Leaves near O and E in ONE, and the bow, show slight wear on the edges.

Surface is still somewhat lustrous.

EXTREMELY FINE *Very light wear on only the highest points.*

EF-45 *Choice*

OBVERSE: Hair well detailed. Wear shows above and below LIBER, on parts of hair above RTY, and on curl in front of ear. Stars are sharp.

REVERSE: Slight wear shows on high points of leaves. The bow and ribbon are slightly rounded.

EF-40 *Typical*

OBVERSE: Wear shows above LIBER and to the right of eye below those letters. Some wear shows on curls at back of head and in front of the ear. Hair cords are sharp.

REVERSE: Slight wear shows on most of the lettering, high parts of leaves, and the bow and ribbon ends.

VERY FINE *Light to moderate even wear. All major features are sharp.*

VF-30 *Choice*

OBVERSE: Hair cord and curl before ear are distinct. High points of hair above coronet are worn but show many details. There is slight flatness in curls on shoulder.

REVERSE: High points of leaves are worn but still show detail. Bow and ribbon ends worn but clear.

VF-20 *Typical*

OBVERSE: High parts of hair worn but show three-quarters detail. Balance of hair and cords are distinct. Curls on shoulder and star details are weak.

REVERSE: Leaves are worn and show only half of details. Bow and lettering are well worn but sharp.

FINE *Moderate to heavy even wear. Entire design clear and bold.*

F-12 OBVERSE: Hair worn from top of head to bottom of neck, but will still show most of detail. Hair cords and LIBERTY worn but bold. Stars have no central detail.

REVERSE: Leaves and bow heavily worn but edges still show some ribbing. Legend is worn but clear.

VERY GOOD *Well worn. Design clear but flat and lacking details.*

VG-8 OBVERSE: About half of the hair detail is visible. Back hair cord and half of inner cord show clearly. The eye and ear are visible. Rim, stars and date are clear.

REVERSE: Only the outline of bow and parts of the leaf stems show. Legend is complete but some letters may be weak.

GOOD *Heavily worn. Design and legend visible but faint in spots.*

G-4 OBVERSE: Hair shows no detail. Parts of LIBERTY and about half of back hair cord show, but ear, eye and rim are worn nearly smooth. Stars weak but visible.

REVERSE: All letters in legend are visible but very weak. Wreath is worn smooth with bow and ribbon outlined.

LARGE CENTS—CORONET 1816–1835

ABOUT GOOD   *Outlined design. Parts of date and legend worn smooth.*

AG-3   OBVERSE: Head is outlined with all details worn away. Date very weak but readable. LIBERTY and stars only partially visible. Stars partially worn away.

REVERSE: Entire design and rim is partially worn away. Most letters in the legend are readable.

Note: Coins of this design were often weakly struck. Characteristic traits listed here to assist in grading must not be confused with actual wear.

1816 Newcomb-2   Randall hoard variety. The point of the coronet, forelock, and forehead are very flat. Some leaves and the bow show weakness.

1817 N-14   Randall hoard variety. Parts of hair detail are not sharp, especially behind the hair cords. The leaves under ICA show flatness.

1819 N-2   Large date. In the later state of the dies, with the rusted reverse, the point of the coronet and the forelock are weakly struck.

1827 N-1   Sometimes seen poorly struck on the forelock, along the coronet line, and hair on top of the head; reverse may show weakness on the wreath.

1829 N-3, N-5, and N-9   Small letter varieties. On most examples, weak striking is seen on the coronet, forelock and throughout the hair. The wreath and some lettering on the reverse will lack detail.

1830 N-6   Small letter variety. Usually the coronet, forelock, hair, wreath and lettering are weakly struck.

1834 N-1   Small 8, large stars, small letters. Weakly struck on the forelock.

REFERENCE

Newcomb, H. R., *United States Copper Cents 1816–1857.* New York, 1944.

MINT STATE *Absolutely no trace of wear.*

MS-70 UNCIRCULATED
A flawless coin exactly as it was minted, with no trace of wear or injury. Must have full mint luster and natural color. Any unusual die or planchet traits must be described.

MS-67 UNCIRCULATED
Virtually flawless but with very minor imperfections.

MS-65 UNCIRCULATED
No trace of wear; nearly as perfect as MS-67 except for some small blemish. Has full mint luster but may be unevenly toned or lightly fingermarked. A few barely noticeable nicks or marks may be present.

MS-63 UNCIRCULATED
A mint state coin with attractive mint luster, but noticeable detracting contact marks or minor blemishes.

MS-60 UNCIRCULATED
A strictly Uncirculated coin with no trace of wear, but with blemishes more obvious than for MS-63. May lack full mint luster; color is usually an even light brown with traces of red.

ABOUT UNCIRCULATED *Small trace of wear visible on highest points.*

AU-58 *Very Choice*

Has some signs of abrasion: hair above ear; bow of ribbon on wreath, high points of leaves.

AU-55 *Choice*
OBVERSE: Hair shows trace of wear above and to right of the ear.
REVERSE: High points on a few leaves show trace of wear.
Considerable mint luster still present.

AU-50 *Typical*
OBVERSE: There are traces of wear near ear, and on high points of curls on neck and below bust.

REVERSE: High points of leaves show slight wear on the edges and ribs. There is a trace of wear on bow.

Surface is still somewhat lustrous.

EXTREMELY FINE *Very light wear on only the highest points.*

EF-45 *Choice*

OBVERSE: Hair well detailed. Wear shows above ear, and on parts of the curls above eye, on neck, and below bust.

REVERSE: Slight wear shows on most of the leaves and on bow.

EF-40 *Typical*

OBVERSE: Wear visible at top of head, above eye, to right of ear, at tip of coronet, and along the high curls on the shoulder.

REVERSE: Slight wear shows on most of the leaves and high parts of the bow.

VERY FINE *Light to moderate even wear. All major features are sharp.*

VF-30 *Choice*

OBVERSE: Hair above ear is weak. Curl below bust is worn. Slight flatness at tip of coronet.

REVERSE: Leaves worn at high points but still show some detail. High points of bow worn but visible.

VF-20 *Typical*

OBVERSE: Parts of hair worn from top of head to upper neck but most details are sharp. Balance of hair and coronet distinct. Shoulder curls are flattened.

REVERSE: Leaves are worn at high points and show only half of the details. Bow is well worn.

FINE   *Moderate to heavy even wear. Entire design clear and bold.*

F-12   OBVERSE: Hair worn from top of head to bottom of neck, but still will show some detail. Coronet shows wear along upper edge. Beads on hair cord sharp and LIBERTY bold. Stars and date worn but sharp.

REVERSE: Leaves and bow heavily worn but edges and some details still show. Legend is worn but bold.

VERY GOOD   *Well worn. Design clear but flat and lacking details.*

VG-8   OBVERSE: Hair shows detail only in spots, mostly around the bun. The coronet is outlined and the hair cord shows clearly. LIBERTY is worn but complete.

REVERSE: Only a bold outline of the leaves, stems, and bow show. Legend is complete but some letters may be weak.

GOOD   *Heavily worn. Design and legend visible but faint in spots.*

G-4   OBVERSE: Hair and bun show very few details. Parts of LIBERTY, the coronet, and the eye show. Hair cord still has some visible beads.

REVERSE: Most of the letters in legend are visible.

ABOUT GOOD   *Outlined design. Parts of date and legend worn smooth.*

AG-3   OBVERSE: Head is outlined with nearly all details worn away. Stars and date very weak but visible.

REVERSE: Entire design is partially worn away. Only half of the letters in legend are readable.

Note: The characteristic traits listed here to assist in grading must not be confused with actual wear.

1835   Type of 1836, all varieties. Weakly struck in the hair, and behind the hair cords. Slight weakness on the coronet line and the forelock.

1837 N-1   Plain hair cord, large letters. General weakness is seen in details on both obverse and reverse.

1837 N-5   Plain hair cord, small letters. Hair detail is not sharp on the lower curls. Leaves under OF are weakly struck.

1844 44 over 81, Newcomb 2   Weakly struck on the coronet line, on hair braids above the eye on the ear and on hair over the ear.

1855 Upright 5's, N-12   Hair behind the neck lacks detail.

1856 Slanting 5's, N-14   Hair braids above eye, upper parts of coronet, hair lines on top of head, the ribbon, and parts of the lower wreath are weakly struck. The fifth through eighth stars are less sharp than usual.

1857 Small date, N-4   Weakly struck on the upper part of coronet, the forelock, and the hair behind hair cords. The ribbon and some leaves are not sharp.

REFERENCE

Newcomb, H. R., *United States Copper Cents 1816–1857.* New York, 1944.

MINT STATE   *Absolutely no trace of wear.*

MS-70   UNCIRCULATED
A flawless coin exactly as it was minted, with no trace of wear or injury. Must have full mint luster and brilliance or light toning. Any unusual die or planchet traits must be described.

MS-67   UNCIRCULATED
Virtually flawless but with very minor imperfections.

MS-65   UNCIRCULATED
No trace of wear; nearly as perfect as MS-67 except for some small blemish. Has full mint luster but may be unevenly toned or lightly fingermarked. A few barely noticeable nicks or marks may be present.

MS-63   UNCIRCULATED
A mint state coin with attractive mint luster, but noticeable detracting contact marks or minor blemishes.

MS-60   UNCIRCULATED
A strictly Uncirculated coin with no trace of wear, but with blemishes more obvious than for MS-63. May lack full mint luster, and surface may be dull or spotted.

ABOUT UNCIRCULATED   *Small trace of wear visible on highest points.*

AU-58   *Very Choice*

Has some signs of abrasion: feathers on eagle's breast, wing tips.

AU-55   *Choice*
OBVERSE: Only a trace of wear shows on the breast and left wing tip.
REVERSE: A trace of wear shows on the bow.
   Three-quarters of the mint luster is still present.

AU-50   *Typical*
OBVERSE: Traces of wear show on the breast, left wing tip, and head.
REVERSE: Traces of wear show on the leaves and bow.
   Half of the mint luster is still present.

EXTREMELY FINE *Very light wear on only the highest points.*

EF-45 *Choice*
OBVERSE: Wear shows on breast, wing tips and head. All feathers are very plain.
REVERSE: High points of the leaves and bow are lightly worn.
Traces of mint luster still show.

EF-40 *Typical*
OBVERSE: Feathers in wings and tail are plain. Wear shows on breast, wing tips, head and thigh.
REVERSE: High points of the leaves and bow are worn.

VERY FINE *Light to moderate even wear. All major features are sharp.*

VF-30 *Choice*
OBVERSE: Small flat spots of wear show on breast and thigh. Feathers in wings still show nearly full details. Head worn but sharp.
REVERSE: Ends of leaves and bow worn almost smooth.

VF-20 *Typical*
OBVERSE: Breast shows considerable flatness. Over half of the details are visible in feathers of the wings. Head worn but bold. Thigh smooth, but feathers in tail are complete.
REVERSE: Ends of leaves and bow worn smooth.

FINE *Moderate to heavy even wear. Entire design clear and bold.*

F-12   OBVERSE: Some details show at breast, head, and tail. Outlines of feathers in right wing and tail show with no ends missing.

REVERSE: Some details visible in the wreath. Bow is very smooth.

VERY GOOD   *Well worn. Design clear but flat and lacking details.*

VG-8   OBVERSE: Outline of feathers in right wing ends show but some are smooth. Legend and date are visible. The eye shows clearly.

REVERSE: Slight detail in wreath shows, but the top is worn smooth. Very little outline showing in the bow.

GOOD   *Heavily worn. Design and legend visible but faint in spots.*

G-4   OBVERSE: Entire design well worn with very little detail remaining. Legend and date are weak but visible.

REVERSE: Wreath is worn flat but completely outlined. Bow merges with wreath.

ABOUT GOOD   *Outlined design. Parts of date and legend worn smooth.*

AG-3   OBVERSE: Eagle is outlined with all details worn away. Legend and date readable but very weak and merging into rim.

REVERSE: Entire design partially worn away. Bow is merged with the wreath.

Note: The Flying Eagle cents of 1857 and 1858 are sometimes weakly struck at the eagle's head and tail. The 1858, 8 over 7 variety is usually weak at upper right obverse and often at the date, and has a broken wing tip at the point between F and A.

SMALL CENTS—INDIAN HEAD 1859–1909

MINT STATE *Absolutely no trace of wear.*

MS-70 UNCIRCULATED
A flawless coin exactly as it was minted, with no trace of wear or injury. Must have full mint luster and brilliance or light toning. Any unusual die or planchet traits must be described.

MS-67 UNCIRCULATED
Virtually flawless but with very minor imperfections.

MS-65 UNCIRCULATED
No trace of wear; nearly as perfect as MS-67 except for some small blemish. Has full mint luster but may be unevenly toned or lightly fingermarked. A few barely noticeable nicks or marks may be present.

MS-63 UNCIRCULATED
A mint state coin with attractive mint luster, but noticeable detracting contact marks or minor blemishes.

MS-60 UNCIRCULATED
A strictly Uncirculated coin with no trace of wear, but with blemishes more obvious than for MS-63. May lack full mint luster, and surface may be dull or spotted.

ABOUT UNCIRCULATED *Small trace of wear visible on highest points.*

AU-58 *Very Choice*

Has some signs of abrasion: hair above ear, curl to right of ribbon; bow knot.

AU-55 *Choice*
OBVERSE: Only a trace of wear shows on the hair above the ear.
REVERSE: A trace of wear shows on the bow knot.
Three-quarters of the mint luster is still present.

AU-50 *Typical*
OBVERSE: Traces of wear show on the hair above ear and curl to right of ribbon.

REVERSE: Traces of wear show on the leaves and bow knot. Half of the mint luster is still present.

EXTREMELY FINE *Very light wear on only the highest points.*

EF-45 *Choice*

OBVERSE: Wear shows on hair above ear, curl to right of ribbon and on the ribbon end. All of the diamond design and letters in LIBERTY are very plain.

REVERSE: High points of the leaves and bow are lightly worn.

Traces of mint luster still show.

EF-40 *Typical*

OBVERSE: Feathers well defined and LIBERTY is bold. Wear shows on hair above ear, curl to right of ribbon and on the ribbon end. Most of the diamond design shows plainly.

REVERSE: High points of the leaves and bow are worn.

VERY FINE *Light to moderate even wear. All major features are sharp.*

VF-30 *Choice*

OBVERSE: Small flat spots of wear on tips of feathers, ribbon and hair ends. Hair still shows half of details. LIBERTY slightly worn but all letters are sharp.

REVERSE: Leaves and bow worn but fully detailed.

VF-20 *Typical*

OBVERSE: Headdress shows considerable flatness. Nearly half of the details still show in hair and on ribbon. Head slightly worn but bold.

REVERSE: Leaves and bow are almost fully detailed.

SMALL CENTS—INDIAN HEAD 1859–1909

FINE *Moderate to heavy even wear. Entire design clear and bold.*

F-12 OBVERSE: One-quarter of details show in the hair. Ribbon is worn smooth. LIBERTY shows clearly with no letters missing.

REVERSE: Some details visible in the wreath and bow. Tops of leaves are worn smooth.

VERY GOOD *Well worn. Design clear but flat and lacking details.*

VG-8 OBVERSE: Outline of feather ends show but some are smooth. Legend and date are visible. At least three letters in LIBERTY show clearly, but any combination of two full letters and parts of two others are sufficient.

REVERSE: Slight detail in wreath shows, but the top is worn smooth. Very little outline showing in the bow.

GOOD *Heavily worn. Design and legend visible but faint in spots.*

G-4 OBVERSE: Entire design well worn with very little detail remaining. Legend and date are weak but visible.

REVERSE: Wreath is worn flat but completely outlined. Bow merges with wreath.

ABOUT GOOD   *Outlined design. Parts of date and legend worn smooth.*

AG-3   OBVERSE: Head is outlined with nearly all details worn away. Legend and date readable but very weak and merging into rim.

REVERSE: Entire design partially worn away. Bow is merged with the wreath.

Note: The copper-nickel cents of 1859 through 1864 are often weakly struck and lack sharp details.

The 1864 L variety must show the L clearly even for the grade of About Good. Many of the 1909-S Indian cents are weakly struck.

Coins with full sharp diamond designs on ribbon are unusual because this feature is often weak even on Uncirculated coins.

Cleaned Indian Head cents, including Proofs, are often encountered. They can usually be identified by their unnaturally bright, orange color.

MINT STATE *Absolutely no trace of wear.*

MS-70   UNCIRCULATED
A flawless coin exactly as it was minted, with no trace of wear or injury. Must have full mint luster and brilliance or light toning. Any unusual die or planchet traits must be described.

MS-67   UNCIRCULATED
Virtually flawless but with very minor imperfections.

MS-65   UNCIRCULATED
No trace of wear; nearly as perfect as MS-67 except for some small blemish. Has full mint luster but may be unevenly toned or lightly fingermarked. A few barely noticeable nicks or marks may be present.

MS-63   UNCIRCULATED
A mint state coin with attractive mint luster, but noticeable detracting contact marks or minor blemishes.

MS-60   UNCIRCULATED
A strictly Uncirculated coin with no trace of wear, but with blemishes more obvious than for MS-63. May lack full mint luster, and surface may be dull or spotted.

ABOUT UNCIRCULATED *Small trace of wear visible on highest points.*

AU-58   *Very Choice*
Has some signs of abrasion: high points of cheek and jaw; tips of wheat stalks.

AU-55   *Choice*
OBVERSE: Only a trace of wear shows on the highest point of the jaw.
REVERSE: A trace of wear shows on the top of wheat stalks.
    Almost all of the mint luster is still present.

AU-50   *Typical*
OBVERSE: Traces of wear show on the cheek and jaw.

REVERSE: Traces of wear show on the wheat stalks.
Three-quarters of the mint luster is still present.

EXTREMELY FINE   *Very light wear on only the highest points.*

EF-45   *Choice*
OBVERSE: Slight wear shows on hair above ear, the cheek, and on the jaw.
REVERSE: High points of wheat stalks are lightly worn, but each line is
clearly defined.
   Half of the mint luster still shows.

EF-40   *Typical*
OBVERSE: Wear shows on hair above ear, the cheek, and on the jaw.
REVERSE: High points of wheat stalks are worn, but each line is clearly
defined.
   Traces of mint luster still show.

VERY FINE   *Light to moderate even wear. All major features are sharp.*

VF-30   *Choice*
OBVERSE: There are small flat spots of wear on cheek and jaw. Hair still
shows details. Ear and bow tie slightly worn but show clearly.
REVERSE: Lines in wheat stalks are lightly worn but fully detailed.

VF-20   *Typical*
OBVERSE: Head shows considerable flatness. Nearly all the details still show
in hair and on the face. Ear and bow tie worn but bold.
REVERSE: Lines in wheat stalks are worn but plain and without weak spots.

FINE *Moderate to heavy even wear. Entire design clear and bold.*

F-12 OBVERSE: Some details show in the hair. Cheek and jaw are worn nearly smooth. LIBERTY shows clearly with no letters missing. The ear and bow are visible.

REVERSE: Most details are visible in the stalks. Top wheat lines are worn but separated.

VERY GOOD *Well worn. Design clear but flat and lacking details.*

VG-8 OBVERSE: Outline of hair shows but most details are smooth. Cheek and jaw are smooth. More than half of bow tie is visible. Legend and date are clear.

REVERSE: Wheat shows some details and about half of the lines at the top.

GOOD *Heavily worn. Design and legend visible but faint in spots.*

G-4 OBVERSE: Entire design well worn with very little detail remaining. Legend and date are weak but visible.

REVERSE: Wheat is worn nearly flat but is completely outlined. Some grains are visible.

SMALL CENTS—LINCOLN 1909 TO DATE

ABOUT GOOD   *Outlined design. Parts of date and legend worn smooth.*

AG-3   OBVERSE: Head is outlined with nearly all details worn away. Legend and date readable but very weak and merging into rim.

REVERSE: Entire design partially worn away. Parts of wheat and motto merged with the rim.

Note: The Memorial cents from 1959 to date can be graded by using the obverse descriptions.

The following characteristic traits will assist in grading but must not be confused with actual wear on the coins:

Matte Proof cents of 1909 through 1916 are often spotted or stained.

Branch mint cents of the 1920's are usually not as sharply struck as later dates.

Many of the early dates of Lincoln cents are weakly struck on the obverse and/or the reverse, especially the following dates: 1911-D, 1914-D, 1917-D, 1918-D, S, 1921, 1921-S, 1922-D, 1923, 1923-S, 1924, 1924-S, 1925-D, S, 1926-S, 1927-D, S, 1928-S, 1929-D, S, 1930-S and 1935-D, S.

1922 "No D" is weakly struck at the head, has a small I and joined RT in LIBERTY. The most reliable variety has a weak obverse and a strong reverse. On two other varieties that sometimes show a "Weak D" the wheat heads are weak on the reverse.

1924-D usually has a weak mint mark.

1931-S is sometimes unevenly struck.

1936 Proof cents: early strikes are less brilliant than those made later that year.

1955 doubled die: hair details are less sharp than most cents of the period.

Uncirculated cents before 1935 should not be expected in bright, red condition. They are usually toned to various shades.

TWO CENTS—1864–1873

MINT STATE *Absolutely no trace of wear.*

MS-70 UNCIRCULATED
A flawless coin exactly as it was minted, with no trace of wear or injury. Must have full mint luster and brilliance or light toning. Any unusual die or planchet traits must be described.

MS-67 UNCIRCULATED
Virtually flawless but with very minor imperfections.

MS-65 UNCIRCULATED
No trace of wear; nearly as perfect as MS-67 except for some small blemish. Has full mint luster but may be unevenly toned or lightly fingermarked. A few barely noticeable nicks or marks may be present.

MS-63 UNCIRCULATED
A mint state coin with attractive mint luster, but noticeable detracting contact marks or minor blemishes.

MS-60 UNCIRCULATED
A strictly Uncirculated coin with no trace of wear, but with blemishes more obvious than for MS-63. May lack full mint luster, and surface may be dull or spotted.

ABOUT UNCIRCULATED *Small trace of wear visible on highest points.*

AU-58 *Very Choice*

Has some signs of abrasion: tips of leaves, arrow points, the word WE.

AU-55 *Choice*
OBVERSE: Only a trace of wear shows on the word WE.
REVERSE: A trace of wear shows on the ribbons.
    Three-quarters of the mint luster is still present.

AU-50 *Typical*
OBVERSE: Traces of wear show on the word WE and at tips of the leaves.

REVERSE: Traces of wear show on leaves and ribbons.
Half of the mint luster is still present.

EXTREMELY FINE *Very light wear on only the highest points.*

EF-45 *Choice*

OBVERSE: Slight wear shows on the word WE, and at tips of leaves and arrows. There is a trace of wear on horizontal lines of the shield.

REVERSE: High points of leaves and wheat are lightly worn.

Traces of mint luster still show.

EF-40 *Typical*

OBVERSE: WE worn but well defined and bold. Slight wear shows on horizontal lines of the shield. High points of leaves and arrows are worn but show all details.

REVERSE: Leaves and wheat are worn but all details are visible.

VERY FINE *Light to moderate even wear. All major features are sharp.*

VF-30 *Choice*

OBVERSE: Entire motto is worn but each letter is visible. Leaves and arrows show nearly full details. Vertical lines of shield are worn but sharp and separated.

REVERSE: Ends of leaves and bow worn. Wheat grains show plainly.

VF-20 *Typical*

OBVERSE: WE shows considerable flatness, but all letters in motto are clear. Over half the details still show in leaves. Shield worn but bold.

REVERSE: Leaves and ribbon are worn. Wheat grains are all visible.

TWO CENTS—1864–1873

FINE *Moderate to heavy even wear. Entire design clear and bold.*

F-12 OBVERSE: Some details show in leaves and shield lines. Entire motto is plain but WE is very weak.

REVERSE: Some details visible in the wreath. Bow is very smooth but ribbons are distinct.

VERY GOOD *Well worn. Design clear but flat and lacking details.*

VG-8 OBVERSE: Outline of leaves and arrows shows but parts are smooth. Motto is weak and WE is incomplete. Only a few vertical shield lines show separations.

REVERSE: Slight detail in wreath shows, but the knot is still clear. Very little outline showing in bow.

GOOD *Heavily worn. Design and legend visible but faint in spots.*

G-4 OBVERSE: Entire design well worn with very little detail remaining. IN GOD and TRUST are very weak but visible.

REVERSE: Wreath is worn nearly flat but is completely outlined. Legend is weak but readable.

ABOUT GOOD   *Outlined design. Parts of date and legend worn smooth.*

AG-3   OBVERSE: Design is outlined with nearly all details worn away. Date readable but very weak and merging into rim.
REVERSE: Entire design partially worn away. Bow is merged with wreath. Only parts of the legend are visible.

Note: Two-cent pieces are occasionally seen weakly struck, and with the horizontal lines joined even on Uncirculated specimens.

Red Uncirculated coins are much scarcer than the usual toned or brown pieces. 1864 and 1865 Proof coins are frequently dull.
   Cleaned Two-Cent pieces, including Proofs, are often encountered. They can usually be identified by their unnaturally bright, orange color.

THREE CENTS—SILVER 1851–1873

The first three-cent silver pieces had no lines bordering the six-pointed star. From 1854 through 1858 there were three lines, while issues of the last fifteen years show only two lines. Issues from 1854 through 1873 have an olive sprig over the III and a bundle of three arrows beneath.

MINT STATE *Absolutely no trace of wear.*

MS-70 UNCIRCULATED
A flawless coin exactly as it was minted, with no trace of wear or injury. Must have full mint luster and brilliance or light toning. Any unusual die or striking traits must be described.

MS-67 UNCIRCULATED
Virtually flawless but with very minor imperfections.

MS-65 UNCIRCULATED
No trace of wear; nearly as perfect as MS-67 except for some small blemish. Has full mint luster but may be unevenly toned or lightly fingermarked. A few barely noticeable nicks or marks may be present.

MS-63 UNCIRCULATED
A mint state coin with attractive mint luster, but noticeable detracting contact marks or minor blemishes.

MS-60 UNCIRCULATED
A strictly Uncirculated coin with no trace of wear, but with blemishes more obvious than for MS-63. May lack full mint luster, and surface may be dull or spotted.

ABOUT UNCIRCULATED *Small trace of wear visible on highest points.*

AU-58 *Very Choice*
Has some signs of abrasion: points and ridges of star; high parts of Roman numeral III.

AU-55 *Choice*
OBVERSE: Only a trace of wear shows on top ridges of star.

REVERSE: A trace of wear shows on Roman numeral.

Three-quarters of the mint luster is still present.

AU-50 *Typical*

OBVERSE: Traces of wear show on star ridges and points. Edges are distinct on five of the six star points.

REVERSE: Traces of wear show on leaves and Roman numeral.

Half of the mint luster is still present.

EXTREMELY FINE *Very light wear on only the highest points.*

EF-45 *Choice*

OBVERSE: Slight wear shows on star points and ridges. There is a trace of wear on shield.

REVERSE: High points of numeral and diamond pattern are lightly worn.

Traces of mint luster still show.

EF-40 *Typical*

OBVERSE: Slight wear shows on outer edge of the shield. High points of the star points and ridges are worn but show all details.

REVERSE: Entire central design is lightly worn but all details are visible.

VERY FINE *Light to moderate even wear. All major features are sharp.*

VF-30 *Choice*

OBVERSE: Entire design is worn but every detail is visible. Shield shows nearly full details. Vertical lines of shield are worn but sharp and separated.

REVERSE: Numeral and stars show signs of wear. Design within C shows plainly.

VF-20 *Typical*

OBVERSE: Shield shows considerable flatness, but all features are clear. Over half the details show in star edges. Legend worn but bold.

REVERSE: Numeral, C, and stars are worn. Design within C is all visible.

FINE *Moderate to heavy even wear. Entire design clear and bold.*

F-12 OBVERSE: Some details show in scroll and outer shield lines; central shield lines are nearly all visible. The entire star is plain but very weak.

REVERSE: All details are visible in the C. Numeral is very smooth and stars are well worn.

VERY GOOD *Well worn. Design clear but flat and lacking details.*

VG-8 OBVERSE: Outline of star and shield shows but parts are smooth. Shield lines are weak and incomplete. Only a few vertical shield lines show separations.

REVERSE: Design in C is complete but very weak. Numeral and stars well worn but fully outlined. Most of rim is visible.

GOOD *Heavily worn. Design and legend visible but faint in spots.*

G-4 OBVERSE: Entire design well worn with very little detail remaining. Half the shield lines are weak but visible. Rim merges with legend.

REVERSE: Design is worn nearly flat but is completely outlined. Design in C is weak but visible. Stars merge with rim.

ABOUT GOOD   *Outlined design. Parts of date and legend worn smooth.*

AG-3   OBVERSE: Design is outlined with nearly all details worn away. Date and legend readable but very weak and merging into rim.

REVERSE: Entire design partially worn away. Rim is merged with the stars. Only parts of the design in C are visible.

Note: Three-cent pieces of 1854 through 1858 are usually weakly struck and have incomplete shield lines and date even on Uncirculated specimens.

The coins from 1863 to 1872 are all much rarer in Uncirculated than in Proof. On some coins, ascertaining whether a coin is Mint State or Proof is difficult. Consequently, care should be exercised to determine the business strike status of all alleged mint state specimens.

1851–1853 (Type 1) coins are 75% silver composition. Surfaces are often dull; luster not as frosted as with 90% silver coinage. The obverse shield is typically softly struck.

1851–O occasionally seen in higher grades with lamination marks (black streaks). Striking quality is usually weak.

MINT STATE *Absolutely no trace of wear.*

MS-70 UNCIRCULATED
A flawless coin exactly as it was minted, with no trace of wear or injury. Must have full mint luster but this may range from brilliant to frosty. Any extreme striking weakness or unusual die wear must be described.

MS-67 UNCIRCULATED
Virtually flawless but with very minor imperfections.

MS-65 UNCIRCULATED
No trace of wear; nearly as perfect as MS-67 except for some small blemish. Has full mint luster but may be unevenly toned, frosty, or lightly finger-marked. A few barely noticeable nicks, carbon spots, or marks may be present.

MS-63 UNCIRCULATED
A mint state coin with attractive mint luster, but noticeable detracting contact marks or minor blemishes.

MS-60 UNCIRCULATED
A strictly Uncirculated coin with no trace of wear, but with blemishes more obvious than for MS-63. May lack full mint luster, and surface may be dull or spotted. May have some weakness in LIBERTY or on the numeral III.

ABOUT UNCIRCULATED *Small trace of wear visible on highest points.*

AU-58 *Very Choice*
Has some signs of abrasion: high points of cheek, hair curls, and hair above forehead.

AU-55 *Choice*
OBVERSE: Only a trace of wear shows on the highest points of hair over forehead.
REVERSE: A trace of wear shows on wreath.
Half of the mint luster is still present.

AU-50 *Typical*

OBVERSE: Traces of wear show on the curls and hair above forehead.

REVERSE: Traces of wear show on wreath and numeral III.

Part of the mint luster is still present.

EXTREMELY FINE *Very light wear on only the highest points.*

EF-45 *Choice*

OBVERSE: Slight wear shows on hair above forehead, on the cheek, and on curls at back of neck.

REVERSE: High points of leaves are lightly worn. Lines in III are clearly defined.

Traces of mint luster may still show.

EF-40 *Typical*

OBVERSE: Wear shows on hair above forehead, on the cheek, and on curls.

REVERSE: High points of leaves are worn, but each line is clearly defined. Numeral shows some wear.

VERY FINE *Light to moderate even wear. All major features are sharp.*

VF-30 *Choice*

OBVERSE: Three-quarters of hair details show. The coronet has a partially beaded upper edge.

REVERSE: Leaves are worn but some of the ribs are visible. Most of the lines in the numeral are clear unless weakly struck.

VF-20 *Typical*

OBVERSE: Over half the details still show in hair and curls. Head worn but bold. Coronet is partially beaded on upper edge.

REVERSE: Leaves are worn but some of the ribs are visible. Most of the lines in the numeral are clear unless weakly struck.

FINE *Moderate to heavy even wear. Entire design clear and bold.*

F-12 OBVERSE: Some details show in curls and hair at top of ear. Beading worn smooth at top of coronet.
REVERSE: Some details visible in wreath. About half the lines in the numeral are clear.

VERY GOOD *Well worn. Design clear but flat and lacking details.*

VG-8 OBVERSE: Top edge of coronet and most hair details are worn smooth. Legend and date are clear. Rim is complete.
REVERSE: Slight detail in wreath shows, but half the leaves are separated. Some lines in the numeral are visible. Rim is complete.

GOOD *Heavily worn. Design and legend visible but faint in spots.*

G-4 OBVERSE: Entire design well worn with very little detail remaining. Legend and date are weak but visible.
REVERSE: Wreath is worn flat but completely outlined. Roman numeral is worn smooth.

THREE CENTS—NICKEL 1865–1889

ABOUT GOOD   *Outlined design. Parts of date and legend worn smooth.*

AG-3   OBVERSE: Head is outlined with nearly all details worn away. Legend and date readable but very weak and merging into rim.
REVERSE: Entire design partially worn away. Rim is merged with the wreath.

Note: Nickel three-cent pieces are sometimes difficult to grade because so many were weakly struck or made from worn dies. The word LIBERTY, and the Roman numeral III, are often very weak or incomplete even on Uncirculated coins. The rims, lettering, date, or parts of the hair may show similar weaknesses because of coining difficulties.

The appearance of mint luster on Uncirculated pieces varies from brilliant to frosty.

Many dates in the 1860's show clash marks in the fields on one or both sides of the coin.

Pieces dated in the 1870's are often uneven and softly struck.

MINT STATE *Absolutely no trace of wear.*

MS-70 UNCIRCULATED
A flawless coin exactly as it was minted, with no trace of wear or injury. Must have full mint luster or attractive light toning. Any unusual die or striking traits must be described.

MS-67 UNCIRCULATED
Virtually flawless but with very minor imperfections.

MS-65 UNCIRCULATED
No trace of wear; nearly as perfect as MS-67 except for some small weakness or blemish. Has full mint luster but may be unevenly toned or lightly finger-marked. A few barely noticeable nicks or marks may be present.

MS-63 UNCIRCULATED
A mint state coin with attractive mint luster, but noticeable detracting contact marks or minor blemishes.

MS-60 UNCIRCULATED
A strictly Uncirculated coin with no trace of wear, but with blemishes more obvious than for MS-63. May lack full mint luster, and surface may be dull or spotted.

ABOUT UNCIRCULATED *Small trace of wear visible on highest points.*

AU-58 *Very Choice*
Has some signs of abrasion: tips of leaves, high points of shield. Shallow or weak spots in the relief, particularly in the numeral 5, are usually caused by improper striking and not wear.

AU-55 *Choice*
OBVERSE: Only a trace of wear shows on the cross.
REVERSE: A trace of wear shows on the numeral.
    Half of the mint luster is still present.

AU-50 *Typical*
OBVERSE: Traces of wear show on the cross and at tips of the leaves.
REVERSE: Traces of wear show on numeral and stars.
    Traces of mint luster still show.

EXTREMELY FINE *Very light wear on only the highest points.*

EF-45 *Choice*

OBVERSE: Slight wear shows on the cross and at tips of leaves. There is a trace of wear on the horizontal lines of the shield.

REVERSE: High points of the numeral and stars are lightly worn.

EF-40 *Typical*

OBVERSE: Cross is lightly worn but well defined and bold. Slight wear shows on horizontal lines of the shield. High points of leaves are worn but show all details.

REVERSE: Numeral and stars are worn but all details are visible.

VERY FINE *Light to moderate even wear. All major features are sharp.*

VF-30 *Choice*

OBVERSE: Leaves show nearly full details. Vertical lines of shield are worn but sharp and separated.

REVERSE: Numeral and stars worn. Most star centers show plainly.

VF-20 *Typical*

OBVERSE: Shield shows considerable flatness, but half of the horizontal lines are clear. Parts of the details still show in leaves. Cross worn but outlined.

REVERSE: Numeral and stars are worn. Star centers show half of details.

FINE *Moderate to heavy even wear. Entire design clear and bold.*

NICKEL FIVE CENTS—SHIELD 1866–1883

F-12 OBVERSE: Some details show in leaves and shield lines. The entire motto is plain but very weak.

REVERSE: Some details visible in stars. Numeral is very smooth but distinct.

VERY GOOD *Well worn. Design clear but flat and lacking details.*

VG-8 OBVERSE: Outline of leaves and cross shows but parts are smooth. Motto is weak but visible. Only a few vertical shield lines show separations.

REVERSE: Slight detail shows in stars. The rim is clear. Numeral is worn nearly flat but is completely outlined.

GOOD *Heavily worn. Design and legend visible but faint in spots.*

G-4 OBVERSE: Entire design is well worn with very little detail remaining. Motto is weak and incomplete.

REVERSE: Numeral nearly flat but is outlined. Legend is weak but readable. Rim worn to tops of letters.

ABOUT GOOD *Outlined design. Parts of date and legend worn smooth.*

AG-3 OBVERSE: Design is outlined with nearly all details worn away. Date and motto partially readable but very weak and merging into rim.

REVERSE: Entire design partially worn away. Rim is merged with the letters. Only parts of stars and legend are visible.

Note: Shield nickels are occasionally seen weakly struck, and with the horizontal lines joined even on Uncirculated specimens. Many of the early dates are unevenly struck with weak spots in details.

Brilliant Uncirculated coins are much scarcer than the usual dull or frosty pieces. The surface is often marred with small black spots.

NICKEL FIVE CENTS—LIBERTY HEAD 1883–1912

MINT STATE *Absolutely no trace of wear.*

MS-70 UNCIRCULATED
A flawless coin exactly as it was minted, with no trace of wear or injury. Must have full mint luster but this may range from brilliant to frosty. Any unusual die or striking traits must be described.

MS-67 UNCIRCULATED
Virtually flawless but with very minor imperfections.

MS-65 UNCIRCULATED
No trace of wear; nearly as perfect as MS-67 except for some small weakness or blemish. Has full mint luster but may be unevenly toned, frosty, or lightly fingermarked. A few barely noticeable nicks or marks may be present.

MS-63 UNCIRCULATED
A mint state coin with attractive mint luster, but noticeable detracting contact marks or minor blemishes.

MS-60 UNCIRCULATED
A strictly Uncirculated coin with no trace of wear, but with blemishes more obvious than for MS-63. May lack full mint luster, and surface may be dull or spotted.

ABOUT UNCIRCULATED *Small trace of wear visible on highest points.*

AU-58 *Very Choice*

Has some signs of abrasion: high points of hair left of ear and at forehead; corn ears at bottom of wreath.

AU-55 *Choice*

OBVERSE: Only a trace of wear shows on the highest points of hair left of ear.
REVERSE: A trace of wear shows on corn ears.
Half of the mint luster is still present.

NICKEL FIVE CENTS—LIBERTY HEAD 1883–1912

AU-50   *Typical*
OBVERSE: Traces of wear show on hair left of ear and at forehead.
REVERSE: Traces of wear show on the wreath and corn ears.
Part of the mint luster is still present.

EXTREMELY FINE   *Very light wear on only the highest points.*

EF-45   *Choice*
OBVERSE: Slight wear shows on high points of hair from forehead to the ear.
REVERSE: High points of wreath are lightly worn. Lines in corn are clearly defined.
Traces of mint luster may still show.

EF-40   *Typical*
OBVERSE: Wear shows on hair from forehead to ear, the cheek, and on curls.
REVERSE: High points of wreath are worn, but each line is clearly defined.
Corn shows some wear.

VERY FINE   *Light to moderate even wear. All major features are sharp.*

VF-30   *Choice*
OBVERSE: Three-quarters of hair details show. The coronet has full bold lettering.
REVERSE: Leaves are worn but most of the ribs are visible. Some of the lines in the corn are clear unless weakly struck.

VF-20   *Typical*
OBVERSE: Over half the details still show in hair and curls. Head worn but bold. Every letter on coronet is plainly visible.
REVERSE: Leaves are worn but some of the ribs are visible. Most details in the wreath are clear unless weakly struck.

FINE   *Moderate to heavy even wear. Entire design clear and bold.*

F-12   OBVERSE: Some details show in curls and hair at top of head. All letters of LIBERTY are visible.

REVERSE: Some details visible in wreath. Letters in the motto are worn but clear.

VERY GOOD   *Well worn. Design clear but flat and lacking details.*

VG-8   OBVERSE: Bottom edge of coronet and most hair details are worn smooth. At least three letters in LIBERTY are clear. Rim is complete.

REVERSE: Wreath shows only bold outline. Some letters in the motto are very weak. Rim is complete.

GOOD   *Heavily worn. Design and legend visible but faint in spots.*

G-4   OBVERSE: Entire design well worn with very little detail remaining. Stars and date are weak but visible.

REVERSE: Wreath is worn flat and not completely outlined. Legend and motto are worn nearly smooth.

NICKEL FIVE CENTS—LIBERTY HEAD 1883–1912

ABOUT GOOD   *Outlined design. Parts of date and legend worn smooth.*

AG-3   OBVERSE: Head is outlined with nearly all details worn away. Date readable but very weak and merging into rim.
REVERSE: Entire design partially worn away.

Note: Liberty nickels are subject to laminations and rough planchets. Carbon spots are typical as are lint marks on the Proofs.

Not all Proofs of this series are of the same brilliance. Some dates in the 80's and 90's merely have a frosty appearance but can be identified as Proofs by their sharp edge.

The 1912-D, 1912-S, and 1883 "no cents" variety are often weakly struck. Because the obverse design is in higher relief than the reverse, all dates appear to be more worn on the reverse in low grades.

NICKEL FIVE CENTS—BUFFALO 1913–1938

MINT STATE   *Absolutely no trace of wear.*

MS-70   UNCIRCULATED
A flawless coin exactly as it was minted, with no trace of wear or injury. Must have full mint luster. Any unusual die or striking traits must be described.

MS-67   UNCIRCULATED
Virtually flawless but with very minor imperfections.

MS-65   UNCIRCULATED
No trace of wear; nearly as perfect as MS-67 except for some small weakness or blemish. Has full mint luster but may be unevenly toned or lightly finger-marked. A few barely noticeable nicks or marks may be present.

MS-63   UNCIRCULATED
A mint state coin with attractive mint luster, but noticeable detracting contact marks or minor blemishes.

MS-60   UNCIRCULATED
A strictly Uncirculated coin with no trace of wear, but with blemishes more obvious than for MS-63. May lack full mint luster and surface may be dull or spotted.

ABOUT UNCIRCULATED   *Small trace of wear visible on highest points.*

AU-58   *Very Choice*
Has some signs of abrasion: high points of Indian's cheek; hip bone, flank. Shallow or weak spots in the relief are usually caused by improper striking and not wear.

AU-55   *Choice*
OBVERSE: Only a trace of wear shows on high point of cheek.
REVERSE: A trace of wear shows on the hip.
   Half of the mint luster is still present.

AU-50   *Typical*
OBVERSE: Traces of wear show on hair above and to left of forehead, and at the cheekbone.

NICKEL FIVE CENTS—BUFFALO 1913-1938

REVERSE: Traces of wear show on tail, hip and hair above and around the horn.

Traces of mint luster still show.

EXTREMELY FINE   *Very light wear on only the highest points.*

EF-45   *Choice*

OBVERSE: Slight wear shows on the hair above the braid. There is a trace of wear on the temple and hair near cheekbone.

REVERSE: High points of hip and thigh are lightly worn. The horn and tip of tail are sharp and nearly complete.

EF-40   *Typical*

OBVERSE: Hair and face are lightly worn but well defined and bold. Slight wear shows on lines of hair braid.

REVERSE: Horn and end of tail are worn but all details are visible.

VERY FINE   *Light to moderate even wear. All major features are sharp.*

VF-30   *Choice*

OBVERSE: Hair shows nearly full details. Feathers and braid are worn but sharp.

REVERSE: Head, front leg and hip are worn. Tail shows plainly. Horn is worn but full.

VF-20   *Typical*

OBVERSE: Hair and cheek show considerable flatness, but all details are clear. Feathers still show partial detail.

REVERSE: Hair on head is worn. Tail and point of horn are visible.

FINE *Moderate to considerable even wear. Entire design clear and bold.*

F-12 OBVERSE: Three-quarters of details show in hair and braid. LIBERTY is plain.

REVERSE: Major details visible along the back. Horn and tail are smooth but three-quarters visible.

VERY GOOD *Well worn. Design clear but flat and lacking details.*

VG-8 OBVERSE: Outline of hair is visible at temple and near cheekbone. LIBERTY merges with rim. Date is clear.

REVERSE: Some detail shows in head. Lettering is all clear. Horn is worn nearly flat but is partially visible.

GOOD *Heavily worn. Design and legend visible but faint in spots.*

G-4 OBVERSE: Entire design well worn with very little detail remaining in central part. LIBERTY is weak and merged with rim.

REVERSE: Buffalo is nearly flat but is well outlined. Horn does not show. Legend is weak but readable. Rim worn to tops of letters.

NICKEL FIVE CENTS—BUFFALO 1913-1938

ABOUT GOOD *Outlined design. Parts of date and legend worn smooth.*

AG-3 OBVERSE: Design is outlined with nearly all details worn away. Date and motto partially readable but very weak and merging into rim.
REVERSE: Entire design partially worn away. Rim is merged with the letters.

Note: Buffalo nickels were often weakly struck, and lack details even on Uncirculated specimens. The following dates are usually unevenly struck with weak spots in the details:

1913-S I and II, 1917-D, S, 1918-D, S, 1919-D, S, 1920-D, S, 1921-S, 1923-S, 1924-D, S, 1925-D, S, 1926-D, S, 1927-D, S, 1928-D, S, 1929-D, 1931-S, 1934-D and 1935-D. Nickels dated 1919-S, 1920-S, 1923-S, 1925-S and especially 1926-D are seldom found with full details.

1913 through 1916 Matte Proof coins are sometimes spotted or stained.

1937-D three-legged buffalo, entire design is always weak because of excessive die polishing.

NICKEL FIVE CENTS—JEFFERSON 1938 TO DATE

MINT STATE *Absolutely no trace of wear.*

MS-70 UNCIRCULATED
A flawless coin exactly as it was minted, with no trace of wear or injury. Must have full mint luster and brilliance. Any unusual striking or planchet traits must be described.

MS-67 UNCIRCULATED
Virtually flawless but with very minor imperfections.

MS-65 UNCIRCULATED
No trace of wear; nearly as perfect as MS-67 except for some small weakness or blemish. Has full mint luster but may be unevenly toned or lightly finger-marked. A few barely noticeable nicks or marks may be present.

MS-63 UNCIRCULATED
A mint state coin with attractive mint luster, but noticeable detracting contact marks or minor blemishes.

MS-60 UNCIRCULATED
A strictly Uncirculated coin with no trace of wear, but with weaknesses and blemishes more obvious than for MS-63. May lack full mint luster and surface may be dull or spotted.

ABOUT UNCIRCULATED *Small trace of wear visible on highest points.*

AU-58 *Very Choice*

Has some signs of abrasion: cheekbone and high points of hair, collar, triangular roof above pillars. Shallow or weak spots in the relief, particularly in the steps below pillars, are usually caused by improper striking and not wear.

AU-55 *Choice*
OBVERSE: Only a trace of wear shows on cheekbone.
REVERSE: A trace of wear shows on the beam above pillars.
Three-quarters of the mint luster is still present.

NICKEL FIVE CENTS—JEFFERSON 1938 TO DATE

AU-50 *Typical*

OBVERSE: Traces of wear show on cheekbone and high points of hair.

REVERSE: Traces of wear show on the beam and triangular roof above pillars.
Half of the mint luster is still present.

EXTREMELY FINE *Very light wear on only the highest points.*

EF-45 *Choice*

OBVERSE: Slight wear shows on cheekbone and central portion of hair. There
is a trace of wear at bottom of the bust.

REVERSE: High points of the triangular roof and beam are lightly worn.
Traces of mint luster still show.

EF-40 *Typical*

OBVERSE: Hair is lightly worn but well defined and bold. Slight wear shows
on cheekbone and bottom of the bust. High points of hair are worn but show
all details.

REVERSE: Triangular roof and beam are worn but all details are visible.

VERY FINE *Light to moderate even wear. All major features are sharp.*

VF-30 *Choice*

OBVERSE: Hair worn but shows nearly full details. Cheek line and bottom
of bust are worn but sharp.

REVERSE: Triangular roof and beam worn nearly flat. Most of the pillar lines
show plainly.

VF-20 *Typical*

OBVERSE: Cheek line shows considerable flatness. Over half the hair lines are
clear. Parts of the details still show in collar.

REVERSE: Pillars are worn but clearly defined. Triangular roof is partially
visible.

FINE *Moderate to heavy even wear. Entire design clear and bold.*

F-12 OBVERSE: Some details show in hair around face. Cheek line and collar plain but very weak.

REVERSE: Some details visible behind pillars. Triangular roof is very smooth and indistinct.

VERY GOOD *Well worn. Design clear but flat and lacking details.*

VG-8 OBVERSE: Cheek line is visible but parts are worn smooth. Collar is weak but visible. Only a few hair lines show separations.

REVERSE: Slight detail shows throughout building. The arch is worn away. Pillars are weak but visible.

GOOD *Heavily worn. Design and legend visible but faint in spots.*

G-4 OBVERSE: Entire design well worn with very little detail remaining. Motto is weak and merged with rim.

REVERSE: Building is nearly flat but is well outlined. Pillars are worn flat. Rim worn to tops of letters.

NICKEL FIVE CENTS—JEFFERSON 1938 TO DATE

ABOUT GOOD *Outlined design. Parts of date and legend worn smooth.*

AG-3 OBVERSE: Design is outlined with nearly all details worn away. Date and legend readable but very weak and merging into rim.
REVERSE: Entire design partially worn away. Rim is merged with the letters.

Note: Jefferson nickels are frequently seen weakly struck, and with the horizontal step lines joined even on Uncirculated specimens. Many of the 1950 and 1955 nickels are unevenly struck with weak spots in the details. 1953-S and 1954-S were often struck from worn dies.

MINT STATE *Absolutely no trace of wear.*

MS-70 UNCIRCULATED
A flawless coin exactly as it was minted, with no trace of wear or injury. Must have full mint luster and brilliance or light toning. Any unusual die or striking traits must be described.

MS-67 UNCIRCULATED
Virtually flawless but with very minor imperfections.

MS-65 UNCIRCULATED
No trace of wear; nearly as perfect as MS-67 except for some small blemish. Has full mint luster but may be unevenly toned or lightly fingermarked. A few barely noticeable nicks or adjustment file marks may be present.

MS-63 UNCIRCULATED
A mint state coin with attractive mint luster, but noticeable detracting contact marks or minor blemishes.

MS-60 UNCIRCULATED
A strictly Uncirculated coin with no trace of wear, but with blemishes more obvious than for MS-63. May lack full mint luster, and surface may be dull, spotted or heavily toned.

ABOUT UNCIRCULATED *Small trace of wear visible on highest points.*

AU-58 *Very Choice*
Has some signs of abrasion: high points of hair left of ear and at forehead; eagle's head, breast and top edges of wings. Shallow or weak spots in the relief are usually caused by improper striking and not wear.

AU-55 *Choice*
OBVERSE: Only a trace of wear shows on the highest points of hair above forehead.
REVERSE: A trace of wear shows on the breast.
Three-quarters of the mint luster is still present.

AU-50   *Typical*

OBVERSE: Traces of wear show on hair left of ear and at forehead.
REVERSE: Traces of wear show on breast, head, and the top edges of wings.
Half of the mint luster is still present.

EXTREMELY FINE   *Very light wear on only the highest points.*

EF-45   *Choice*

OBVERSE: Slight wear shows on high points of hair from forehead to the ear.
REVERSE: High points of the wings, breast and head are lightly worn. Lines in feathers are clearly defined.
Part of the mint luster is still present.

EF-40   *Typical*

OBVERSE: Wear shows on hair from forehead to ear, and lightly on the cheek.
REVERSE: High points of the eagle are worn, but each detail is clearly defined.
Traces of mint luster may still show.

VERY FINE   *Light to moderate even wear. All major features are sharp.*

VF-30   *Choice*

OBVERSE: Three quarters of flowing hair details show. Hair above forehead is worn but has some bold features.
REVERSE: Feathers are worn but most of the details are visible. Some of the lines in leaves are clear unless weakly struck.

VF-20   *Typical*

OBVERSE: Over half the details still show in hair. Above forehead, hair worn but bold. Every letter and star is plainly visible.
REVERSE: Head and breast are worn, but some feathers are visible. Most of the details in wings are clear unless weakly struck.

FINE *Moderate to heavy even wear. Entire design clear and bold.*

F-12 OBVERSE: Some details show in hair ends, and at left of forehead. All letters, date and stars are visible.

REVERSE: Some details visible in wings and tail. Letters in legend are worn but clear.

VERY GOOD *Well worn. Design clear but flat and lacking details.*

VG-8 OBVERSE: Entire head is weak, and most hair details are worn smooth. The date and LIBERTY are weak but clear.

REVERSE: Eagle shows only bold outline. Some of the letters are very weak.

GOOD *Heavily worn. Design and legend visible but faint in spots.*

G-4 OBVERSE: Entire design well worn with very little detail remaining. Legend, stars and date are weak but visible.

REVERSE: Eagle is worn flat and not completely outlined. Tops of letters are worn nearly smooth.

HALF DIMES—FLOWING HAIR 1794–1795

ABOUT GOOD   *Outlined design. Parts of date and legend worn smooth.*

AG-3   OBVERSE: Head is outlined with nearly all details worn away. Date readable but very weak. Stars merging into rim.

REVERSE: Entire design partially worn away. Letters very weak but visible.

Note: Coins of this design are often weakly struck, particularly on the hair behind the ear, and on the eagle's breast and feathers. File adjustment marks are common, and a normal part of the manufacturing process.

HALF DIMES—DRAPED BUST 1796–1797

MINT STATE   *Absolutely no trace of wear.*

MS-70   UNCIRCULATED
A flawless coin exactly as it was minted, with no trace of wear or injury. Must have full mint luster and brilliance or light toning. Any unusual die or striking traits must be described.

MS-67   UNCIRCULATED
Virtually flawless but with very minor imperfections.

MS-65   UNCIRCULATED
No trace of wear; nearly as perfect as MS-67 except for some small blemish. Has full mint luster but may be unevenly toned or lightly fingermarked. A few barely noticeable nicks or adjustment file marks may be present.

MS-63   UNCIRCULATED
A mint state coin with attractive mint luster, but noticeable detracting contact marks or minor blemishes.

MS-60   UNCIRCULATED
A strictly Uncirculated coin with no trace of wear, but with blemishes more obvious than for MS-63. May lack full mint luster, and surface may be dull, spotted or heavily toned.

ABOUT UNCIRCULATED   *Small trace of wear visible on highest points.*

AU-58   *Very Choice*
Has some signs of abrasion: high points of bust, shoulder, and hair above ear and at forehead; eagle's head and top edges of wings. Shallow or weak spots in the relief are usually caused by defective planchets or improper striking and not wear.

AU-55   *Choice*
OBVERSE: Only a trace of wear shows on the highest points of hair above forehead.
REVERSE: A trace of wear shows on the breast.
Three-quarters of the mint luster is still present.

[120]

HALF DIMES—DRAPED BUST 1796-1797

AU-50 *Typical*

OBVERSE: Traces of wear show on hair above forehead. Drapery has trace of wear at shoulder and bustline.

REVERSE: Traces of wear show on breast, head, and the top edges of wings. Half of the mint luster is still present.

EXTREMELY FINE *Very light wear on only the highest points.*

EF-45 *Choice*

OBVERSE: Slight wear shows on high points of hair from forehead to the ear. Drapery is worn at shoulder and bustline.

REVERSE: High points of wings, breast and head are lightly worn. Lines in feathers are clearly defined.

Part of the mint luster is still present.

EF-40 *Typical*

OBVERSE: Wear shows on hair from forehead to ear, and lightly on the cheek. Drapery lightly worn at neckline in spots.

REVERSE: High points of the eagle are worn, but each detail is clearly defined. Head and breast are weak.

Traces of mint luster may still show.

VERY FINE *Light to moderate even wear. All major features are sharp.*

VF-30 *Choice*

OBVERSE: Hair above forehead is worn but has some bold features. Flowing hair is well detailed.

REVERSE: Feathers are worn but most of the details are visible. Some of the details in head and breast are clear unless weakly struck.

VF-20 *Typical*

OBVERSE: Hair above forehead worn almost smooth. Three-quarters of the details still show in flowing hair. Every letter and star is plainly visible. Left side of drapery is indistinct.

REVERSE: Head and breast are worn, but some of the feathers are visible. Most of the details in wings are clear unless weakly struck.

[121]

FINE *Moderate to heavy even wear. Entire design clear and bold.*

F-12 OBVERSE: Some details show in hair ends, and at left of ear. All letters, date and stars are visible.

REVERSE: Half the feathers are visible in the wings. Letters in legend are worn but clear.

VERY GOOD *Well worn. Design clear but flat and lacking details.*

VG-8 OBVERSE: Entire head is weak, and most hair details are worn smooth. Date and LIBERTY are weak but clear.

REVERSE: Eagle shows only bold outline. Some letters are very weak.

GOOD *Heavily worn. Design and legend visible but faint in spots.*

G-4 OBVERSE: Entire design well worn with very little detail remaining. Legend, stars and date are weak but visible.

REVERSE: Eagle is worn flat and not completely outlined. Tops of some letters are worn nearly smooth.

HALF DIMES—DRAPED BUST 1796-1797

ABOUT GOOD   *Outlined design. Parts of date and legend worn smooth.*

AG-3   OBVERSE: Head is outlined with nearly all details worn away. Date readable but very weak. Stars merging into rim.
REVERSE: Entire design partially worn away.

Note: Coins of this design are often weakly struck, particularly in the drapery lines, on the hair at left of neck, and on the eagle's breast and feathers. File adjustment marks are occasionally seen, and are a normal part of the manufacturing process.

MINT STATE   *Absolutely no trace of wear.*

MS-70   UNCIRCULATED
A flawless coin exactly as it was minted, with no trace of wear or injury. Must have full mint luster and brilliance or light toning. Any unusual die or striking traits must be described.

MS-67   UNCIRCULATED
Virtually flawless but with very minor imperfections.

MS-65   UNCIRCULATED
No trace of wear; nearly as perfect as MS-67 except for some small blemish. Has full mint luster but may be unevenly toned or lightly fingermarked. A few barely noticeable nicks or adjustment file marks may be present.

MS-63   UNCIRCULATED
A mint state coin with attractive mint luster, but noticeable detracting contact marks or minor blemishes.

MS-60   UNCIRCULATED
A strictly Uncirculated coin with no trace of wear, but with blemishes more obvious than for MS-63. May lack full mint luster, and surface may be dull, spotted or heavily toned.

ABOUT UNCIRCULATED   *Small trace of wear visible on highest points.*

AU-58   *Very Choice*
Has some signs of abrasion: high points of bust, shoulder, and hair above ear and at forehead; eagle's head and top edges of wings. Shallow or weak spots in the relief are usually caused by improper striking and not wear.

AU-55   *Choice*
OBVERSE: Only a trace of wear shows on the highest points of hair above forehead.
REVERSE: A trace of wear shows on feathers above shield and on edges of wings.
     Three-quarters of the mint luster is still present.

HALF DIMES—HERALDIC EAGLE 1800–1805

AU-50 *Typical*

OBVERSE: Traces of wear show on hair above forehead. Drapery has trace of wear at shoulder and bustline.
REVERSE: Traces of wear show on shield, head, and top wing edges. Half of the mint luster is still present.

EXTREMELY FINE   *Very light wear on only the highest points.*

EF-45 *Choice*

OBVERSE: Slight wear shows on high points of hair from forehead to the ear. Drapery is worn at shoulder and bustline.
REVERSE: High points of wings, shield, tail and head are lightly worn. Lines in feathers are clearly defined.
Part of the mint luster is still present.

EF-40 *Typical*

OBVERSE: Wear shows on hair from forehead to ear, and lightly on the cheek. Drapery lightly worn at neckline in spots.
REVERSE: High points of the eagle are worn, but each detail is clearly defined. Tail and feathers above shield are very weak.
Traces of mint luster may still show.

VERY FINE   *Light to moderate even wear. All major features are sharp.*

VF-30 *Choice*

OBVERSE: Hair above forehead is worn but has some bold features. Flowing hair is well detailed.
REVERSE: Feathers are worn but most details are visible. Some details above shield and in the tail are clear unless weakly struck.

VF-20 *Typical*

OBVERSE: Hair above forehead worn almost smooth. Three-quarters of the details still show in flowing hair. Every letter and star is plainly visible. Left side of drapery is indistinct.
REVERSE: Head and tail are worn, but some of the feathers are visible. Most of the details in wings are clear unless weakly struck. The motto is weak but complete.

FINE   *Moderate to heavy even wear. Entire design clear and bold.*

F-12   OBVERSE: Some details show in hair ends, and at left of ear. All letters, date and stars are visible.

REVERSE: Half the feathers are visible in wings. Letters in legend are worn but clear. Parts of motto are very weak.

VERY GOOD   *Well worn. Design clear but flat and lacking details.*

VG-8   OBVERSE: Entire head is weak, and most hair details are worn smooth. Date and LIBERTY are weak but clear.

REVERSE: Eagle shows bold outline with only a few feathers visible. Some letters in legend are very weak. Motto is only partially visible.

GOOD   *Heavily worn. Design and legend visible but faint in spots.*

G-4   OBVERSE: Entire design well worn with very little detail remaining. Legend, stars and date are weak but visible.

REVERSE: Eagle is worn flat but is completely outlined. Tops of some letters, head, and motto are worn nearly smooth.

HALF DIMES—HERALDIC EAGLE 1800-1805

ABOUT GOOD   *Outlined design. Parts of date and legend worn smooth.*

AG-3   OBVERSE: Head is outlined with nearly all details worn away. Date readable but very weak. Stars merging into rim.
REVERSE: Entire design partially worn away.

Note: Coins of this design are often weakly struck, particularly in the drapery lines, on the hair at left of neck, and on the eagle's shield and feathers. File adjustment marks are occasionally seen, and are a normal part of the manufacturing process.

HALF DIMES—CAPPED BUST 1829–1837

MINT STATE   *Absolutely no trace of wear.*

MS-70   UNCIRCULATED
A flawless coin exactly as it was minted, with no trace of wear or injury. Must have full mint luster and brilliance or light toning. Any unusual die or striking traits must be described.

MS-67   UNCIRCULATED
Virtually flawless but with very minor imperfections.

MS-65   UNCIRCULATED
No trace of wear; nearly as perfect as MS-67 except for some small blemish. Has full mint luster but may be unevenly toned or lightly fingermarked. A few barely noticeable nicks or marks may be present.

MS-63   UNCIRCULATED
A mint state coin with attractive mint luster, but noticeable detracting contact marks or minor blemishes.

MS-60   UNCIRCULATED
A strictly Uncirculated coin with no trace of wear, but with blemishes more obvious than for MS-63. May lack full mint luster, and surface may be dull, spotted or heavily toned.

ABOUT UNCIRCULATED   *Small trace of wear visible on highest points.*

AU-58   *Very Choice*

Has some signs of abrasion: drapery at tip of bust, shoulder clasp, and hair above eye and at forehead; eagle's claws, neck, and edges of wings. Shallow or weak spots in the motto are usually caused by improper striking and not wear.

AU-55   *Choice*

OBVERSE: Only a trace of wear shows on the highest points of hair above eye.
REVERSE: A trace of wear shows on the talons.
    Three-quarters of the mint luster is still present.

AU-50 *Typical*

OBVERSE: Traces of wear show on hair above eye and over the ear. Drapery has trace of wear at tip of bust.

REVERSE: Traces of wear show on talons, head, and edges of wings.

Half of the mint luster is still present.

EXTREMELY FINE *Very light wear on only the highest points.*

EF-45 *Choice*

OBVERSE: Slight wear shows on high points of hair above eye and over the ear. Drapery is worn at shoulder and bustline.

REVERSE: High points of wings, shield, talons and head are lightly worn. Lines in feathers are clearly defined.

Part of the mint luster is still present.

EF-40 *Typical*

OBVERSE: Wear shows on hair above eye and ear, and lightly on curls. Drapery lightly worn at neckline in spots. The eye and shoulder clasp are very sharp.

REVERSE: High points of the eagle are worn, but each detail is clearly defined. Head, neck feathers, and leg feathers are very lightly worn.

Traces of mint luster may still show.

VERY FINE *Light to moderate even wear. All major features are sharp.*

VF-30 *Choice*

OBVERSE: Hair above forehead is worn almost smooth. Balance of hair is well detailed. Ear and shoulder clasp show clearly.

REVERSE: Feathers are worn but most details are visible. Some of the details in the head, shield, and tail are worn nearly flat.

VF-20 *Typical*

OBVERSE: Over half the details still show in hair. Drapery and lower curls worn but bold. Ear, clasp and star centers are all plainly visible.

REVERSE: Head and leg are worn, but some feathers are visible. Most of the details in the wings are clear unless weakly struck. Motto is complete.

FINE *Moderate to heavy even wear. Entire design clear and bold.*

F-12 OBVERSE: About half the details show in hair ends, and at left of ear. All letters, and parts of ear and clasp are visible.

REVERSE: Half of the feathers are visible in the wings. Letters in motto are worn but clear.

VERY GOOD *Well worn. Design clear but flat and lacking details.*

VG-8 OBVERSE: Entire head is weak, and most hair details are worn smooth. Date and LIBERTY are weak but clear.

REVERSE: Eagle is boldly outlined with some feathers showing in wings. Some letters in the motto are very weak or partially missing.

GOOD *Heavily worn. Design and legend visible but faint in spots.*

G-4 OBVERSE: Entire design well worn with very little detail remaining. Half the letters in LIBERTY are worn away. Stars and date are weak but visible.

REVERSE: Eagle is worn nearly flat but is completely outlined. Tops of some letters are worn nearly smooth and may merge with rim.

ABOUT GOOD *Outlined design. Parts of date and legend worn smooth.*

AG-3 OBVERSE: Head is outlined with nearly all details worn away. Date readable but very weak. Stars merging into rim.

REVERSE: Entire design partially worn away.

Note: Coins of this design are sometimes weakly struck, particularly in the drapery, clasp, hair, on the motto above the eagle, and wings close to the shield.

HALF DIMES—LIBERTY SEATED 1837–1859

MINT STATE *Absolutely no trace of wear.*

MS-70 UNCIRCULATED
A flawless coin exactly as it was minted, with no trace of wear or injury. Must have full mint luster and brilliance or light toning. Any unusual die or striking traits must be described.

MS-67 UNCIRCULATED
Virtually flawless but with very minor imperfections.

MS-65 UNCIRCULATED
No trace of wear; nearly as perfect as MS-67 except for some small blemish. Has full mint luster but may be unevenly toned or lightly fingermarked. A few barely noticeable nicks or marks may be present.

MS-63 UNCIRCULATED
A mint state coin with attractive mint luster, but noticeable detracting contact marks or minor blemishes.

MS-60 UNCIRCULATED
A strictly Uncirculated coin with no trace of wear, but with blemishes more obvious than for MS-63. May lack full mint luster, and surface may be dull, spotted or heavily toned.

ABOUT UNCIRCULATED *Small trace of wear visible on highest points.*

AU-58 *Very Choice*
Has some signs of abrasion: high points of breast and knees; ribbon bow and tips of leaves. Weak spots in the horizontal shield lines are usually caused by striking and not wear.

AU-55 *Choice*
OBVERSE: Only a trace of wear shows on highest points of knees.
REVERSE: A trace of wear shows on ribbon bow.
Three-quarters of the mint luster is still present.

AU-50 *Typical*

OBVERSE: Traces of wear show on knees, right shoulder and hairline.
REVERSE: Traces of wear show on ribbon bow, and tips of leaves.
Half of the mint luster is still present.

EXTREMELY FINE *Very light wear on only the highest points.*

EF-45 *Choice*

OBVERSE: Slight wear shows on high points of knees and hairline. Drapery
is worn at shoulder and bustline. LIBERTY is sharp and scroll edges are
raised.
REVERSE: High points of wreath and bow lightly worn. Lines in leaves are
clearly defined.
Part of the mint luster is still present.

EF-40 *Typical*

OBVERSE: Wear shows on knees, head and shoulder. Gown lightly worn at
neckline in spots. LIBERTY is complete and scroll edges are raised.
REVERSE: High points of wreath and bow are worn, but all details are clearly
defined.
Traces of mint luster may still show.

VERY FINE *Light to moderate even wear. All major features are sharp.*

VF-30 *Choice*

OBVERSE: Wear spots show on shoulder, breast, knee and legs. The head is
weak but has some visible details. LIBERTY and scroll are complete.
REVERSE: Leaves are worn but almost all the details are visible. Most of the
details in the ribbon bow are clear.

VF-20 *Typical*

OBVERSE: Over half the details still show in the gown. Hair worn but bold.
Every letter in LIBERTY is visible.
REVERSE: The ribbon is worn, but some details are visible. Half the details
in the leaves are clear.

HALF DIMES—LIBERTY SEATED 1837–1859

FINE *Moderate to heavy even wear. Entire design clear and bold.*

F-12 OBVERSE: Some details show in cap and at the shoulder and breast. All letters in LIBERTY are weak but visible.
REVERSE: Half the details in leaves are visible. Bow is outlined but flat. Letters in the legend are worn but clear.

VERY GOOD *Well worn. Design clear but flat and lacking details.*

VG-8 OBVERSE: Entire shield is weak, and most of the gown details are worn smooth. Three letters in LIBERTY are clear.
REVERSE: Wreath shows only bold outline. Some of the bow is very weak.

GOOD *Heavily worn. Design and legend visible but faint in spots.*

G-4 OBVERSE: Entire design well worn with very little detail remaining. Date is weak but visible.
REVERSE: Wreath is worn flat but is completely outlined. Tops of some letters are worn nearly smooth.

HALF DIMES—LIBERTY SEATED 1837–1859

ABOUT GOOD   *Outlined design. Parts of date and legend worn smooth.*

AG-3   OBVERSE: Liberty is outlined with nearly all details worn away. Date readable but very weak. Stars merging into rim.

REVERSE: Entire design partially worn away.

Note: Coins of this design are sometimes weakly struck, particularly in the horizontal lines of the shield.

Pieces dated 1856 through 1858 are usually weak at central drapery and head. New Orleans coins of 1840–1857 rarely show full head and are often weakly struck.

HALF DIMES—LIBERTY SEATED 1860–1873

MINT STATE *Absolutely no trace of wear.*

MS-70 UNCIRCULATED
A flawless coin exactly as it was minted, with no trace of wear or injury. Must have full mint luster and brilliance or light toning. Any unusual die or striking traits must be described.

MS-67 UNCIRCULATED
Virtually flawless but with very minor imperfections.

MS-65 UNCIRCULATED
No trace of wear; nearly as perfect as MS-67 except for some small blemish. Has full mint luster but may be unevenly toned or lightly fingermarked. A few barely noticeable nicks or marks may be present.

MS-63 UNCIRCULATED
A mint state coin with attractive mint luster, but noticeable detracting contact marks or minor blemishes.

MS-60 UNCIRCULATED
A strictly Uncirculated coin with no trace of wear, but with blemishes more obvious than for MS-63. May lack full mint luster, and surface may be dull, spotted or heavily toned.

ABOUT UNCIRCULATED *Small trace of wear visible on highest points.*

AU-58 *Very Choice*
Has some signs of abrasion: high points of breast and knees; ribbon bow and tips of leaves.

AU-55 *Choice*
OBVERSE: Only a trace of wear shows on highest points of knees.
REVERSE: A trace of wear shows on the ribbon bow.
 Three-quarters of the mint luster is still present.

AU-50 *Typical*
OBVERSE: Traces of wear show on knees, right shoulder, and edge of hairline.
REVERSE: Traces of wear show on ribbon bow and tips of leaves.
 Half of the mint luster is still present.

EXTREMELY FINE *Very light wear on only the highest points.*

EF-45 *Choice*

OBVERSE: Slight wear shows on high points of knees and hairline. Drapery is worn at shoulder and bustline. LIBERTY is sharp and scroll edges are raised.

REVERSE: High points of the wreath and bow lightly worn. Lines in leaves are clearly defined.

Part of the mint luster is still present.

EF-40 *Typical*

OBVERSE: Wear shows on knees, head and shoulder. Gown lightly worn at neckline in spots. LIBERTY is complete and scroll edges are raised.

REVERSE: High points of wreath and bow are worn, but all details are clearly defined.

Traces of mint luster may still show.

VERY FINE *Light to moderate even wear. All major features are sharp.*

VF-30 *Choice*

OBVERSE: Wear spots show on shoulder, breast, knee and legs. The head is weak but has some visible details. LIBERTY and scroll are complete.

REVERSE: Wear shows on the two bottom leaves but most of the details are visible. Nearly all the details in the ribbon bow are clear.

VF-20 *Typical*

OBVERSE: Over half the details still show in the gown. Hair worn but bold. Every letter in LIBERTY is visible. Details in cap are visible.

REVERSE: The ribbon is worn, but some of the details are visible. Half the details in the leaves are clear. Bottom leaves and upper stalks show wear spots.

FINE *Moderate to heavy even wear. Entire design clear and bold.*

F-12 OBVERSE: Some details show in cap and at the shoulder and breast. All letters in LIBERTY are weak but visible. Clasp is worn away.

REVERSE: Some details in the upper leaves and corn are visible. Bow is nearly all outlined but flat. Letters in legend are worn but clear.

VERY GOOD *Well worn. Design clear but flat and lacking details.*

VG-8 OBVERSE: Entire shield is weak, and most details in the gown, knee and legs are worn smooth. Three letters in LIBERTY are clear. Rim is complete.

REVERSE: Wreath shows only a small amount of detail. Corn and grain are flat. Some of the bow merges with wreath.

GOOD *Heavily worn. Design and legend visible but faint in spots.*

G-4 OBVERSE: Entire design well worn with very little detail remaining. Date is weak but visible. LIBERTY is worn away.

REVERSE: Wreath is worn flat but is completely outlined. Corn and grains are worn nearly smooth.

HALF DIMES—LIBERTY SEATED 1860–1873

ABOUT GOOD   *Outlined design. Parts of date and legend worn smooth.*

AG-3   OBVERSE: Liberty is outlined with nearly all details worn away. Date readable but worn. Legend merging into rim.

REVERSE: Entire design partially worn away.

Note: Coins of this design are sometimes weakly struck, particularly in the horizontal lines of the shield and at the top of the wreath.

REFERENCES

Newlin, H.P. *The Early Half-Dimes of the United States.* Philadelphia, 1883. (reprinted 1975).

Valentine, D.W. *"The United States Half Dimes."* New York, 1931 (reprinted 1975).

MINT STATE *Absolutely no trace of wear.*

MS-70 UNCIRCULATED
A flawless coin exactly as it was minted, with no trace of wear or injury. Must have full mint luster and brilliance or light toning. Any unusual die, planchet or striking traits must be described.

MS-67 UNCIRCULATED
Virtually flawless but with very minor imperfections.

MS-65 UNCIRCULATED
No trace of wear; nearly as perfect as MS-67 except for some small blemish. Has full mint luster but may be unevenly toned or lightly fingermarked. A few barely noticeable nicks or adjustment file marks may be present.

MS-63 UNCIRCULATED
A mint state coin with attractive mint luster, but noticeable detracting contact marks or minor blemishes.

MS-60 UNCIRCULATED
A strictly Uncirculated coin with no trace of wear, but with blemishes more obvious than for MS-63. May lack full mint luster, and surface may be dull, spotted or heavily toned.

ABOUT UNCIRCULATED *Small trace of wear visible on highest points.*

AU-58 *Very Choice*
Has some signs of abrasion: high points of bust, shoulder, and hair above ear and at forehead; eagle's head and top edges of wings. Shallow or weak spots in the relief are usually caused by improper striking and not wear.

AU-55 *Choice*
OBVERSE: Only a trace of wear shows on the highest points of hair above forehead.
REVERSE: A trace of wear shows on the breast.
Three-quarters of the mint luster is still present.

DIMES—DRAPED BUST 1796-1797

AU-50   *Typical*

OBVERSE: Traces of wear show on the hair above ear and at forehead. Drapery has trace of wear at shoulder and bustline.

REVERSE: Traces of wear show on breast, head, and top wing edges.

Half of the mint luster is still present.

EXTREMELY FINE   *Very light wear on only the highest points.*

EF-45   *Choice*

OBVERSE: Slight wear shows on high points of hair from forehead to the ear. Drapery is worn at shoulder and bustline.

REVERSE: High points of wings, breast and head are lightly worn. Lines in feathers are clearly defined.

Part of the mint luster is still present.

EF-40   *Typical*

OBVERSE: Wear shows on hair from forehead to ear, and lightly on the cheek. Drapery lightly worn at neckline in spots.

REVERSE: High points of the eagle are worn, but major details are clearly defined. Head and breast are very weak.

Traces of mint luster may still show.

VERY FINE   *Light to moderate even wear. All major features are sharp.*

VF-30   *Choice*

OBVERSE: Hair above forehead is worn but has some bold features. Flowing hair is well detailed.

REVERSE: Feathers are worn but most of the details are visible. Some of the details in head and breast are clear unless weakly struck.

VF-20   *Typical*

OBVERSE: Hair above forehead worn almost smooth. Three-quarters of the details still show in flowing hair. Every letter and star is plainly visible. Left side of drapery is indistinct.

REVERSE: Head and breast are worn, but some of the feathers are visible. Most of the details in wings are clear unless weakly struck.

FINE   *Moderate to heavy even wear. Entire design clear and bold.*

F-12   OBVERSE: Some details show in hair ends, and at left of ear. All letters, date and stars are visible.

REVERSE: Half the feathers are visible in the wings. Letters in legend are worn but clear.

VERY GOOD   *Well worn. Design clear but flat and lacking details.*

VG-8   OBVERSE: Entire head is weak, and most hair details are worn smooth. The date and LIBERTY are weak but clear.

REVERSE: Eagle is boldly outlined with only a few details showing in wings. Some of the letters are very weak.

GOOD   *Heavily worn. Design and legend visible but faint in spots.*

G-4   OBVERSE: Entire design well worn with very little detail remaining. Legend, stars and date are weak but visible.

REVERSE: Eagle is worn flat and not completely outlined. Tops of some letters are worn nearly smooth.

DIMES—DRAPED BUST 1796–1797

ABOUT GOOD   *Outlined design. Parts of date and legend worn smooth.*

AG-3   OBVERSE: Head is outlined with nearly all details worn away. Date readable but very weak. Stars merging into rim.
REVERSE: Entire design partially worn away. Letters very weak but visible.

Note: Coins of this design are often weakly struck, particularly in the drapery lines, on the hair at left of neck, and on the eagle's breast and feathers. File adjustment marks are occasionally seen, and are a normal part of the manufacturing process. Pieces dated 1796 are known with proof-like surface. One of the most common of the 1796 shows a lumpy die break at left of date.

REFERENCES

Ahwash, Kamal M. *Encyclopedia of United States Liberty Seated Dimes 1837–1891.* Kamal Press, 1977.

Davis, David. et al. *Early United States Dimes 1796–1837.* Ypsilanti, Michigan, 1984.

Kosoff, A. *United States Dimes from 1796.* New York, 1945.

DIMES—HERALDIC EAGLE 1798–1807

MINT STATE *Absolutely no trace of wear.*

MS-70 UNCIRCULATED
A flawless coin exactly as it was minted, with no trace of wear or injury. Must have full mint luster and brilliance or light toning. Any unusual die or striking traits must be described.

MS-67 UNCIRCULATED
Virtually flawless but with very minor imperfections.

MS-65 UNCIRCULATED
No trace of wear; nearly as perfect as MS-67 except for some small blemish. Has full mint luster but may be unevenly toned or lightly fingermarked. Small nicks or adjustment file marks may be present.

MS-63 UNCIRCULATED
A mint state coin with attractive mint luster, but noticeable detracting contact marks or minor blemishes.

MS-60 UNCIRCULATED
A strictly Uncirculated coin with no trace of wear, but with blemishes more obvious than for MS-63. May lack full mint luster, and surface may be dull, spotted or heavily toned.

ABOUT UNCIRCULATED *Small trace of wear visible on highest points.*

AU-58 *Very Choice*
Has some signs of abrasion: high points of bust, shoulder, and hair above ear and at forehead; eagle's head and top edges of wings. Shallow or weak spots in the relief are usually caused by improper striking and not wear.

AU-55 *Choice*
OBVERSE: Only a trace of wear shows on highest points of hair above forehead.
REVERSE: A trace of wear shows on feathers above shield and on edges of wings.
Three-quarters of the mint luster is still present.

AU-50 *Typical*
OBVERSE: Traces of wear show on hair above ear and at forehead. Drapery

[143]

has trace of wear at shoulder and bustline.

REVERSE: Traces of wear show on shield, head, tail, and the top edges of wings.

Half of the mint luster is still present.

EXTREMELY FINE *Very light wear on only the highest points.*

EF-45 *Choice*

OBVERSE: Slight wear shows on high points of hair from forehead to the ear. Drapery is worn at shoulder and bustline.

REVERSE: High points of wings, shield, tail and head are lightly worn. Lines in feathers are clearly defined.

Part of the mint luster is still present.

EF-40 *Typical*

OBVERSE: Wear shows on hair from forehead to ear, and lightly on the cheek. Drapery lightly worn at neckline in spots.

REVERSE: High points of the eagle are worn, but each detail is clearly defined. Tail and feathers above shield are very weak.

Traces of mint luster may still show.

VERY FINE *Light to moderate even wear. All major features are sharp.*

VF-30 *Choice*

OBVERSE: Hair above forehead is worn but has some bold features. Flowing hair is well detailed.

REVERSE: Feathers are worn but most of the details are visible. Some of the details in tail and above shield are clear unless weakly struck.

VF-20 *Typical*

OBVERSE: Hair above forehead worn almost smooth. Three-quarters of the details still show in flowing hair. Every letter and star is plainly visible. Left side of drapery is indistinct.

REVERSE: Head and tail are worn, but some of the feathers are visible. Most of the details in wings are clear unless weakly struck. The motto is weak but complete.

FINE *Moderate to heavy even wear. Entire design clear and bold.*

F-12 OBVERSE: Some details show in hair ends, and at left of ear. All letters, date and stars are visible.

REVERSE: Half the feathers are visible in the wings. Letters in legend are worn but clear. Parts of motto are very weak.

VERY GOOD *Well worn. Design clear but flat and lacking details.*

VG-8 OBVERSE: Entire head is weak, and most hair details are worn smooth. Date and LIBERTY are weak but clear.

REVERSE: Eagle shows bold outline with only a few feathers visible. Some of the letters in legend are very weak. Motto is only partially visible.

GOOD *Heavily worn. Design and legend visible but faint in spots.*

G-4 OBVERSE: Entire design well worn with very little detail remaining. Legend, stars and date are weak but visible.

REVERSE: Eagle is worn flat but is completely outlined. Tops of some letters, head, and motto are worn nearly smooth.

ABOUT GOOD *Outlined design. Parts of date and legend worn smooth.*

AG-3 OBVERSE: Head is outlined with nearly all details worn away. Date readable but very weak. Stars merging into rim.

REVERSE: Entire design partially worn away.

Note: Coins of this design are often weakly struck, particularly in the drapery lines, on the hair at left of neck, and on the eagle's shield and feathers. File adjustment marks are occasionally seen, and are a normal part of the manufacturing process.

1798 over 7, 16 stars reverse.   Usually weak at right border, parts of curls and on eagle's breast.

1798 over 7, 13 stars reverse.   Has central weakness and heavy obverse clash marks.

1798, small 8.   Usually struck weakly and with uneven surface.

1800, large A's.   Often weak at upper right reverse and near borders on both sides.

1801   Always unevenly struck, weak in centers.

1802   Usually weak in centers.

1803   Usually weak in centers.

1804, 13 stars reverse.   Planchets are frequently defective, with pitted appearance. Reverse is always weak, the die having been drastically polished.

1804, 14 stars reverse.   Reverse is often weak at the left; later bulged at ERICA.

1807   Usually with heavy and numerous clash marks, and weak border. On late strikes the legend is not readable, and still later most of the date is gone.

DIMES—CAPPED BUST 1809–1837

MINT STATE *Absolutely no trace of wear.*

MS-70 UNCIRCULATED
A flawless coin exactly as it was minted, with no trace of wear or injury. Must have full mint luster and brilliance or light toning. Any unusual die or striking traits must be described.

MS-67 UNCIRCULATED
Virtually flawless but with very minor imperfections.

MS-65 UNCIRCULATED
No trace of wear; nearly as perfect as MS-67 except for some small blemish. Has full mint luster but may be unevenly toned or lightly fingermarked. A few barely noticeable nicks or marks may be present.

MS-63 UNCIRCULATED
A mint state coin with attractive mint luster, but noticeable detracting contact marks or minor blemishes.

MS-60 UNCIRCULATED
A strictly Uncirculated coin with no trace of wear, but with blemishes more obvious than for MS-63. May lack full mint luster, and surface may be dull, spotted or heavily toned.

ABOUT UNCIRCULATED *Small trace of wear visible on highest points.*
AU-58 *Very Choice*
Has some signs of abrasion: drapery at front of bust, shoulder clasp, and hair above ear and at forehead; eagle's claws, neck, and edges of wings. Shallow or weak spots in the design are usually caused by improper striking and not wear.

AU-55 *Choice*
OBVERSE: Only a trace of wear shows on highest points of hair above eye.
REVERSE: A trace of wear shows on the talons.
    Three-quarters of the mint luster is still present.

AU-50 *Typical*
OBVERSE: Traces of wear show on hair above eye and over the ear. Drapery has trace of wear at tip of bust.

REVERSE: Traces of wear show on talons, head, and edges of wings. Half of the mint luster is still present.

EXTREMELY FINE   *Very light wear on only the highest points.*

EF-45   *Choice*

OBVERSE: Slight wear shows on high points of hair above eye and over the ear. Drapery is worn at shoulder and bustline. Trace of wear visible on lowest curl.

REVERSE: High points of wings, shield, talons and head are lightly worn. Lines in feathers are clearly defined.

Part of the mint luster is still present.

EF-40   *Typical*

OBVERSE: Wear shows on hair above eye and ear, and lightly on the curls. Drapery lightly worn at neckline in spots. The ear and shoulder clasp are very sharp. Eye is well defined.

REVERSE: High points of the eagle are worn, but each detail is clearly defined. Neck and leg feathers are very lightly worn. Talons and olive branch show slight wear.

Traces of mint luster may still show.

VERY FINE   *Light to moderate even wear. All major features are sharp.*

VF-30   *Choice*

OBVERSE: Hair above eye is worn almost smooth. Balance of hair is well detailed. Ear and shoulder clasp show clearly. LIBERTY and eye are well defined.

REVERSE: Feathers are worn but most of the details are visible. Some of the details in neck, shield, and talons are well worn.

VF-20   *Typical*

OBVERSE: Over half the details still show in hair. Drapery and lower curls worn but bold. Ear, clasp and LIBERTY are all plainly visible.

REVERSE: Head and leg are worn, but some of the feathers are visible. Most details in the wings are clear unless weakly struck. Motto is complete. Talons are separated.

DIMES—CAPPED BUST 1809–1837

FINE *Moderate to heavy even wear. Entire design clear and bold.*

F-12 OBVERSE: Nearly half the details show in hair, drapery, and cap. All letters, and parts of ear and clasp are visible. Eyelid is flattened. Parts of rim are worn flat.

REVERSE: Half the feathers are visible in the wings. Letters in the motto are weak but clear. Head is nearly smooth but eye and some feathers show.

VERY GOOD *Well worn. Design clear but flat and lacking details.*

VG-8 OBVERSE: Entire head outlined with most hair details worn smooth. Eye, ear, and clasp are barely visible. At least three letters in LIBERTY are clear.

REVERSE: Eagle is boldly outlined with some feathers showing in wings. Some of the letters in motto are very weak. Head and olive branch are smooth.

GOOD *Heavily worn. Design and legend visible but faint in spots.*

G-4 OBVERSE: Entire design well worn with very little detail remaining. Most of the letters in LIBERTY are worn away. Stars and date are weak but visible and may merge with rim.

REVERSE: Eagle is worn nearly flat but is completely outlined. Tops of some letters are worn nearly smooth and may merge with rim. Eye and motto are only partially visible.

ABOUT GOOD   *Outlined design. Parts of date and legend worn smooth.*

AG-3   OBVERSE: Head is outlined with nearly all details worn away. Date readable but very weak. Stars merging into rim.

REVERSE: Entire design partially worn away.

Note: Coins of this design are sometimes weakly struck, particularly in the drapery, clasp, hair, and on the motto above the eagle. In grading, some allowance must be made for planchet defects, varying thickness, and broken dies. These characteristics are common to pieces made prior to introduction of the closed collar process in 1828.

1809 usually has weakly struck stars on left side of obverse.

1811 over 9 is very unevenly struck.

1814 is usually bold but flat on high points of the obverse.

1823 and 1828 usually have very poorly struck obverses.

DIMES—LIBERTY SEATED 1837-1859

MINT STATE *Absolutely no trace of wear.*

MS-70 UNCIRCULATED

A flawless coin exactly as it was minted, with no trace of wear or injury. Must have full mint luster and brilliance or light toning. Any unusual die or striking traits must be described.

MS-67 UNCIRCULATED

Virtually flawless but with very minor imperfections.

MS-65 UNCIRCULATED

No trace of wear; nearly as perfect as MS-67 except for some small blemish. Has full mint luster but may be unevenly toned or lightly fingermarked. A few barely noticeable nicks or marks may be present.

MS-63 UNCIRCULATED

A mint state coin with attractive mint luster, but noticeable detracting contact marks or minor blemishes.

MS-60 UNCIRCULATED

A strictly Uncirculated coin with no trace of wear, but with blemishes more obvious than for MS-63. May lack full mint luster, and surface may be dull, spotted or heavily toned.

ABOUT UNCIRCULATED *Small trace of wear visible on highest points.*

AU-58 *Very Choice*

Has some signs of abrasion: high points of breast and knees; ribbon bow and tips of leaves. Weak spots in the design are usually caused by striking and not wear.

AU-55 *Choice*

OBVERSE: Only a trace of wear shows on highest points of the knees.

REVERSE: A trace of wear shows on the ribbon bow.

Three-quarters of the mint luster is still present.

DIMES—LIBERTY SEATED 1837–1859

AU-50   *Typical*

OBVERSE: Traces of wear show on knees, right shoulder, and edge of hairline.

REVERSE: Traces of wear show on ribbon bow, and tips of leaves.

Half of the mint luster is still present.

EXTREMELY FINE   *Very light wear on only the highest points.*

EF-45   *Choice*

OBVERSE: Slight wear shows on high points of knees and hair at forehead. Drapery is worn at shoulder and bustline. LIBERTY is sharp and scroll edges are raised.

REVERSE: High points of wreath and bow lightly worn. Lines in leaves are clearly defined.

Part of the mint luster is still present.

EF-40   *Typical*

OBVERSE: Wear shows on knees, head and shoulder. Gown lightly worn at neckline in spots. LIBERTY is complete and scroll edges are raised.

REVERSE: High points of wreath and bow are worn, but all details are clearly defined.

Traces of mint luster may still show.

VERY FINE   *Light to moderate even wear. All major features are sharp.*

VF-30   *Choice*

OBVERSE: Wear spots show on shoulder, breast, knee and legs. The head is weak but has some visible details. LIBERTY and scroll are complete.

REVERSE: Leaves are worn but most details are visible. Nearly all the details in the ribbon bow are clear.

VF-20   *Typical*

OBVERSE: Over half the details still show in the gown. Hair, shoulder, and legs are worn but bold. Every letter in LIBERTY is visible.

REVERSE: The ribbon is worn, but some details are visible. Half the details in the leaves are clear.

DIMES—LIBERTY SEATED 1837–1859

FINE *Moderate to heavy even wear. Entire design clear and bold.*

F-12   OBVERSE: Some details show in hair, cap, and at the shoulder and breast. All letters in LIBERTY are weak but visible.

REVERSE: Some of the details in leaves are visible. Bow is outlined but flat. Leaves are separated. Letters in legend are worn but clear.

VERY GOOD *Well worn. Design clear but flat and lacking details.*

VG-8   OBVERSE: Entire shield is weak, and most gown details are worn smooth. Three letters in LIBERTY are clear. Rim is complete.

REVERSE: Wreath shows only bold outline. Some of the bow is very weak.

GOOD *Heavily worn. Design and legend visible but faint in spots.*

G-4   OBVERSE: Entire design well worn with very little detail remaining. Date is weak but visible.

REVERSE: Wreath is worn flat but is completely outlined. Tops of some letters are worn nearly smooth.

ABOUT GOOD   *Outlined design. Parts of date and legend worn smooth.*

AG-3   OBVERSE: Liberty is outlined with nearly all details worn away. Date readable but very weak. Stars merging into rim.
REVERSE: Entire design partially worn away.

Note: Coins of this design are sometimes weakly struck, particularly in the head, drapery and horizontal lines of the shield.

DIMES—LIBERTY SEATED 1860–1891

MINT STATE   *Absolutely no trace of wear.*

MS-70   UNCIRCULATED
A flawless coin exactly as it was minted, with no trace of wear or injury. Must have full mint luster and brilliance or light toning. Any unusual die or striking traits must be described.

MS-67   UNCIRCULATED
Virtually flawless but with very minor imperfections.

MS-65   UNCIRCULATED
No trace of wear; nearly as perfect as MS-67 except for some small blemish. Has full mint luster but may be unevenly toned or lightly fingermarked. A few barely noticeable nicks or marks may be present.

MS-63   UNCIRCULATED
A mint state coin with attractive mint luster, but noticeable detracting contact marks or minor blemishes.

MS-60   UNCIRCULATED
A strictly Uncirculated coin with no trace of wear, but with blemishes more obvious than for MS-63. May lack full mint luster, and surface may be dull, spotted or heavily toned.

ABOUT UNCIRCULATED   *Small trace of wear visible on highest points.*

AU-58   *Very Choice*
Has some signs of abrasion: high points of breast and knees; ribbon bow and tips of leaves.

AU-55   *Choice*
OBVERSE: Only a trace of wear shows on highest points of the knees.
REVERSE: A trace of wear shows on the ribbon bow.
   Three-quarters of the mint luster is still present.

AU-50   *Typical*
OBVERSE: Traces of wear show on knees, right shoulder, and edge of hairline.
REVERSE: Traces of wear show on ribbon bow and tips of leaves.
   Half of the mint luster is still present.

EXTREMELY FINE *Very light wear on only the highest points.*

EF-45 *Choice*

OBVERSE: Slight wear shows on high points of knees and hairline. Drapery is worn at shoulder and bustline. LIBERTY is sharp and scroll edges are raised.

REVERSE: High points of wreath and bow lightly worn. Lines in leaves are clearly defined.

Part of the mint luster is still present.

EF-40 *Typical*

OBVERSE: Wear shows on knees, head and shoulder. Gown lightly worn at neckline in spots. LIBERTY is complete and scroll edges are raised.

REVERSE: High points of wreath and bow are worn, but all details are clearly defined.

Traces of mint luster may still show.

VERY FINE *Light to moderate even wear. All major features are sharp.*

VF-30 *Choice*

OBVERSE: Wear spots show on shoulder, breast, knee and legs. The head is weak but has some visible details. LIBERTY and scroll are complete.

REVERSE: Wear shows on the two bottom leaves but most details are visible. Nearly all the details in the ribbon bow are clear.

VF-20 *Typical*

OBVERSE: Over half the details still show in the gown. Hair, shoulder, and legs are worn but bold. Every letter in LIBERTY is visible. Details in cap are visible.

REVERSE: The ribbon is worn, but some details are visible. Half of the details in leaves are clear. Bottom leaves and upper stalks show wear spots.

FINE *Moderate to heavy even wear. Entire design clear and bold.*

F-12 OBVERSE: Some details show in hair, cap, and at the shoulder and breast. All letters in LIBERTY are weak but visible. Clasp is worn away.
REVERSE: Some details in upper leaves and corn are visible. Bow is outlined but flat. Letters in are worn but clear.

VERY GOOD *Well worn. Design clear but flat and lacking details.*

VG-8 OBVERSE: Entire shield is weak, and most details in the gown, knee and legs are worn smooth. Three letters in LIBERTY are clear. Rim is complete.
REVERSE: Wreath shows only a small amount of details. Corn and grain are flat. Some of the bow is very weak.

GOOD *Heavily worn. Design and legend visible but faint in spots.*

G-4 OBVERSE: Entire design well worn with very little detail remaining. Date is weak but visible. LIBERTY is worn away.
REVERSE: Wreath is worn flat but is completely outlined. Corn and grain are worn nearly smooth.

ABOUT GOOD   *Outlined design. Parts of date and legend worn smooth.*

AG-3   OBVERSE: Liberty is outlined with nearly all details worn away. Date readable but worn. Legend merging into rim.
REVERSE: Entire design partially worn away.

Note: Coins of this design are sometimes weakly struck, particularly in the head, mint mark, horizontal lines of the shield, and at the top of the wreath.

1860-O   Usually porous, granular or with many tiny planchet defects.

1862-S   Mint mark often very weak.

1865-S   Usually weakly struck.

1866-S   Mint mark usually weak; one reverse has a strong, filled mint mark.

1871-S   Head and parts of wreath usually weak.

1871-CC, 1872-CC   Usually weak and uneven.

1873-CC with arrows, 1874-CC   Granular or porous surface is common.

1879, 1880, 1881   Uncirculated pieces usually have prooflike surfaces.

1887-S   Mint mark usually partly or wholly filled.

DIMES—BARBER 1892–1916

MINT STATE   *Absolutely no trace of wear.*

MS-70   UNCIRCULATED
A flawless coin exactly as it was minted, with no trace of wear or injury. Must have full mint luster and brilliance or light toning. Any unusual die or striking traits must be described.

MS-67   UNCIRCULATED
Virtually flawless but with very minor imperfections.

MS-65   UNCIRCULATED
No trace of wear; nearly as perfect as MS-67 except for some small blemish. Has full mint luster but may be unevenly toned or lightly fingermarked. A few barely noticeable nicks or marks may be present.

MS-63   UNCIRCULATED
A mint state coin with attractive mint luster, but noticeable detracting contact marks or minor blemishes.

MS-60   UNCIRCULATED
A strictly Uncirculated coin with no trace of wear, but with blemishes more obvious than for MS-63. May lack full mint luster, and surface may be dull, spotted or heavily toned.

ABOUT UNCIRCULATED   *Small trace of wear visible on highest points.*

AU-58   *Very Choice*
Has some signs of abrasion: high points of cheek, and hair below LIBERTY; ribbon bow and tips of leaves.

AU-55   *Choice*
OBVERSE: Only a trace of wear shows on highest points of hair below LIBERTY.
REVERSE: A trace of wear shows on ribbon bow, wheat grains, and leaf near O.
   Three-quarters of the mint luster is still present.

AU-50   *Typical*
OBVERSE: Traces of wear show on cheek, top of forehead, and hair below LIBERTY.

REVERSE: Traces of wear show on ribbon bow, wheat grains, and tips of leaves.

Half of the mint luster is still present.

EXTREMELY FINE *Very light wear on only the highest points.*

EF-45 *Choice*

OBVERSE: Slight wear shows on high points of upper leaves, cheek, and hair above forehead. LIBERTY is sharp and band edges are bold.

REVERSE: High points of the wreath and bow lightly worn. Lines in leaves are clearly defined.

Part of the mint luster is still present.

EF-40 *Typical*

OBVERSE: Light wear shows on leaves, cheek, cap and hair above forehead. LIBERTY is sharp and band edges are clear.

REVERSE: High points of wreath and bow are worn, but all details are clearly defined.

Traces of mint luster may still show.

VERY FINE *Light to moderate even wear. All major features are sharp.*

VF-30 *Choice*

OBVERSE: Wear spots show on leaves, cap, hair and cheek. Bottom row of leaves is weak but has some visible details. LIBERTY and band are complete.

REVERSE: Wear shows on the two bottom leaves but most details are visible. Nearly all the details in the ribbon bow and corn kernels are clear.

VF-20 *Typical*

OBVERSE: Over half the details still show in leaves. Hair worn but bold. Every letter in LIBERTY is visible.

REVERSE: The ribbon is worn, but some details are visible. Half the details in leaves are clear. Bottom leaves and upper stalks show wear spots.

DIMES—BARBER 1892–1916

FINE   *Moderate to heavy even wear. Entire design clear and bold.*

F-12   OBVERSE: Some details show in hair, cap, and facial features. All letters in LIBERTY are weak but visible. Upper row of leaves is outlined, but bottom row is worn smooth.

       REVERSE: Some details in the lower leaf clusters are plainly visible. Bow is outlined but flat. Letters are worn but clear.

VERY GOOD   *Well worn. Design clear but flat and lacking details.*

VG-8   OBVERSE: Entire head weak, and most of the details in the face are worn smooth. Three letters in LIBERTY are clear. Rim is complete.

       REVERSE: Wreath shows only a small amount of detail. Corn and grain are flat. Some of the bow is very weak.

GOOD   *Heavily worn. Design and legend visible but faint in spots.*

G-4   OBVERSE: Entire design well worn with very little detail remaining. Legend is weak but visible. LIBERTY is worn away.

       REVERSE: Wreath is worn flat but is completely outlined. Corn and grains are worn nearly smooth.

ABOUT GOOD   *Outlined design. Parts of date and legend worn smooth.*

AG-3   OBVERSE: Head is outlined with nearly all details worn away. Date readable but partially worn away. Legend merging into rim.
REVERSE: Entire wreath partially worn away and merging into rim.

Note: New Orleans issues, in particular, are occasionally softly struck.

1907-O   Liberty's brow and hair are very softly struck.

MINT STATE   *Absolutely no trace of wear.*

MS-70   UNCIRCULATED
A flawless coin exactly as it was minted, with no trace of wear or injury. Must have full mint luster and brilliance or light toning. Any unusual die or striking traits must be described.

MS-67   UNCIRCULATED
Virtually flawless but with very minor imperfections.

MS-65   UNCIRCULATED
No trace of wear; nearly as perfect as MS-67 except for some small blemish. Has full mint luster but may be unevenly toned or lightly fingermarked. A few barely noticeable nicks or marks may be present.

MS-63   UNCIRCULATED
A mint state coin with attractive mint luster, but noticeable detracting contact marks or minor blemishes.

MS-60   UNCIRCULATED
A strictly Uncirculated coin with no trace of wear, but with blemishes more obvious than for MS-63. May lack full mint luster, and surface may be dull, spotted or heavily toned.

ABOUT UNCIRCULATED   *Small trace of wear visible on highest points.*

AU-58   *Very Choice*
Has some signs of abrasion: high points of hair and in front of ear; diagonal bands on fasces.

AU-55   *Choice*
OBVERSE: Only a trace of wear shows on highest points of hair above forehead and in front of ear.
REVERSE: A trace of wear shows on the horizontal and diagonal fasces bands.
Three-quarters of the mint luster is still present.

AU-50   *Typical*
OBVERSE: Traces of wear show on hair along face, above forehead, and in front of ear.

[163]

REVERSE: Traces of wear show on the fasces bands but edges are sharply defined.

Half of the mint luster is still present.

EXTREMELY FINE *Very light wear on only the highest points.*

EF-45 *Choice*

OBVERSE: Slight wear shows on high points of feathers and at hairline. Hair along face is sharp and detailed.

REVERSE: High points of the diagonal fasces bands are lightly worn. Horizontal lines are clearly defined but not fully separated.

Part of the mint luster is still present.

EF-40 *Typical*

OBVERSE: Wear shows on high points of feathers, hair, and at neckline.

REVERSE: High points of fasces bands are worn, but all details are clearly defined and partially separated.

Traces of mint luster may still show.

VERY FINE *Light to moderate even wear. All major features are sharp.*

VF-30 *Choice*

OBVERSE: Wear spots show on hair along face, cheek and neckline. Feathers are weak but have nearly full details.

REVERSE: Wear shows on the two diagonal bands but most details are visible. All vertical lines are sharp. All details in the branch are clear.

VF-20 *Typical*

OBVERSE: Three-quarters of the details still show in feathers. Hair worn but bold. Some details in hair braid are visible.

REVERSE: Wear shows on the two diagonal bands but most details are visible. All vertical lines are sharp. All details in the branch are clear.

FINE *Moderate to considerable even wear. Entire design clear and bold.*

F-12 OBVERSE: Some details show in hair. All feathers are weak but partially visible. Hair braid is nearly worn away.

REVERSE: Vertical lines are all visible but lack sharpness. Diagonal bands show on fasces but one is worn smooth at midpoint.

VERY GOOD *Well worn. Design clear but flat and lacking details.*

VG-8 OBVERSE: Entire head is weak, and most details in the wing are worn smooth. All letters and date are clear. Rim is complete.

REVERSE: About half the vertical lines in the fasces are visible. Rim is complete.

GOOD *Heavily worn. Design and legend visible but faint in spots.*

G-4 OBVERSE: Entire design well worn with very little detail remaining. Legend and date are weak but visible. Rim is visible.

REVERSE: Fasces is worn nearly flat but is completely outlined. Sticks and bands are worn smooth.

DIMES—MERCURY 1916–1945

ABOUT GOOD   *Outlined design. Parts of date and legend worn smooth.*

AG-3   OBVERSE: Head is outlined with nearly all details worn away. Date readable but worn. Legend merging into rim.

REVERSE: Entire design partially worn away. Rim worn half way into the legend.

Note: Coins of this design are sometimes weakly struck in spots, particularly in the lines and horizontal bands of the fasces.

The following dates are usually found poorly struck and lacking full details regardless of condition: 1916-D, 1918-S, 1919-S, 1920-S, 1921, 1921-D, 1923-S, 1924-S, 1925-D, S, 1926-S, 1927-D, S, 1928-S, 1930-S, 1931-S, 1934 and 1939-S.

1920 and 1920-D usually show the zero joined to the rim.

1921 usually has a weakly struck date, especially the last two digits.

1923 often has the bottom of the three weakly struck and joined to the rim.

1945 is rarely seen with full cross bands on the fasces.

DIMES—ROOSEVELT 1946 TO DATE

MINT STATE   *Absolutely no trace of wear.*

MS-70   UNCIRCULATED
A flawless coin exactly as it was minted, with no trace of wear or injury. Must have full mint luster and brilliance or light toning. Any unusual striking traits must be described.

MS-67   UNCIRCULATED
Virtually flawless but with very minor imperfections.

MS-65   UNCIRCULATED
No trace of wear; nearly as perfect as MS-67 except for some small blemish. Has full mint luster but may be unevenly toned or lightly fingermarked. A few barely noticeable nicks or marks may be present.

MS-63   UNCIRCULATED
A mint state coin with attractive mint luster, but noticeable detracting contact marks or minor blemishes.

MS-60   UNCIRCULATED
A strictly Uncirculated coin with no trace of wear, but with blemishes more obvious than for MS-63. Has full mint luster, but surface may be dull, spotted or toned.

ABOUT UNCIRCULATED   *Small trace of wear visible on highest points.*

AU-58   *Very Choice*
Has some signs of abrasion: high points of cheek, and hair above ear; tops of leaves, and details in flame.

AU-55   *Choice*
OBVERSE: Only a trace of wear shows on highest points of hair above ear.
REVERSE: A trace of wear shows on .highest spots of the flame.
   Three-quarters of the mint luster is still present.

AU-50   *Typical*
OBVERSE: Traces of wear show in hair above ear.
REVERSE: Traces of wear show on flame but details are sharply defined.
   Half of the mint luster is still present.

EXTREMELY FINE *Very light wear on only the highest points.*

EF-45 *Choice*

OBVERSE: Slight wear shows on high points of hair above ear. Ear is sharp and detailed.

REVERSE: High points of flame are lightly worn. Torch lines are clearly defined and fully separated.

Part of the mint luster is still present.

EF-40 *Typical*

OBVERSE: Wear shows on high points of hair, and at cheek line. Ear shows slight wear on the upper tip.

REVERSE: High points of flame, torch, and leaves are worn, but all details are clearly defined and partially separated.

Traces of mint luster may still show.

VERY FINE *Light to moderate even wear. All major features are sharp.*

VF-30 *Choice*

OBVERSE: Wear spots show on hair, ear, cheek and chin. Hair lines are weak but have nearly full visible details.

REVERSE: Wear shows on flame but some details are visible. All vertical lines are plain. Most details in the torch and leaves are clear.

VF-20 *Typical*

OBVERSE: Three-quarters of the details still show in hair. Face worn but bold. Some details in the ear are visible.

REVERSE: Wear shows on the flame but a few lines are visible. All torch lines are worn but bold. Most details in leaves are clear.

DIMES—ROOSEVELT 1946 TO DATE

FINE   *Moderate to heavy even wear. Entire design clear and bold.*

F-12   OBVERSE: Half the details show in hair. All of the face is weak but boldly visible. Half of inner edge of ear is worn away.

REVERSE: Vertical lines are all visible, but horizontal bands are worn smooth. Leaves show some detail. Flame is nearly smooth.

VERY GOOD   *Well worn. Design clear but flat and lacking details.*

VG-8   OBVERSE: Entire head is weak, and most of the details in hair and inner edge of ear are worn smooth. All letters and date are clear. Rim is complete.

REVERSE: About half the outer vertical lines in torch are visible. Flame is only outlined. Leaves show very little detail. Rim is complete.

GOOD   *Heavily worn. Design and legend visible but faint in spots.*

G-4   OBVERSE: Entire design well worn with very little detail remaining. Ear is completely outlined. Legend and date are weak but visible. Rim is visible.

REVERSE: Torch is worn nearly flat but is completely outlined. Leaves are worn smooth. Legend is all visible.

ABOUT GOOD   *Outlined design. Parts of date and legend worn smooth.*

AG-3   OBVERSE: Head is outlined with nearly all details worn away. Date readable but worn. Legend merging into rim.

REVERSE: Entire design partially worn away. Rim merges into the legend.

Note: Many of the clad pieces are weakly struck in several spots.

MINT STATE *Absolutely no trace of wear.*

MS-70 UNCIRCULATED
A flawless coin exactly as it was minted, with no trace of wear or injury. Must have full mint luster and brilliance or light toning. Any unusual die or striking traits must be described.

MS-67 UNCIRCULATED
Virtually flawless but with very minor imperfections.

MS-65 UNCIRCULATED
No trace of wear; nearly as perfect as MS-67 except for some small blemish. Has full mint luster but may be unevenly toned, frosty, or lightly finger-marked. A few barely noticeable nicks or marks may be present.

MS-63 UNCIRCULATED
A mint state coin with attractive mint luster, but noticeable detracting contact marks or minor blemishes.

MS-60 UNCIRCULATED
A strictly Uncirculated coin with no trace of wear, but with blemishes more obvious than for MS-63. May lack full mint luster, and surface may be dull, spotted or heavily toned.

ABOUT UNCIRCULATED *Small trace of wear visible on highest points.*

AU-58 *Very Choice*
Has some signs of abrasion: high points of the head, breast, and knees; eagle's breast and top of wings.

AU-55 *Choice*
OBVERSE: Only a trace of wear shows on highest points of head and knees. The clasp is raised and gown has bold lines.
REVERSE: A trace of wear shows on eagle's breast.
Three-quarters of the mint luster is still present.

AU-50 *Typical*
OBVERSE: Traces of wear show on head, breast, knees, and arm. Clasp is very bold.

TWENTY CENTS—1875–1878

REVERSE: Traces of wear show on breast, and tops of wings. Half of the mint luster is still present.

EXTREMELY FINE *Very light wear on only the highest points.*

EF-45 *Choice*

OBVERSE: Slight wear shows on high points of head, breast, knees and arms. Drapery above clasp shows wear.

REVERSE: High points of breast and head lightly worn. Lines in wings are clearly defined.

Part of the mint luster is still present.

EF-40 *Typical*

OBVERSE: Wear shows on knees, head, breast, arms and shoulder. LIBERTY is sharp and scroll edges are raised. Cap shows wear but details are plain.

REVERSE: High points of breast and head are worn, but all details are clearly defined. Wings show wear at top.

Traces of mint luster may still show.

VERY FINE *Light to moderate even wear. All major features are sharp.*

VF-30 *Choice*

OBVERSE: Wear spots show on shoulder, breast, knees and legs. The head is weak but about half the details in hair are visible. LIBERTY and scroll are complete although slightly worn.

REVERSE: Wear shows on breast feathers and wing edges but most details are visible. Most details in head are flat but clear.

VF-20 *Typical*

OBVERSE: Less than half the details show in the hair. Head, shoulder, breast, and legs are worn but bold. Every letter in LIBERTY is visible.

REVERSE: Wings are worn, but three-quarters of the details are visible. Half the details in breast feathers are clear. Head is flat.

FINE   *Moderate to heavy even wear. Entire design clear and bold.*

F-12   OBVERSE: Some details show in gown, shield, and at the shoulder and breast. Three or more letters in LIBERTY must be visible. Clasp is worn. Head and hair are flat.

REVERSE: Half the details in wings and legs visible. Head is outlined but flat; eye is visible. Letters in legend are worn but clear.

VERY GOOD   *Well worn. Design clear but flat and lacking details.*

VG-8   OBVERSE: Entire head is weak, and most details in the gown, knee and legs are worn smooth. One or two letters in LIBERTY may show. Some details show near right arm.

REVERSE: Breast shows only a small amount of detail. Eye is very weak. Head and wing edges are flat. Less than half the feathers' are visible.

GOOD   *Heavily worn. Design and legend visible but faint in spots.*

G-4   OBVERSE: Entire design well worn with very little detail remaining. Shield is weak but partially visible. LIBERTY is worn away.

REVERSE: Eagle is worn flat but is completely outlined and some feathers are visible. Head and breast are worn nearly smooth.

TWENTY CENTS—1875-1878

ABOUT GOOD *Outlined design. Parts of date and legend worn smooth.*

AG-3   OBVERSE: Liberty is outlined with nearly all details worn away. Date readable but worn. Stars merging into rim.

REVERSE: Entire design partially worn away. Legend readable although merged with rim.

Note: Coins of this design are sometimes weakly struck, particularly on the obverse, and at the top of the eagle's right wing.

1875-S usually shows flatness on eagle's breast.

1875-CC usually shows flatness on eagle's breast and upper left wing.

MINT STATE *Absolutely no trace of wear.*

MS-70 UNCIRCULATED
A flawless coin exactly as it was minted, with no trace of wear or injury. Must have full mint luster and brilliance or light toning. Any unusual die or striking traits must be described.

MS-67 UNCIRCULATED
Virtually flawless but with very minor imperfections.

MS-65 UNCIRCULATED
No trace of wear; nearly as perfect as MS-67 except for some small blemish. Has full mint luster but may be unevenly toned or lightly fingermarked. A few barely noticeable nicks or adjustment file marks may be present.

MS-63 UNCIRCULATED
A mint state coin with attractive mint luster, but noticeable detracting contact marks or minor blemishes.

MS-60 UNCIRCULATED
A strictly Uncirculated coin with no trace of wear, but with blemishes more obvious than for MS-63. May lack full mint luster, and surface may be dull, spotted or heavily toned.

ABOUT UNCIRCULATED *Small trace of wear visible on highest points.*

AU-58 *Very Choice*
Has some signs of abrasion: high points of bust, shoulder, and hair above forehead; eagle's breast and top edges of wings. Shallow or weak spots in the relief are usually caused by improper striking and not wear.

AU-55 *Choice*
OBVERSE: Only a trace of wear shows on highest points of hair above forehead.
REVERSE: A trace of wear shows on breast.
Three-quarters of the mint luster is still present.

AU-50 *Typical*
OBVERSE: Traces of wear show on hair above ear and at forehead. Drapery

QUARTERS—DRAPED BUST, SMALL EAGLE 1796

has trace of wear at shoulder and bustline.

REVERSE: Traces of wear show on breast, and top edges of wings.
Half of the mint luster is still present.

EXTREMELY FINE   *Very light wear on only the highest points.*

EF-45   *Choice*

OBVERSE: Slight wear shows on high points of hair from forehead to the ear.
Drapery is worn at shoulder and bustline.

REVERSE: High points of wings, breast and head are lightly worn. Lines in
feathers are clearly defined.

Part of the mint luster is still present.

EF-40   *Typical*

OBVERSE: Wear shows on hair from forehead to ear, and lightly on the cheek
and bust. Drapery lightly worn at neckline in spots.

REVERSE: High points of eagle are worn, but each detail is clearly defined.
Head and breast are very weak.

Traces of mint luster may still show.

VERY FINE   *Light to moderate even wear. All major features are sharp.*

VF-30   *Choice*

OBVERSE: Hair above forehead is worn but has some bold features. Flowing
hair is well detailed.

REVERSE: Feathers are worn but most details are visible. Some of the details
in head and breast are clear unless weakly struck.

VF-20   *Typical*

OBVERSE: Hair above forehead worn almost smooth. Three-quarters of the
details still show in flowing hair. Every letter and star is plainly visible. Left
side of drapery is indistinct.

REVERSE: Head and breast are worn, but some feathers are visible. Most
details in wings are clear unless weakly struck.

FINE   *Moderate to heavy even wear. Entire design clear and bold.*

F-12   OBVERSE: Some details show in hair ends and at left of ear. All letters, date and stars are visible. The eye and eyebrow are clear.

REVERSE: Half the feathers are visible in the wings. Breast is smooth. Letters in the legend are worn but clear.

VERY GOOD   *Well worn. Design clear but flat and lacking details.*

VG-8   OBVERSE: Entire head is weak, but most hair details are worn smooth. Date and LIBERTY are weak but clear. Parts of the eye and eyebrows are visible.

REVERSE: Eagle is boldly outlined with only a few details showing in wings. Breast is smooth. Some letters are very weak.

GOOD   *Heavily worn. Design and legend visible but faint in spots.*

G-4   OBVERSE: Entire design well worn with very little detail remaining. Legend, stars and date are partially worn away but visible.

REVERSE: Eagle is worn flat and not completely outlined. Tops of some letters are worn nearly smooth.

Draped Bust quarters, small eagle 1796 series continued on page 193.

CHARACTERISTICS OF UNCIRCULATED COINS

This chapter illustrates examples of various coins that are typical Uncirculated specimens. It shows in detail some of the important points discussed in other parts of this book. The related chapters should be read and followed to better understand how these coins exemplify the elements of luster, eye appeal, surface and strike.Uncirculated coins are graded differently than circulated pieces because they are free from wear or loss of detail from circulation. The various levels of Uncirculated coins range from MS-60 to MS-70, and the differences in grade are more a matter of eye appeal than concern for physical abuse.

This 1887 Morgan dollar grades only MS-60 because of excessive contact marks.

Elements that affect the value of an Uncirculated coin are: Quality of luster; Surface marks; Eye appeal; and Fullness of strike. A full description of these features is given in the chapter on Basic Grading Techniques on pages 29-34. The importance of these elements cannot be overstated as they are essential to determining the quality, and thus the grade and value of all uncirculated coins.

A Morgan dollar with attractive rainbow tones, and the colorful Mercury dime are both candidates for higher than normal grades because of their exceptional eye appeal.

Descriptions of the Uncirculated grade for each type of United States coins are given in the applicable section in chronological and denominational order. Also included are special notes on the quality of strike and other individual characteristics where appropriate. Of special importance are the charts and line drawings used to describe the Walking Liberty half dollars, Morgan and Peace dollars, and Liberty and St. Gaudens $20 gold pieces.

With but a few modifications, most Uncirculated coins can be graded with the same standards. The significant differences have to do with the location of prime focal areas of the designs (which have a bearing on eye appeal), and the color variations of copper coins and silver coins that are toned.

The other elements that must be considered are the size and weight of the coin. Small, light coins like three cent silver pieces will not have the same kind of surface marks as a large, silver dollar. Gold coins that are made of a much softer but heavier metal are more subject to marks than their silver counterparts.

Liberty Standing quarter with nearly full head.
Details are missing on typical weak strike piece.

The principles used for grading coins shown in this section can be applied to most other Uncirculated coins if one uses the charts and comments in each appropriate section of the book to determine variations of focal areas, severity of contact marks, normal luster and strike characteristics.

Additional details and guidelines for grading Uncirculated coins will be found throughout this book. An ideal pictorial supplement for learning the nuances of this topic can be seen in the video *Grading Mint-State Coins* with J.P. Martin, available through the American Numismatic Association.

This 88 minute video presentation gives an in-depth look at all aspects of grading with detailed color illustrations describing in detail types of luster, strike, toning, eye appeal, lighting and magnification.

GRADING UNCIRCULATED COINS

The difference in appearance between an uncirculated coin and one barely touched by friction from circulation or handling is slight. On the scale from one to seventy, all uncirculated coins range from 60 to 70, and the circulated pieces are 58 or below. The two point spread from one category to the other is slight.

Gold coin showing light band (cartwheel) on an Uncirculated specimen.

Beyond the physical distinction of actual wear on a coin, there is the consideration of eye appeal that also must be taken into account when evaluating borderline pieces. In practice an AU-58 coin that has only a slight break in luster, but otherwise has the appearance of MS-62, is far more attractive than a technically uncirculated coin that is noticeably marred by contact marks or other disfigurements. In most cases the more attractive About Uncirculated coin will be valued higher than its less attractive Uncirculated counterpart.

Eye appeal, or the esthetic quality of a coin, is very much a personal consideration, but some elements are universally accepted as being more attractive than others. Charts and quantifying comments in this book are designed to assist in understanding those borderline considerations that can sway a grading determination by a point or two in either direction. The color pictures in this section will bemost helpful in this regard.

Notice the exceptional toning and eye appeal of this quarter.

LUSTER

Fine-line differences in grading become important when there is a difference of hundreds or even thousands of dollars in value between coins of superior quality. Of all the esthetic considerations none is more important than the quality and originality of luster. To evaluate the luster of a coin one must be able to judge its appearance against a perfect coin of the same date and mint. That is not always possible, but one can usually distinguish between three basic kinds of luster, and judge quality based on the remaining brilliance.

Differences between incandescent (left) and florescent (right) lighting.

The best way to examine mint luster is to hold a coin close to an incandescent light source and rotate it so that a band of light will be reflected across the surface. The strength, brilliance and sharpness of this band will help to determine the quality and originality of remaining luster.

Luster is the reflection of light from microscopic erosion or flow lines on a coin's surface. Although luster manifests itself in a multitude of variations, it is grouped into four categories: Frosty, Brilliant, Satin and Prooflike.

Examples of Frosty luster and Brilliant luster.

Dies are generally polished before being put into service. Those with the highest degree of polishing initially produce coins similar to today's proofs.

Those surfaces show a high degree of reflectivity. Technically, those coins have little or no luster. As each coin is struck, erosion lines develop on the die, producing coins that have normal luster.

As flow line develop, the coins produced have surface with reduced ability to mirror images. This degradation of the prooflike surface can be measured by the distance a reflected image can be accurately depicted.

Dies which are not polished tend to produce coins with a soft sheen or uniform reflection of light. This luster type is called Satin. These coins lack the strong reaction to light typical of other types of luster.

Prooflike luster is unnatural for circulation coins. It is produced from dies which are heavily polished and highly reflective. Normal production eventually erodes this to a frosty luster, which is the most prevalent type. Satin and Prooflike surfaces are much scarcer and are typical of early striking or low mintage runs.

Examples of Satin and Frosty Luster.

Styles of luster typified by coins:
Frosty Luster - Peace Dollars, Franklin Half Dollars.
Brilliant Luster - 1879-1882-S Morgan Dollars.
Satin Luster - 1936 Proof Cents and Nickels.
Prooflike Luster - Special Mint Sets issued 1965-1967.
Cameo Prooflike - All modern U.S. Proofs since 1974.

Example of Cameo Prooflike Dollar.   *Uncirculated coin with luster removed by dipping or cleaning.*

Diminished or dull luster is usually a result of cleaning by chemical means (dipping) that has destroyed some of the brilliance of a coin's normal luster by reducing the reflectivity of the flow lines. If all the luster has been striped away, the coin will grade no better than AU-50.

[180]

MINTING CHARACTERISTICS

The mints create anomalies on coins by design and defect. The method in which dies are prepared or polished may greatly affect the appearance of the coin. Dies are polished to remove die erosion, cracks or clashings.

There are also characteristics which develop with die use or overuse, such as die erosion, cracking and clashes. Unclean working conditions may result in "strike throughs" or contaminated planchets.

Dies are polished to remove die erosion. They show up on the fields of coins as raised lines. They are common and accepted as a normal part of production.

"Strike throughs", occur when foreign material lands between the dies and planchet during minting.

Die cracking is the common result of minting. Die cracks generally do not affect grade or value.

Planchet defects such as scratches, clips, striations, rollouts or uneven surfaces may not be struck out in the minting process and affect the appearance and grade of the coin.

Planchet scratches (left) or rollouts (right) may affect grade depending on their severity.

The roughness on the face of Liberty is due to a pitted planchet.

CONTACT MARKS

The effect of contact marks on the grade of a coin is well defined in charts and wording throughout each specific section of this book. Of equal importance is the location of such marks. A prime focal area is one in which your eye is immediately drawn to when viewing a coin. Prime focal areas draw attention to marks that might otherwise be considered unimportant. A small mark hidden in a busy design is not nearly as offensive as the same size mark on the end of Liberty's nose. A portrait coin's prime focal area is the face and the area directly in front of it.

Note: The circled prime focal area. The Morgan dollar grades MS-60 due to excessive contact marks.

Study the drawings that accompany descriptions of the following coins to better understand the effect that marks have when they are located in either prime focal areas or secondary zones: Liberty Walking 50¢ (a non portrait type); Morgan dollars (portrait types); Liberty Head $20 gold and St. Gaudens $20 gold pieces. The illustrations shown here depict coins at various grade levels with typical marks for these types of coins.

No single set of rules can apply to the consideration of eye appeal when it comes to location and severity of contact marks. The size of the marks in relation to a coin's overall surface is as important as where the marks are located.

STRIKE

The quality of "strike" is another subjective quality that must be judged carefully to determine the grade of a coin. In strictest terms, strike is not a factor of technical grading, but in the commercial world it can cause a significant difference in value, and thus the way in which a coin is judged according to eye appeal. A weakly struck coin is usually unattractive and thus graded lower than a sharply struck piece.

Walking Liberty with a weak strike and one with strong details.

Strike, like luster, is a factor that can only be judged by comparison to other, perfect, coins. Some pieces like half dollars from the San Francisco Mint made during the years 1940-41 are nearly always weakly struck. A choice well struck example of one of these is so desirable that it might be given an extra grade point or so because of superior eye appeal.

Comparison of a weak strike and perfect Proof details.

The Morgan dollar of 1884 shown here is a weak strike. Still, it is uncirculated. It's value would be about the same as an AU coin of the same date. Comparison of a typical 1884-O dollar with a fully struck 1896 Proof shows the differences in detail that have been lost to a weak strike.

Coins like the Standing Liberty quarter and Winged Liberty dime are identified by the strength or weakness of the head on the quarter, and the bands of the fasces on the reverse of the dime. The middle band binding the fasces is the last area to fully strike up.

This coin does not display bands.

This dime displays fully split center bands known as full bands.

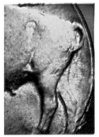

Die erosion near rim of Buffalo nickel.

Quality of dies is another subjective factor of eye appeal, and thus has a bearing on the desirability of a coin and its grade. The die for this Buffalo nickel was used to the point that it shows considerable erosion. Loss of detail, luster and surface defects can reduce its grade by one to several points.

COLOR

When copper or bronze coins are freshly made they have a brilliant luster that varies from red to orange, or gold depending on the alloy. With time the color usually fades to more subtle hues or becomes dull and dark. Improper storage, moisture or cleaning will accelerate the change in color.

Even (l) and uneven (r) coloring on early copper cents.

Copper coins are generally referred to as being either Red, Red/Brown, or Brown in color. These terms are relative and imply originality more than actual color. In each case, a coin can be considered Uncirculated regardless of its color if the underlying luster is still present and unbroken. Study the accompanying pictures that show examples of even and uneven coloring, along with cents that have been dipped and cleaned.

Copper cents with Red, Red/Brown and Brown colors.

TONING

Silver coins react similarly to copper pieces in that they too tend to darken or lose their original brilliance and change color with time. Unlike copper coins, the variety of colors taken on by silver coins can be very attractive. Some collectors (and grading services) consider unusual rainbow hues as added eye appeal and tend to grade such coins higher than untoned pieces.

Artificial toning on Walker and original toning on Franklin half dollars.

Technically, toned coins have been subjected to possibly harmful effects of tarnish or oxidation, or worse yet they may have been artificially enhanced to add to their market value. The subjective value of toned coins is questionable at best and a matter of personal preference.

Indian Head cents with toned and natural red color.   *Artificial toning.*

The toned Liberty Standing quarter shown on page 179 has great eye appeal and would command a premium price. Most professional grading services would add a point or more to its grade because it is so attractive. Compare it to the artificial toning on the reverse of this Morgan dollar. Also study the effects of cleaning, and contamination of luster caused by improper storage in PVC holders.

The large cent of 1831 shown here has been cleaned. The 1864 cent is still original and brilliant.

Cleaned and retoned 1831 cent, and original 1864 bronze cent.

CLEANING AND RESTORATION

Pilgrim half dollar original (l) and cleaned (r) showing differences in luster.

Once a coin has been stripped of original surface and luster it can never be fully restored or made Uncirculated again. Examine the Pilgrim half dollar illustrations showing a coin that has been cleaned, and an uncleaned example to see the difference in luster. Also take a close look at the Morgan dollar photos showing a coin that has been "thumbed" to hide surface marks. In this case oils from a finger have been rubbed on the surface of the coin in an effort to cover old scratches. The artificial frosting that has been applied to the reverse of the Morgan dollar does not carefully follow the outline of the design.

Morgan dollars: Thumbed. Artificial frosting.

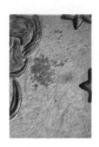

This 1931-S cent has been dipped and its luster dimished leaving an unnatural pink color.

PVC residue which has a blue green color, can turn corrosive. It is removable by use of solvents but can leave areas of corrosion.

Whizzed coins are most easily detected by an unnatural look to the "luster" which has been simulated by polishing with a brush. Under magnification you can see that there are ridges on the edges of some letters and raised design. The Stone Mountain commemorative half illustration is a good example of whizzing.

Details of a Stone Mountain half dollar showing whizzing with a rotating brush.

GOLD COINS

Gold coins are graded somewhat differently than copper and silver. Gold is a relatively soft metal and subject to more handling marks. Further, gold was usually stored in bags and frequently transported in quantity. The large size of these heavy gold coins, and the rough handling produced marks and blemishes not found on most other coins. Because of this it is usual to find uncirculated coins with slight breaks in luster on the high points where coins hit together in bags.

Typical copper spots on gold coins.

Luster breaks on otherwise uncirculated gold coins are often accepted in grades up to MS-63. Gold coins are also notorious for dark streaks known as "copper spots." These are caused by impurities in the metal. They can not be removed or diminished, and are considered unattractive. A gold coin should not be downgraded for such a blemish, but the lower eye appeal will usually lessen the coin's value. They are usually not accepted in grades above MS-63, depending on location and severity.

COMPARISON OF TYPICAL UNCIRCULATED GRADES

LIBERTY WALKING HALF DOLLARS

The design of this coin fills most of the available space and leaves little open field area to absorb contact marks. It is typical of many American coins and an example of how eye appeal is affected by blemishes that are noticeable in open areas, or are obscured by design elements.

MS-65 Coins are strictly Uncirculated with no trace of wear, but are not perfect. They may show light scattered marks in the design, but nothing of consequence in prime focal areas.

MS-63 Is a mint state coin with attractive mint luster but with noticeable detracting contact marks or minor blemishes. Scuffing along the head and breast is usually a result of roll handling and not wear.

MS-60 Strictly Uncirculated with no wear but with excessive blemishes, or poor luster. There may be heavy contact marks in prime areas. Eye appeal is poor.

COMPARISON OF TYPICAL UNCIRCULATED GRADES
MORGAN DOLLARS

Morgan dollars are similar in design to the Barber series, Indian Head cents and other coins displaying a head on the obverse and an eagle within open areas on the reverse. The diagrams on page 271 identify prime focal areas that are of concern to eye appeal to these coins.

MS-65 Coins have no trace of wear and are nearly as perfect as MS-67 coins except for a few additional bag marks. These pieces must have full luster but may be unevenly toned. An excessively weak strike may lower the eye appeal and affect the grade.

MS-63 A mint state coin with attractive mint luster, but noticeable detracting contact marks or minor blemishes. The obverse is of prime concern and usually determines the grade of this type of coin if there is a slight difference in the reverse.

MS-60 No trace of wear, but may show numerous contact marks, poor luster, spotting or heavy toning. Will have poor eye appeal.

COMPARISON OF TYPICAL UNCIRCULATED GRADES
PEACE DOLLARS

Peace dollars are unusual in that they are struck in low relief, and have a rather subdued luster. There are no prooflike specimens of this coinage, and the few proof coins that were struck have a satin to frosty finish. Expect good luster to be highly reflective, but not brilliant like a Morgan dollar.

MS-65 Will have light and scattered contact marks. A few may be in prime focal areas but should not be distracting. Some light hairlines may be seen. The eye appeal will be pleasing and luster bright and original.

MS-63 Coins are attractive and have full luster with no major distracting marks. Scattered blemishes will be seen in the field.

MS-60 A strictly Uncirculated coin with no trace of wear, but with bag marks and other abrasions. May have a few small rim marks and may be weakly struck. May lack original luster and may be spotted or toned.

COMPARISON OF TYPICAL UNCIRCULATED GRADES
EXAMPLES OF PROOFLIKE, SATIN, AND TONED DOLLARS

A wide range of differences are possible for the eye appeal and quality of luster seen on Morgan and Peace dollars. Appearance may vary from subdued to blazing, or Cameo Prooflike. The value of each of these coins varies according to overall eye appeal and grade.

Deep mirror proof-likes with cameo contrast is considered very appealing.

Cameo prooflike coins are the result of die finishing and can occur on weakly struck coins such as this 1884-O dollar.

Peace dollar dies were not polished or refinished, and usually begin producing satin luster coins.

Coins stored in paper rolls can produce attractively toned coins.

Colorful toning such as seen on this bag-toned dollar is attractive and highly sought after.

COMPARISON OF TYPICAL UNCIRCULATED GRADES

LIBERTY HEAD TWENTY DOLLAR GOLD PIECES

The Twenty Dollar gold coin is typical of most others with a large head on the obverse and eagle on the reverse. All gold pieces are heavy for their size and subject to more contact marks than silver or copper pieces. Light friction from bulk storage is common and not considered wear.

MS-65 No trace of wear and only the lightest friction can be detected on high points. Small blemishes or contact marks are usually present, but coin will have good eye appeal. Full luster and brilliance are necessary, but it may show slight discoloration.

MS-63 Slightly more friction is allowable on the high points but coin must be in strictly Uncirculated condition with good eye appeal. Copper spots are allowable if they do not distract from overall appearance. Some contact marks are noticeable in prime focal areas.

MS-60 An Uncirculated coin with no trace of wear, but with blemishes more obvious than for MS-63. Has mint luster but may lack brilliance. Surface is usually marred by minor bag marks and abrasions. Poor eye appeal.

COMPARISON OF TYPICAL UNCIRCULATED GRADES

SAINT-GAUDENS TWENTY DOLLAR GOLD PIECES

The Standing Liberty design on the Saint-Gaudens twenty dollar coin is a good example of a non-portrait type coin struck in a soft, heavy metal. As such it is subject to more contact marks than pieces in other metals, and those marks are apt to occur in open areas of the field. Storage and handling of these coins over a long period of time has left many of them with unattractive blemishes.

MS-65 No trace of wear, but may show slight luster breaks on the head, breast and leg from bag storage. Good eye appeal, and no noticeable blemishes in any of the prime focal areas. Full and brilliant mint luster is a requirement.

MS-63 May have noticeable scuff marks on head, breast and leg but no detectable wear. Contact marks may show in prime focal areas, but overall the coin is rather attractive with brilliant luster. A few copper spots may be present.

MS-60 A strictly Uncirculated coin with no trace of wear, but with blemishes more obvious than for MS-63. Has full mint luster but may lack brilliance. Surface may be lightly marred by friction, contact marks and abrasions.

QUARTERS—DRAPED BUST, SMALL EAGLE 1796

ABOUT GOOD   *Outlined design. Parts of date and legend worn smooth.*

AG-3   OBVERSE: Head is outlined with nearly all details worn away. Date readable but very weak. Stars merging into rim.
REVERSE: Entire design partially worn away. Letters very weak but visible.

Note: Uncirculated examples of this design are known to exist with either a brilliant prooflike surface, or frosty mint luster. These coins are often weakly struck, particularly on the eagle's head, breast and feathers. File adjustment marks are occasionally seen, and are a normal part of the manufacturing process.

REFERENCES

Browning, A. W. *The Early Quarter Dollars of the United States 1796–1838.* New York, 1925.

Cline, J. H. *Standing Liberty Quarters.* 1976.

Duphorne, R. *The Early Quarter Dollars of the United States.* 1975.

Haseltine, J. W. *Type Table of United States Dollars, Half Dollars and Quarter Dollars.* Philadelphia, 1881 (reprinted 1927, 1968).

Kelman, Keith N. *Standing Liberty Quarters,* N.H., 1976.

MINT STATE   *Absolutely no trace of wear.*

MS-70   UNCIRCULATED
A flawless coin exactly as it was minted, with no trace of wear or injury. Must have full mint luster and brilliance or light toning. Any unusual die or striking traits must be described.

MS-67   UNCIRCULATED
Virtually flawless but with very minor imperfections.

MS-65   UNCIRCULATED
No trace of wear; nearly as perfect as MS-67 except for some small blemish. Has full mint luster but may be unevenly toned or lightly fingermarked. A few barely noticeable nicks or adjustment file marks may be present.

MS-63   UNCIRCULATED
A mint state coin with attractive mint luster, but noticeable detracting contact marks or minor blemishes.

MS-60   UNCIRCULATED
A strictly Uncirculated coin with no trace of wear, but with blemishes more obvious than for MS-63. May lack full mint luster, and surface may be dull, spotted or heavily toned.

ABOUT UNCIRCULATED   *Small trace of wear visible on highest points.*

AU-58   *Very Choice*
Has some signs of abrasion: high points of bust, shoulder, and hair above forehead; eagle's head and top edges of wings. Shallow or weak spots in the relief are usually caused by improper striking and not wear.

AU-55   *Choice*
OBVERSE: Only a trace of wear shows on highest points of hair above forehead.
REVERSE: A trace of wear shows on head feathers and tips of wings.
   Three-quarters of the mint luster is still present.

AU-50   *Typical*
OBVERSE: Traces of wear show on hair above forehead. Drapery has trace

of wear at shoulder and bustline.

REVERSE: Traces of wear show on head, tail, and top edges of wings. Half of the mint luster is still present.

EXTREMELY FINE *Very light wear on only the highest points.*

EF-45 *Choice*

OBVERSE: Slight wear shows on high points of hair from forehead to the ear. Drapery is worn at shoulder and bustline.

REVERSE: High points of wings, shield, tail and head are lightly worn. Lines in feathers are clearly defined.

Part of the mint luster is still present.

EF-40 *Typical*

OBVERSE: Wear shows on hair from forehead to ear, and lightly on the cheek and bust. Drapery lightly worn at neckline in spots.

REVERSE: High points of eagle are worn, but each detail is clearly defined. Tail and feathers above shield are very weak. Wear spots show on ribbon and clouds.

Traces of mint luster may still show.

VERY FINE *Light to moderate even wear. All major features are sharp.*

VF-30 *Choice*

OBVERSE: Hair above forehead is worn but has some bold features. Flowing hair is well detailed.

REVERSE: Feathers are worn but three-quarters of details are visible. Some details in the tail and above shield are clear unless weakly struck. Motto is weak but complete.

VF-20 *Typical*

OBVERSE: Hair above forehead worn almost smooth. Three-quarters of the details still show in flowing hair. Every letter and star is plainly visible. Left side of drapery is indistinct.

REVERSE: Head and tail are worn, but some feathers are visible. Most details in wings are clear unless weakly struck. The motto is weak but complete.

FINE *Moderate to heavy even wear. Entire design clear and bold.*

F-12 OBVERSE: Some details show in drapery, hair ends, and at left of ear. All letters, date and stars are visible. Star centers are smooth.

REVERSE: Half the feathers are visible in wings. Letters in legend are worn but clear. Parts of motto are very weak. Tail feathers show separations.

VERY GOOD *Well worn. Design clear but flat and lacking details.*

VG-8 OBVERSE: Entire head is weak, and most hair details are worn smooth. Date and LIBERTY are weak but clear.

REVERSE: Eagle shows bold outline with only a few feathers visible. Some letters in legend are very weak. Motto is only partially visible.

GOOD *Heavily worn. Design and legend visible but faint in spots.*

G-4 OBVERSE: Entire design well worn with very little detail remaining. Legend, stars and date are weak but visible.

REVERSE: Eagle is worn flat but is completely outlined. Tops of some letters, head, and motto are worn nearly smooth.

ABOUT GOOD   *Outlined design. Parts of date and legend worn smooth.*

AG-3   OBVERSE: Head is outlined with nearly all details worn away. Date readable but very weak. Stars merging into rim.
REVERSE: Entire design partially worn away. Lettering merges with rim.

Note: Coins of this design are often weakly struck, particularly in the drapery lines, on the hair at left of neck, and on the eagle's feathers, shield, and motto. File adjustment marks are occasionally seen, and are a normal part of the manufacturing process.
The characteristic traits listed here to assist in grading must not be confused with actual wear.

1805 Obverse stars are sometimes weakly struck. Drapery at shoulder is not always sharp. Clouds and stars below ES are usually weak.

1806 Weaknesses in striking are often seen at stars, border, hair behind forehead and ear, and in drapery at shoulder. The central portion of the reverse is frequently flatly struck.

1807 Weakness around edges is common. Obverse border and stars are often flat. Tops of letters may appear to merge with the rim.

MINT STATE *Absolutely no trace of wear.*

MS-70 UNCIRCULATED
A flawless coin exactly as it was minted, with no trace of wear or injury. Must have full mint luster and brilliance or light toning. Any unusual die or striking traits must be described.

MS-67 UNCIRCULATED
Virtually flawless but with very minor imperfections.

MS-65 UNCIRCULATED
No trace of wear; nearly as perfect as MS-67 except for some small blemish. Has full mint luster but may be unevenly toned or lightly fingermarked. A few minute nicks or marks may be present.

MS-63 UNCIRCULATED
A mint state coin with attractive mint luster, but noticeable detracting contact marks or minor blemishes.

MS-60 UNCIRCULATED
A strictly Uncirculated coin with no trace of wear, but with blemishes more obvious than for MS-63. May lack full mint luster, and surface may be dull, spotted or heavily toned.

ABOUT UNCIRCULATED *Small trace of wear visible on highest points.*

AU-58 *Very Choice*
Has some signs of abrasion: drapery at front of bust, shoulder clasp, and hair above eye and at tips of curls; eagle's claws, neck, and edges of wings. Shallow or weak spots in the design are usually caused by improper striking and not wear.

AU-55 *Choice*
OBVERSE: Only a trace of wear shows on highest points of hair above eye.
REVERSE: A trace of wear shows on talons and arrowheads.
    Three-quarters of the mint luster is still present.

AU-50 OBVERSE: Traces of wear show on hair above eye and over the ear. Drapery clasp is clear and bold.

REVERSE: Traces of wear show on talons, arrowheads, and edges of wings. Half of the mint luster is still present.

EXTREMELY FINE   *Very light wear on only the highest points.*

EF-45   *Choice*

OBVERSE: Slight wear shows on high points of clasp, and hair above eye and over the ear. Drapery is worn at shoulder and bustline. Trace of wear on lowest curl.

REVERSE: High points of wings, head, talons and arrowheads are lightly worn. Lines in feathers are clearly defined.

Part of the mint luster is still present.

EF-40   *Typical*

OBVERSE: Wear shows on hair above eye and ear, and lightly on the cap and curls. Drapery lightly worn at neckline in spots. Ear and shoulder clasp are bold. Eye is well defined. Star details are complete.

REVERSE: High points of eagle are worn, but each detail is clearly defined. Neck and leg feathers are very lightly worn. Talons, arrows and olive branch show slight wear.

Traces of mint luster may still show.

VERY FINE   *Light to moderate even wear. All major features are sharp.*

VF-30   *Choice*

OBVERSE: Hair above eye and around ear is worn almost smooth. Balance of hair is well detailed. Ear and shoulder clasp show clearly. Drapery and eye are well defined. Star centers are weak.

REVERSE: Feathers are worn but most details are visible. Some details in neck and shield. Talons are well worn. Eyelid is visible. Shield lines flat but separated.

VF-20   *Typical*

OBVERSE: Over half the details still show in hair. Drapery and lower curls

QUARTERS—CAPPED BUST 1815–1828

worn but bold. Ear, clasp and curls are all plainly visible.

REVERSE: Head and leg are worn, but some feathers are visible. Most details in wings are clear unless weakly struck. Motto is complete. Half of the horizontal shield lines are separated.

FINE *Moderate to heavy even wear. Entire design clear and bold.*

F-12 OBVERSE: Nearly half the details show in hair, drapery, and cap. All letters, and parts of ear and clasp are visible. Eyelid is flattened. Parts of star centers are worn flat. LIBERTY is complete.

REVERSE: Half the feathers are visible in the wings. Letters in motto weak but clear. Head is nearly smooth; eye and some feathers show.

VERY GOOD *Well worn. Design clear but flat and lacking details.*

VG-8 OBVERSE: Entire head outlined with most hair details worn smooth. Eye, ear and clasp are barely visible. At least three letters in LIBERTY are clear. Star centers are flat.

REVERSE: Eagle is boldly outlined with some feathers showing in wings. Some letters in motto are very weak or partially worn away. Head, talons and olive branch are nearly smooth. Eye is visible.

GOOD *Heavily worn. Design and legend visible but faint in spots.*

G-4 OBVERSE: Entire design well worn with very little detail remaining. Most of the letters in LIBERTY are worn away. Stars and date are weak but visible and may merge with rim.

QUARTERS—CAPPED BUST 1815–1828

REVERSE: Eagle is worn nearly flat but is completely outlined. Tops of some letters are worn nearly smooth and may merge with rim. Eye and motto are only partially visible.

ABOUT GOOD   *Outlined design. Parts of date and legend worn smooth.*

AG-3   OBVERSE: Head is outlined with nearly all details worn away. Date readable but very weak. Stars merging into rim.

REVERSE: Entire design partially worn away.

Note: Coins of this design are sometimes weakly struck, particularly around the curl on the neck, in the clasp, hair, and on the motto above the neck.

QUARTERS—CAPPED BUST 1831–1838

MINT STATE *Absolutely no trace of wear.*

MS-70 UNCIRCULATED
A flawless coin exactly as it was minted, with no trace of wear or injury. Must have full mint luster and brilliance or light toning. Any unusual die or striking traits must be described.

MS-67 UNCIRCULATED
Virtually flawless but with very minor imperfections.

MS-65 UNCIRCULATED
No trace of wear; nearly as perfect as MS-67 except for some small blemish. Has full mint luster but may be unevenly toned or lightly fingermarked. A few barely noticeable nicks or marks may be present.

MS-63 UNCIRCULATED
A mint state coin with attractive mint luster, but noticeable detracting contact marks or minor blemishes.

MS-60 UNCIRCULATED
A strictly Uncirculated coin with no trace of wear, but with blemishes more obvious than for MS-63. May lack full mint luster, and surface may be dull, spotted or heavily toned.

ABOUT UNCIRCULATED *Small trace of wear visible on highest points.*

AU-58 *Very Choice*
Has some signs of abrasion: top of cap, stars, and hair above ear and at forehead; eagle's claws, arrows, and edges of wings.

AU-55 *Choice*
OBVERSE: Only a trace of wear shows on highest points of hair above eye, at top of cap, and on the stars.
REVERSE: A trace of wear shows on talons and arrowheads.
Three-quarters of the mint luster is still present.

AU-50 *Typical*
OBVERSE: Traces of wear show on the hair above eye and over the ear, at

[202]

top of cap, and on the stars.

REVERSE: Traces of wear show on talons, arrowheads, and edges of wings. Half of the mint luster is still present.

EXTREMELY FINE   *Very light wear on only the highest points.*

EF-45   *Choice*

OBVERSE: Slight wear shows on high points of hair above eye and over the ear. Drapery is worn at shoulder and bustline. Trace of wear shows on cap and stars. Clasp and ear are bold.

REVERSE: High points of wings, shield, talons and beak are lightly worn. Lines in feathers are clearly defined.

Part of the mint luster is still present.

EF-40   *Typical*

OBVERSE: Wear shows on hair above eye and ear, and lightly on the cap, curls, and stars. Drapery lightly worn at neckline in spots. Ear and shoulder clasp are very sharp. Eye is well defined.

REVERSE: High points of eagle are worn, but each detail is clearly defined. Neck and leg feathers are very lightly worn. Talons, arrows and olive branch show slight wear.

Traces of mint luster may still show.

VERY FINE   *Light to moderate even wear. All major features are sharp.*

VF-30   *Choice*

OBVERSE: Hair above eye and around ear is worn almost smooth. Balance of hair is well detailed. Ear and shoulder clasp show clearly. Drapery, cap and eye are well defined. Star centers are weak.

REVERSE: Feathers are worn but most details are visible. Some details in neck and shield. Talons are well worn. All shield lines are separated.

VF-20   *Typical*

OBVERSE: Over half the details still show in hair. Drapery, cap and lower curls worn but bold. Ear, clasp and LIBERTY are all plainly visible. Star centers are partially visible.

QUARTERS—CAPPED BUST 1831–1838

REVERSE: Head, neck, and leg are worn, but some feathers are visible. Most details in wings are clear except for outer edges. Talons and arrowheads are well worn.

FINE   *Moderate to heavy even wear. Entire design clear and bold.*

F-12   OBVERSE: Nearly half the details show in hair, drapery, and cap. All letters, and parts of ear and clasp are visible. Eyelid is flattened. Parts of stars are worn flat.

REVERSE: Half the feathers are visible in wings. Talons, branch and arrows are weak but clear. Head is nearly smooth but eye and some feathers show.

VERY GOOD   *Well worn. Design clear but flat and lacking details.*

VG-8   OBVERSE: Entire head outlined with most hair details worn smooth. Eye, ear and clasp are barely visible. All letters in LIBERTY are clear. Parts of stars are worn flat.

REVERSE: Eagle is boldly outlined with some feathers showing in wings. Some of the letters are very weak. Head and olive branch are smooth. Talons are separated. Eye is visible.

GOOD   *Heavily worn. Design and legend visible but faint in spots.*

G-4   OBVERSE: Entire design well worn with very little detail remaining. Parts of letters in LIBERTY are worn away. Stars and date are weak but visible and may merge with rim.

REVERSE: Eagle is worn nearly flat but is completely outlined and shows a few feathers. Tops of some letters are worn nearly smooth and may merge with rim. Eye and talons are only partially visible.

ABOUT GOOD   *Outlined design. Parts of date and legend worn smooth.*

AG-3   OBVERSE: Head is outlined with nearly all details worn away. Date readable but very weak. Stars merging into rim.

REVERSE: Entire design partially worn away. Parts of talons are visible. Arrowheads and legend merge with rim.

MINT STATE *Absolutely no trace of wear.*

MS-70 UNCIRCULATED
A flawless coin exactly as it was minted, with no trace of wear or injury. Must have full mint luster and brilliance or light toning. Any unusual die or striking traits must be described.

MS-67 UNCIRCULATED
Virtually flawless but with very minor imperfections.

MS-65 UNCIRCULATED
No trace of wear; nearly as perfect as MS-67 except for some small blemish. Has full mint luster but may be unevenly toned or lightly fingermarked. A few barely noticeable nicks or marks may be present.

MS-63 UNCIRCULATED
A mint state coin with attractive mint luster, but noticeable detracting contact marks or minor blemishes.

MS-60 UNCIRCULATED
A strictly Uncirculated coin with no trace of wear, but with blemishes more obvious than for MS-63. May lack full mint luster, and surface may be dull, spotted or heavily toned.

ABOUT UNCIRCULATED *Small trace of wear visible on highest points.*

AU-58 *Very Choice*
Has some signs of abrasion: high points of hair, breast and knees; neck, claws and tops of wings. Weak spots in the design are usually caused by striking and not wear.

AU-55 *Choice*
OBVERSE: Only a trace of wear shows on highest points of hair above eye, breast and right leg.
REVERSE: A trace of wear shows on head, beak and above eye.
Three-quarters of the mint luster is still present.

AU-50 *Typical*
OBVERSE: Traces of wear show on knees, breast and edge of hairline. Foot

is separated from sandal.

REVERSE: Traces of wear show on talons, neck, head and tips of wings. Half of the mint luster is still present.

EXTREMELY FINE   *Very light wear on only the highest points.*

EF-45   *Choice*

OBVERSE: Slight wear shows on high points of knees, breast and hair at forehead. Drapery is worn at shoulder and bustline. LIBERTY is sharp and scroll edges are raised.

REVERSE: High points of eagle and arrows lightly worn. Lines in talons are clearly defined. Neck feathers are fully separated.

Part of the mint luster is still present.

EF-40   *Typical*

OBVERSE: Wear shows on knees, head and shoulder. Gown lightly worn at neckline in spots. LIBERTY is complete and scroll edges are raised.

REVERSE: High points of eagle and arrows are worn, but each detail is clearly defined. Neck feathers and talons are distinct.

Traces of mint luster may still show.

VERY FINE   *Light to moderate even wear. All major features are sharp.*

VF-30   *Choice*

OBVERSE: Wear spots show on shoulder, breast, knee and legs. Center of neckline is weak but has some visible details. LIBERTY and scroll are complete. Fingers at pole are flat but separated.

REVERSE: Leaves are worn but three-quarters of the details are visible. Most details in feathers and talons are clear.

VF-20   *Typical*

OBVERSE: Over half the details still show in the gown. Hair, shoulder and legs are worn but bold. Neckline is incomplete. Every letter in LIBERTY is visible. Horizontal shield lines are weak at center.

REVERSE: Three-quarters of the feathers are visible. Arrowheads and talons are worn, but some details are visible. Half the details in leaves are clear.

FINE *Moderate to even wear. Entire design clear and bold.*

F-12 OBVERSE: Some details show in hair, cap, and at the shoulder and breast. All shield lines and letters in LIBERTY are weak but visible. Foot and sandal are separated.

REVERSE: Some details in feathers are visible. Shield border is partially visible on right side. Talons are flat but separated. Letters in legend are worn but clear.

VERY GOOD *Well worn. Design clear but flat and lacking details.*

VG-8 OBVERSE: Entire shield is weak, and most of the gown details are worn smooth. Three letters in LIBERTY are clear. Rim is complete.

REVERSE: Eagle shows only bold outline. Some of the shield is very weak. Leaves are fully outlined. Legend and rim are clear.

GOOD *Heavily worn. Design and legend visible but faint in spots.*

G-4 OBVERSE: Entire design well worn with very little detail remaining. Date is weak but visible. Shield is worn smooth.

REVERSE: Eagle is worn flat but is completely outlined. Tops of some letters are worn nearly smooth. For coins after 1865, the motto is partially visible.

ABOUT GOOD   *Outlined design. Parts of date and legend worn smooth.*

AG-3   OBVERSE: Liberty is outlined with nearly all details worn away. Date readable but very weak. Stars merging into rim.

REVERSE: Entire design partially worn away. Legend merging into rim.

Note: Coins of this design are sometimes weakly struck, particularly in the lines of the clasp on Liberty's gown. Those dated 1840 through 1852 seldom show full head, and Uncirculated pieces of 1879 through 1891 often have a prooflike surface.

QUARTERS—BARBER 1892-1916

MINT STATE   *Absolutely no trace of wear.*

MS-70   UNCIRCULATED
A flawless coin exactly as it was minted, with no trace of wear or injury. Must have full mint luster and brilliance or light toning. Any unusual die or striking traits must be described.

MS-67   UNCIRCULATED
Virtually flawless but with very minor imperfections.

MS-65   UNCIRCULATED
No trace of wear; nearly as perfect as MS-67 except for some small blemish. Has full mint luster but may be unevenly toned or lightly fingermarked. A few barely noticeable nicks or marks may be present.

MS-63   UNCIRCULATED
A mint state coin with attractive mint luster, but noticeable detracting contact marks or minor blemishes.

MS-60   UNCIRCULATED
A strictly Uncirculated coin with no trace of wear, but with blemishes more obvious than for MS-63. May lack full mint luster, and surface may be dull, spotted or heavily toned.

ABOUT UNCIRCULATED   *Small trace of wear visible on highest points.*

AU-58   *Very Choice*
Has some signs of abrasion: high points of cheek and hair below LIBERTY; eagle's head and tips of tail and wings.

AU-55   *Choice*
OBVERSE: Only a trace of wear shows on highest points of hair below BER in LIBERTY.
REVERSE: A trace of wear shows on head, tip of tail and tips of wings.
    Three-quarters of the mint luster is still present.

AU-50   *Typical*
OBVERSE: Traces of wear show on cheek, tips of leaves, and hair below LIBERTY.

REVERSE: Traces of wear show on head, neck, tail, and tips of wings. Half of the mint luster is still present.

EXTREMELY FINE   *Very light wear on only the highest points.*

EF-45   *Choice*

OBVERSE: Slight wear shows on high points of upper leaves, cheek, and hair above forehead. LIBERTY is sharp and band edges are bold.

REVERSE: High points of head, neck, wings and talons lightly worn. Lines in center tail feathers are clearly defined.

Part of the mint luster is still present.

EF-40   *Typical*

OBVERSE: Light wear shows on leaves, cheek, cap and hair above forehead. LIBERTY is sharp and band edges are clear.

REVERSE: High points of head, neck, wings, and tail are lightly worn, but all details are clearly defined. Leaves show trace of wear at edges.

Traces of mint luster may still show.

VERY FINE   *Light to moderate even wear. All major features are sharp.*

VF-30   *Choice*

OBVERSE: Wear spots show on leaves, cap, hair and cheek. Bottom row of leaves is weak but has some visible details. LIBERTY and band are complete. Folds in cap are distinct.

REVERSE: Wear shows on shield but all details are visible. Most of the details in neck and tail are clear. Motto is complete.

VF-20   *Typical*

OBVERSE: Over half the details still show in leaves. Hair and ribbon worn but bold. Every letter in LIBERTY is visible.

REVERSE: The shield is worn, but most details are visible. Half the details in feathers are clear. Wings and legs show wear spots. Motto is clear.

FINE *Moderate to heavy even wear. Entire design clear and bold.*

F-12 OBVERSE: Some details show in hair, cap, and facial features. All letters in LIBERTY are weak but visible. Upper row of leaves is outlined, but bottom row is worn nearly smooth. Rim is full and bold.

REVERSE: Half of the feathers are plainly visible. Wear spots show in center of neck, motto, and arrows. Horizontal shield lines are merged; vertical lines are separated. Letters in legend are worn but clear.

VERY GOOD *Well worn. Design clear but flat and lacking details.*

VG-8 OBVERSE: Entire head weak, and most details in face are worn smooth. Three letters in LIBERTY are clear. Rim is complete.

REVERSE: Eagle shows only a small amount of detail. Arrows and leaves are flat. Most of the shield is very weak. Part of the eye is visible.

GOOD *Heavily worn. Design and legend visible but faint in spots.*

G-4 OBVERSE: Entire design well worn with very little detail remaining. Legend is weak but visible. LIBERTY is worn away.

REVERSE: Eagle worn flat but is completely outlined. Ribbon worn nearly smooth. Legend weak but visible. Rim worn to tops of letters.

ABOUT GOOD *Outlined design. Parts of date and legend worn smooth.*

AG-3 OBVERSE: Head is outlined with nearly all details worn away. Date readable but partially worn away. Legend merging into rim.

REVERSE: Entire design partially worn away and legend merges with rim.

Note: Most New Orleans and Denver issues are softly struck, particularly on the eagle's left claw.

QUARTERS—LIBERTY STANDING, VARIETY I
1916–1917

MINT STATE   *Absolutely no trace of wear.*

MS-70   UNCIRCULATED
A flawless coin exactly as it was minted, with no trace of wear or injury. Must have full mint luster and brilliance or light toning. Head details* are an important part of this grade and must be specifically designated. Any other unusual die or striking traits must be described.

MS-67   UNCIRCULATED
Virtually flawless but with very minor imperfections.

MS-65   UNCIRCULATED
No trace of wear; nearly as perfect as MS-67 except for small blemish. Has full mint luster but may be unevenly toned or lightly fingermarked. A few barely noticeable nicks or marks may be present. Head details* may be incomplete.

MS-63   UNCIRCULATED
A mint state coin with attractive mint luster, but noticeable detracting contact marks or minor blemishes.

MS-60   UNCIRCULATED
A strictly Uncirculated coin with no trace of wear, but with blemishes more obvious than for MS-63. May lack full mint luster, and surface may be dull, spotted or heavily toned. Head details* may be incomplete.

ABOUT UNCIRCULATED   *Small trace of wear visible on highest points.*
AU-58   *Very Choice*
Has some signs of abrasion: breast, knee, high points of shield; eagle's breast and wings. Coins of this design frequently show weakly struck spots.

AU-55   *Choice*
OBVERSE: Only a trace of wear shows on highest points of head*, breast, small shield, and right leg above knee.

---

*Full head features: All details in hair are well defined; hairline along face is raised and complete; eyebrow is visible; cheek is rounded. Coins of any grade other than MS-70 can be assumed to lack full head details unless the amount of visible features are specifically designated.

[214]

QUARTERS—LIBERTY STANDING, VARIETY I
1916–1917

REVERSE: A trace of wear shows on edges of wings, breast, and tail feathers.
Three-quarters of the mint luster is still present.

AU-50   *Typical*

OBVERSE: Traces of wear show on head*, breast, knee and high points of shield.

REVERSE: Traces of wear show on wing feathers, at center of breast and on tail feathers.

Half of the mint luster is still present.

EXTREMELY FINE   *Very light wear on only the highest points.*

EF-45   *Choice*

OBVERSE: Small flat spots show on right leg and knee. Most of the gown line crossing thigh is clearly visible. Shield details are bold. Breast is lightly worn but full and rounded.

REVERSE: Small flat spots show on high points of breast, and at right wing bone joint. Feathers on other parts of wings have nearly full details.

Part of the mint luster is still present.

EF-40   *Typical*

OBVERSE: Wear shows on head, breast, and right leg above and below knee. At least half the gown line crossing thigh is visible.

REVERSE: High points of eagle are lightly worn. Central part of edge on right wing is worn flat.

Traces of mint luster may still show.

VERY FINE   *Light to moderate even wear. All major features are sharp.*

*Full head features: All details in hair are well defined; hairline along face is raised and complete; eyebrow is visible; cheek is rounded. Coins of any grade other than MS-70 can be assumed to lack full head details unless the amount of visible features are specifically designated.

[215]

QUARTERS—LIBERTY STANDING, VARIETY I
1916–1917

VF-30   *Choice*

OBVERSE: Wear spots show on head, breast, shield and leg. Right leg is rounded but worn from above knee almost to foot. Gown line crossing thigh is partially visible. Circle around inner shield is complete.

REVERSE: Breast and right wing are worn but clearly separated. Some feathers are visible between breast and leg. Feather ends and folds are visible in right wing.

VF-20   *Typical*

OBVERSE: Right leg is worn nearly flat in central parts. Wear spots show on head, breast, shield and foot. Beads on outer shield are visible, but those next to breast are very weak.

REVERSE: Entire eagle is lightly worn but most major details are visible. Breast, edge of right wing and high parts of left are worn flat.

FINE   *Moderate to considerable even wear. Entire design clear and bold.*

F-12   OBVERSE: Gown details worn nearly smooth across body, but show at sides. Right leg nearly flat and toe is worn. Breast worn but visible. Date is clear and rim is full. Outer edge of shield is complete.

REVERSE: Eagle is evenly worn. Half of the wing feathers are visible although well worn in spots. The rim is full.

VERY GOOD   *Well worn. Design clear but flat and lacking details.*

VG-8   OBVERSE: Entire design is weak, and most details in gown are worn smooth. All letters and date are clear. Rim is complete. Drapery across breast is outlined. Bottom right star is worn flat.

REVERSE: About one-third of the feathers are visible, and large feathers at ends of wings are well separated. Eye is visible. Rim is complete.

QUARTERS—LIBERTY STANDING, VARIETY I
1916–1917

GOOD *Heavily worn. Design and legend visible but faint in spots.*

G-4 OBVERSE: Entire design well worn with very little detail remaining. Legend and date are weak but visible. Top of date may be worn flat. Rim is complete.

REVERSE: Eagle worn nearly flat but is completely outlined. Lettering and stars worn but clearly visible. Rim worn to tops of legend.

ABOUT GOOD *Outlined design. Parts of date and legend worn smooth.*

AG-3 OBVERSE: Figure is outlined with nearly all details worn away. Date readable but partially worn away. Legend weak but readable and may merge into rim.

REVERSE: Entire design partially worn away. Some letters merging into rim.

Note: Coins of this design are sometimes weakly struck in spots, particularly at Liberty's head, breast, knee and shield, and on the eagle's breast and wings.

Specimens with "full head" must show the following features: Well defined details in hair; complete hairline along face; visible eyebrow; rounded cheek. Coins of any grade other than MS-70 can be assumed to lack full head details unless the amount of visible features are specifically designated.

QUARTERS—LIBERTY STANDING, VARIETY II
1917–1930

MINT STATE *Absolutely no trace of wear.*

MS-70   UNCIRCULATED
A flawless coin exactly as it was minted, with no trace of wear or injury. Must have full mint luster and brilliance or light toning. Head details* are an important part of this grade and must be specifically designated. Any other unusual die or striking traits must be described.

MS-67   UNCIRCULATED
Virtually flawless but with very minor imperfections.

MS-65   UNCIRCULATED
No trace of wear; nearly as perfect as MS-67 except for some small blemish. Has full mint luster but may be unevenly toned or lightly fingermarked. May be weakly struck in one small spot. A few barely noticeable nicks or marks may be present. Head details* may be incomplete.

MS-63   UNCIRCULATED
A mint state coin with attractive mint luster, but noticeable detracting contact marks or minor blemishes.

MS-60   UNCIRCULATED
A strictly Uncirculated coin with no trace of wear, but with blemishes more obvious than for MS-63. May lack full mint luster, and surface may be dull, spotted or heavily toned. One or two small spots may be weakly struck. Head details* may be incomplete.

ABOUT UNCIRCULATED   *Small trace of wear visible on highest points.*

AU-58   *Very Choice*

Has some signs of abrasion: mail covering breast, knee, high points of gown and shield; high points of eagle's breast and wings. Coins of this design frequently show weakly struck spots, and usually lack full head details.

---

*Full head details: The leaves in hair are well defined; hairline along brow and across face is complete; small indentation at ear is visible. Coins of any grade other than MS-70 can be assumed to lack full head details unless the amount of visible features are specifically designated.

QUARTERS—LIBERTY STANDING, VARIETY II
1917–1930

AU-55   *Choice*

OBVERSE: Only a trace of wear shows on highest points of mail covering breast, inner shield, and right knee.

REVERSE: A trace of wear shows on breast and edges of wings.

Three-quarters of the mint luster is still present.

AU-50   *Typical*

OBVERSE: Traces of wear show on breast, knee and high points of inner shield.

REVERSE: Traces of wear show on edges of wings and at center of breast. All of the tail feathers are visible.

Half of the mint luster is still present.

EXTREMELY FINE   *Very light wear on only the highest points.*

EF-45   *Choice*

OBVERSE: Light wear spots show on upper right leg and knee. Nearly all of the gown lines are clearly visible. Shield details are bold. Breast is lightly worn and may show small flat spot.

REVERSE: Small flat spots show on high points of breast, and on front wing edges. Tail feathers have nearly full details.

Part of the mint luster is still present.

EF-40   *Typical*

OBVERSE: Wear shows on breast, and right leg above and below knee. Most of the gown lines are visible. Shield details are bold. Breast is well rounded but has small flat spot.

REVERSE: High points of eagle are lightly worn. Central part of edge on right wing is well worn.

Traces of mint luster may still show.

VERY FINE   *Light to moderate even wear. All major features are sharp.*

QUARTERS—LIBERTY STANDING, VARIETY II
1917–1930

VF-30 *Choice*

OBVERSE: Wear spots show on breast, shield and leg. Right leg is rounded but worn from above knee to ankle. Gown line crossing thigh is partially visible. Half of mail covering breast can be seen. Circle around inner shield is complete.

REVERSE: Breast and leg are worn but clearly separated, with some feathers visible between them. Feather ends and folds are visible in right wing.

VF-20 *Typical*

OBVERSE: Right leg is worn nearly flat in central parts. Wear spots show on head, breast, shield and foot. Beads on outer shield are visible, but those next to body are weak. Inner circle of shield is complete.

REVERSE: Entire eagle is lightly worn but most major details are visible. Breast and edge of right wing are worn flat. Top tail feathers are complete.

FINE *Moderate to considerable even wear. Entire design clear and bold.*

F-12 OBVERSE: Gown details worn but show clearly across body. Left leg is lightly worn. Right leg nearly flat and toe is worn. Breast worn but some mail is visible. Date may show some weakness at top. Rim is full. Outer edge of shield is complete.

REVERSE: Breast is worn almost smooth. Half of the wing feathers are visible although well worn in spots. The rim is full.

VERY GOOD *Well worn. Design clear but flat and lacking details.*

VG-8 OBVERSE: Entire design is weak, and most details in gown are worn smooth. All letters and date are clear but tops of numerals may be flat. Rim is complete. Drapery across breast is partially outlined.

REVERSE: About one-third of the feathers are visible, and large feathers at ends of wings are well separated. Eye is visible. Rim is full and all letters are clear.

QUARTERS—LIBERTY STANDING, VARIETY II
1917–1930

GOOD   *Heavily worn. Design and legend visible but faint in spots.*

G-4   OBVERSE: Entire design well worn with very little detail remaining. Legend and date are weak but visible. Top of date may be worn flat. Rim is complete.

REVERSE: Eagle worn nearly flat but is completely outlined. Lettering and stars worn but clearly visible. Rim worn to tops of legend.

ABOUT GOOD   *Outlined design. Parts of date and legend worn smooth.*

AG-3   OBVERSE: Figure is outlined with nearly all details worn away. Legend visible but half worn away and may merge with rim. Date weak but readable.

REVERSE: Entire design partially worn away. Some letters merging into rim.

Note: Coins of this design are sometimes weakly struck in spots, particularly at Liberty's head, breast, knee and shield, and on the eagle's breast and wings. The following dates are often found weakly struck: 1918-D, 1918 over 7-S, 1919-D, 1920-D, 1924-D, 1924-S, 1926-D, 1926-S, 1927-S, 1928-S and 1929-D.

Specimens with "full head" must show the following details: Three well defined leaves in hair; complete hairline along brow and across face; small indentation at ear. Coins of any grade other than MS-70 can be assumed to lack full head details unless the amount of visable features are specifically designated. Coins of 1916-1924 have the date on a raised platform that is easily worn away in lower grades. Coins of 1925-1930 have the date recessed for protection.

QUARTERS—WASHINGTON 1932 TO DATE

MINT STATE   *Absolutely no trace of wear.*

MS-70   UNCIRCULATED
A flawless coin exactly as it was minted, with no trace of wear or injury. Must have full mint luster and brilliance or light toning. Any unusual striking traits must be described.

MS-67   UNCIRCULATED
Virtually flawless but with very minor imperfections.

MS-65   UNCIRCULATED
No trace of wear; nearly as perfect as MS-67 except for some small blemish. Has full mint luster but may be unevenly toned or lightly fingermarked. A few barely noticeable nicks or marks may be present.

MS-63   UNCIRCULATED
A mint state coin with attractive mint luster, but noticeable detracting contact marks or minor blemishes.

MS-60   UNCIRCULATED
A strictly Uncirculated coin with no trace of wear, but with blemishes more obvious than for MS-63. May lack full mint luster, and surface may be dull, spotted or heavily toned.

ABOUT UNCIRCULATED   *Small trace of wear visible on highest points.*

AU-58   *Very Choice*
Has some signs of abrasion: high points of cheek, and hair in front and back of ear; tops of legs, and details in breast feathers.

AU-55   *Choice*
OBVERSE: Only a trace of wear shows on highest points of hair in front and in back of ear.
REVERSE: A trace of wear shows on highest spots of breast feathers.
   Nearly all of the mint luster is still present.

QUARTERS—WASHINGTON 1932 TO DATE

AU-50 *Typical*

OBVERSE: Traces of wear show on hair in front and in back of ear.

REVERSE: Traces of wear show on legs and breast feathers.

Three-quarters of the mint luster is still present.

EXTREMELY FINE *Light wear on most of the highest points.*

EF-45 *Choice*

OBVERSE: Slight wear shows on high points of hair around ear and along hairline up to crown. Hair lines are sharp and detailed.

REVERSE: High points of legs are lightly worn. Breast feathers are worn but clearly defined and fully separated.

Half of the mint luster is still present.

EF-40 *Typical*

OBVERSE: Wear shows on high points of hair around ear and at hairline up to crown.

REVERSE: High points of breast, legs, and claws are lightly worn, but all details are clearly defined and partially separated.

Part of the mint luster is still present.

VERY FINE *Light to moderate even wear. All major features are sharp.*

VF-30 *Choice*

OBVERSE: Wear spots show on hair at forehead and ear, cheek and jaw. Hair lines are weak but have nearly full visible details.

REVERSE: Wear shows on breast but some of the details are visible. All vertical wing feathers are plain. Most details in the legs are worn smooth.

VF-20 *Typical*

OBVERSE: Three-quarters of the lines still show in hair. Cheek lightly worn but bold. Some hair details around the ear are visible.

REVERSE: Wear shows on breast but a few feathers are visible. Legs are worn smooth. Most details in the wings are clear.

FINE *Moderate to considerable even wear. Entire design clear and bold.*

F-12 OBVERSE: Details show only at back of hair. Motto is weak but clearly visible. Part of cheek edge is worn away.

REVERSE: Feathers in breast and legs are worn smooth. Leaves show some detail. Parts of wings are nearly smooth.

VERY GOOD *Well worn. Design clear but flat and lacking details.*

VG-8 OBVERSE: Entire head is weak, and most details in hair are worn smooth. All letters and date are clear. Rim is complete.

REVERSE: About half of the wing feathers are visible. Breast and legs only outlined. Leaves show very little detail. Rim is complete.

GOOD *Heavily worn. Design and legend visible but faint in spots.*

G-4 OBVERSE: Hair is well worn with very little detail remaining. Half of motto is readable. LIBERTY and date are weak but visible. Rim merges with letters.

REVERSE: Eagle is worn nearly flat but is completely outlined. Leaves, breast and legs are worn smooth. Legend is all visible but merges with rim.

QUARTERS—WASHINGTON 1932 TO DATE

ABOUT GOOD   *Outlined design. Parts of date and legend worn smooth.*

AG-3   OBVERSE: Head is outlined with nearly all details worn away. Date readable but worn. Traces of motto are visible. Legend merging into rim.
REVERSE: Entire design partially worn away. Rim merges into legend.

Note: The obverse motto is always weak on coins of 1932 and early issues of 1934.

The obverse rim is especially thick on coins of 1932-35, protecting the obverse and often resulting in split grades (e.g. VG/AG) on well worn specimens.

The reverse rim and lettering has a tendency to be very weak, particularly on coins dated 1934-D, 1935-D and S, 1936-D and S, 1937-D and S (especially), 1938-S, 1939-D, 1940-D, 1940-S, 1941-S, 1943-S and 1944-S.

Clad pieces are often weakly struck in spots.

Bicentennial coins can be graded by the obverse.

The mintmark on many of the earlier issues tends to be filled.

HALF DOLLARS—FLOWING HAIR 1794–1795

MINT STATE   *Absolutely no trace of wear.*

MS-70   UNCIRCULATED
A flawless coin exactly as it was minted, with no trace of wear or injury. Must have full mint luster and brilliance or light toning. Any unusual die, planchet or striking traits must be described.

MS-67   UNCIRCULATED
Virtually flawless but with very minor imperfections.

MS-65   UNCIRCULATED
No trace of wear; nearly as perfect as MS-67 except for some small blemish. Has full mint luster but may be unevenly toned or lightly fingermarked. A few small nicks or adjustment file marks may be present.

MS-63   UNCIRCULATED
A mint state coin with attractive mint luster, but noticeable detracting contact marks or minor blemishes.

MS-60   UNCIRCULATED
A strictly Uncirculated coin with no trace of wear, but with blemishes more obvious than for MS-63. May lack full mint luster, and surface may be dull, spotted or heavily toned.

ABOUT UNCIRCULATED   *Small trace of wear visible on highest points.*

AU-58   *Very Choice*
Has some signs of abrasion: high points of bust, shoulder, and hair above forehead; eagle's breast, head, and top edges of wings. Shallow or weak spots in the relief are usually caused by improper striking and not wear.

AU-55   *Choice*
OBVERSE: Only a trace of wear shows on highest points of hair above forehead.
REVERSE: A trace of wear shows on breast.
   Three-quarters of the mint luster is still present.

HALF DOLLARS—FLOWING HAIR 1794–1795

AU-50   *Typical*
OBVERSE: Traces of wear show on hair above and beside forehead.
REVERSE: Traces of wear show on breast and head.
   Half of the mint luster is still present.

EXTREMELY FINE   *Very light wear on only the highest points.*

EF-45   *Choice*
OBVERSE: Slight wear shows on high points of hair from forehead to neck.
Very light wear at shoulder and bustline. Stars fully detailed.
REVERSE: High points of wings, breast and head are lightly worn. Lines in
feathers are clearly defined.
   Part of the mint luster is still present.

EF-40   *Typical*
OBVERSE: Wear shows on hair from forehead to nec'· ·d lightly on the
cheek and bust. Lightly worn at neckline in spots. ·   ·lly detailed.
REVERSE: High points of eagle are worn, but each d   s clearly defined.
Head and breast are lightly worn.
   Traces of mint luster may still show.

VERY FINE   *Light to moderate even wear. All major features are sharp.*

VF-30   *Choice*
OBVERSE: Three-quarters of flowing hair details show. Hair above forehead
is worn but has some bold features. Parts of star centers are very weak.
REVERSE: Feathers are worn but most of the details are visible. Some of the
details in head and breast are clear unless weakly struck.

VF-20   *Typical*
OBVERSE: Half of the details still show in hair. Forehead and bust are worn
but show some details. Parts of shoulder are smooth. Every letter and star
is plainly visible. Some star centers are nearly flat.
REVERSE: Head and breast are worn, but some feathers are visible. Nearly
half of details in wings are clear.

FINE   *Moderate to heavy even wear. Entire design clear and bold.*

F-12   OBVERSE: Some details show in hair ends and below ear. All letters, date and stars are visible. The eye and eyebrow are clear.

REVERSE: Some feathers are visible in body, wings and tail. Breast and head are smooth. Eye is visible. Letters in legend are worn but clear.

VERY GOOD   *Well worn. Design clear but flat and lacking details.*

VG-8   OBVERSE: Entire head is weak, and most hair details are worn smooth. Date and LIBERTY are weak but clear. Parts of the eye and eyebrow are visible. Stars are outlined.

REVERSE: Eagle is boldly outlined with only a few details showing in wings and tail. Breast is smooth. Some letters are very weak.

GOOD   *Heavily worn. Design and legend visible but faint in spots.*

G-4   OBVERSE: Entire design worn smooth with very little detail remaining. Legend, stars and date are well worn but all visible.

REVERSE: Eagle is worn flat and not completely outlined. Tops of some letters are worn nearly smooth.

ABOUT GOOD   *Outlined design. Parts of date and legend worn smooth.*

AG-3   OBVERSE: Head is outlined with nearly all details worn away. Date readable but very weak. Stars merging into rim.

REVERSE: Entire design partially worn away. Lettering very weak but readable.

Note: Examples of this design are often weakly struck, particularly on the eagle's breast and feathers. File adjustment marks are occasionally seen, and are a normal part of the manufacturing process.

The 1795 variety with three leaves under each wing is always weak at STA and has a heavy die break. The breast and top of right wing are usually flat.

HALF DOLLARS—DRAPED BUST, SMALL EAGLE
1796–1797

MINT STATE   *Absolutely no trace of wear.*

MS-70   UNCIRCULATED
A flawless coin exactly as it was minted, with no trace of wear or injury. Must have full mint luster and brilliance or light toning. Any unusual die or striking traits must be described.

MS-67   UNCIRCULATED
Virtually flawless but with very minor imperfections.

MS-65   UNCIRCULATED
No trace of wear; nearly as perfect as MS-67 except for some small blemish. Has full mint luster but may be unevenly toned or lightly fingermarked. A few barely noticeable nicks or adjustment file marks may be present.

MS-63   UNCIRCULATED
A mint state coin with attractive mint luster, but noticeable detracting contact marks or minor blemishes.

MS-60   UNCIRCULATED
A strictly Uncirculated coin with no traces of wear, but with blemishes more obvious than for MS-63. May lack full mint luster, and surface may be dull, spotted or heavily toned.

ABOUT UNCIRCULATED   *Small trace of wear visible on highest points.*
AU-58   *Very Choice*
Has some signs of abrasion: high points of bust, shoulder, and hair above forehead; eagle's breast and top edges of wings. Shallow or weak spots in the relief are usually caused by improper striking and not wear.

AU-55   *Choice*
OBVERSE: Only a trace of wear shows on highest points of hair above forehead.
REVERSE: A trace of wear shows on breast.
    Three-quarters of the mint luster is still present.

AU-50   *Typical*
OBVERSE: Trace of wear shows on hair above forehead. Drapery has trace

HALF DOLLARS—DRAPED BUST, SMALL EAGLE
1796–1797

of wear at shoulder and bustline.

REVERSE: Traces of wear show on breast.

Half of the mint luster is still present.

EXTREMELY FINE   *Very light wear on only the highest points.*

EF-45   *Choice*

OBVERSE: Slight wear shows on high points of hair from forehead to the ear. Drapery is worn at shoulder and bustline.

REVERSE: High points of wing tips, breast and left leg are lightly worn. Lines in feathers are clearly defined.

Part of the mint luster is still present.

EF-40   *Typical*

OBVERSE: Wear shows on hair from forehead to ear, and lightly on the cheek and bust. Drapery lightly worn at neckline in spots.

REVERSE: High points of wings are worn, but each detail is clearly defined. Left leg and breast are slightly worn.

Traces of mint luster may still show.

VERY FINE   *Light to moderate even wear. All major features are sharp.*

VF-30   *Choice*

OBVERSE: Three-quarters of hair details show. Hair above forehead is worn but has some bold features. Parts of drapery are worn smooth.

REVERSE: Wing edges are worn, but most central details are visible. Some of the details in left leg and breast are clear unless weakly struck.

VF-20   *Typical*

OBVERSE: Over half of the details still show in hair. Forehead and bust are worn but bold. Parts of drapery are smooth. Every letter and star is plainly visible.

REVERSE: Legs and breast are worn, but some feathers are visible. About three-quarters of details in wings are clear.

[231]

FINE *Moderate to heavy even wear. Entire design clear and bold.*

F-12 OBVERSE: Some details show in hair ends, curls and at left of ear. All letters, date and stars are visible. The eye and eyebrow are clear. Bust is worn with few drapery lines remaining.

REVERSE: Half the feathers are visible in wings. Breast and left leg are smooth. Letters in legend are worn but clear.

VERY GOOD *Well worn. Design clear but flat and lacking details.*

VG-8 OBVERSE: Entire head is weak, and most hair details and drapery are worn smooth. Date and LIBERTY are weak but clear. Parts of the eye and eyebrow are visible. Stars are outlined.

REVERSE: Eagle is boldly outlined with only a few details showing in wings. Breast and left leg are smooth. Some letters are very weak.

GOOD *Heavily worn. Design and legend visible but faint in spots.*

G-4 OBVERSE: Entire design worn smooth with very little detail remaining. Legend, stars and date are well worn but visible.

REVERSE: Eagle is worn flat and only outlined. Tops of some letters are worn nearly smooth. Rim is full.

HALF DOLLARS—DRAPED BUST, SMALL EAGLE
1796–1797

ABOUT GOOD   *Outlined design. Parts of date and legend worn smooth.*

AG-3   OBVERSE: Head is outlined with nearly all details worn away. Date readable but very weak. Stars merging into rim.
REVERSE: Entire design partially worn away. Legend merges with rim.

Note: Examples of this design are often weakly struck, particularly on the eagle's breast and feathers. File adjustment marks are occasionally seen, and are a normal part of the manufacturing process.

MINT STATE *Absolutely no trace of wear.*

MS-70 UNCIRCULATED
A flawless coin exactly as it was minted, with no trace of wear or injury. Must have full mint luster and brilliance or light toning. Any unusual die or striking traits must be described.

MS-67 UNCIRCULATED
Virtually flawless but with very minor imperfections.

MS-65 UNCIRCULATED
No trace of wear; nearly as perfect as MS-67 except for some small blemish. Has full mint luster but may be unevenly toned, or lightly fingermarked. A few barely noticeable nicks or adjustment file marks may be present.

MS-63 UNCIRCULATED
A mint state coin with attractive mint luster, but noticeable detracting contact marks or minor blemishes.

MS-60 UNCIRCULATED
A strictly Uncirculated coin with no trace of wear, but with blemishes more obvious than for MS-63. May lack full mint luster, and surface may be dull, spotted or heavily toned.

ABOUT UNCIRCULATED *Small trace of wear visible on highest points.*

AU-58 *Very Choice*
Has some signs of abrasion: high points of bust, shoulder, and hair above forehead; eagle's head, breast, edges of wings and clouds. Shallow or weak spots in the motto are usually caused by improper striking and not wear.

AU-55 *Choice*
OBVERSE: Only a trace of wear shows on highest points of hair above forehead.
REVERSE: A trace of wear shows on the clouds.
   Three-quarters of the mint luster is still present.

HALF DOLLARS—DRAPED BUST, HERALDIC EAGLE
1801–1807

AU-50   *Typical*

OBVERSE: Trace of wear shows on hair above forehead. Drapery has trace of wear at shoulder and bustline.

REVERSE: Traces of wear show on breast feathers and clouds.

Half of the mint luster is still present.

EXTREMELY FINE   *Very light wear on only the highest points.*

EF-45   *Choice*

OBVERSE: Slight wear shows on high points of hair from forehead to the ear. Drapery is worn at shoulder and bustline.

REVERSE: High points of wing edges, breast feathers and clouds are lightly worn. Lines in shield are clearly defined.

Part of the mint luster is still present.

EF-40   *Typical*

OBVERSE: Wear shows on hair from forehead to ear, and lightly on the cheek and bust. Drapery lightly worn at neckline in spots.

REVERSE: High points of clouds and wings are worn, but each detail is clearly defined. Head and breast are slightly worn. Lines in shield are separated.

Traces of mint luster may still show.

VERY FINE   *Light to moderate even wear. All major features are sharp.*

VF-30   *Choice*

OBVERSE: Three-quarters of hair details show. Hair at back of head is worn but has some bold features. Parts of drapery are worn smooth.

REVERSE: Wing edges are worn, but three-quarters of central details are visible. Clouds, head and motto show wear. Horizontal shield lines worn but separated.

[235]

HALF DOLLARS—DRAPED BUST, HERALDIC EAGLE
1801–1807

VF-20 *Typical*

OBVERSE: Over half of the details still show in hair. Forehead and bust are worn but bold. Parts of drapery are smooth. Every letter and star is plainly visible.

REVERSE: Head and breast are worn, but some feathers are visible. Some lines in shield are merged together. About three-quarters of details in wings are clear.

FINE   *Moderate to considerable even wear. Entire design clear and bold.*

F-12   OBVERSE: Some details show in hair ends, curls and at left of ear. All letters, date and stars are visible. The eye and eyebrow are clear. Bust is worn with few drapery lines remaining.

REVERSE: Half the feathers are visible in wings. Breast and head are smooth. Letters in legend are worn but clear. Clouds and top of shield show considerable wear.

VERY GOOD   *Well worn. Design clear but flat and lacking details.*

VG-8   OBVERSE: Entire head is weak, and most hair details and drapery are worn smooth. Date and LIBERTY are weak but clear. Parts of the eye and eyebrow are visible. Stars are outlined with some tips worn flat.

REVERSE: Eagle is boldly outlined with only a few details showing in wings. Clouds, head and top of shield are smooth. Some letters in legend are very weak; parts of motto are missing.

HALF DOLLARS—DRAPED BUST, HERALDIC EAGLE
1801–1807

GOOD   *Heavily worn. Design and legend visible but faint in spots.*

G-4   OBVERSE: Entire design worn smooth with very little detail remaining. Legend, stars and date are well worn but visible.

REVERSE: Eagle is worn flat and only outlined. Tops of some letters are worn nearly smooth. Only half of the stars are completely outlined. Rim is full.

ABOUT GOOD   *Outlined design. Parts of date and legend worn smooth.*

AG-3   OBVERSE: Head is outlined with nearly all details worn away. Date readable but very weak. Stars merging into rim.

REVERSE: Entire design partially worn away. Legend merges with rim.

Note: Examples of this design are often weakly struck, particularly on the motto, shield, clouds and wing feathers. File adjustment marks are occasionally seen, and are a normal part of the manufacturing process.

REFERENCES

Beistle, M. L. *Register of United States Half Dollar Die Varieties and Sub-Varieties.* Shippensburg, Pa., 1929.

Overton, Al C. *Early Half Dollar Die Varieties 1794–1836.* Colorado Springs, 1970.

MINT STATE   *Absolutely no trace of wear.*

MS-70   UNCIRCULATED
A flawless coin exactly as it was minted, with no trace of wear or injury. Must have full mint luster and brilliance or light toning. Any unusual die or striking traits must be described.

MS-67   UNCIRCULATED
Virtually flawless but with very minor imperfections.

MS-65   UNCIRCULATED
No trace of wear; nearly as perfect as MS-67 except for some small blemish. Has full mint luster but may be unevenly toned or lightly fingermarked. A few barely noticeable nicks or marks may be present.

MS-63   UNCIRCULATED
A mint state coin with attractive mint luster, but noticeable detracting contact marks or minor blemishes.

MS-60   UNCIRCULATED
A strictly Uncirculated coin with no trace of wear, but with blemishes more obvious than for MS-63. May lack full mint luster, and surface may be dull, spotted or heavily toned.

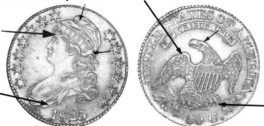

ABOUT UNCIRCULATED   *Small trace of wear visible on highest points.*

AU-58   *Very Choice*
Has some signs of abrasion: drapery at front of bust, cap, shoulder clasp, and hair above eye and at tips of curls; eagle's claws, head, and edges of wings. Shallow or weak spots in the design are usually caused by improper striking and not wear.

AU-55   *Choice*
OBVERSE: Only a trace of wear shows on high points of cap and hair above eye.
REVERSE: A trace of wear shows on wings, head and beak.
   Three-quarters of the mint luster is still present.

AU-50 *Typical*

OBVERSE: Traces of wear show on hair above eye and over the ear. Drapery clasp is clear and bold. Cap and drapery around bust show light signs of wear.

REVERSE: Traces of wear show on head, talons, arrowheads, and edges of wings.

Half of the mint luster is still present.

EXTREMELY FINE *Very light wear on only the highest points.*

EF-45 *Choice*

OBVERSE: Slight wear shows on high points of cap, and hair above eye and over the ear. Drapery is worn at shoulder and bustline. Trace of wear on lowest curl. Star details are full.

REVERSE: High points of wings, head, talons, shield and arrowheads are lightly worn. Lines in feathers are clearly defined.

Part of the mint luster is still present.

EF-40 *Typical*

OBVERSE: Wear shows on hair above eye and ear, and lightly on the cap and curls. Drapery lightly worn at neckline in spots. Ear and shoulder clasp are bold. Star details are complete.

REVERSE: High points of eagle and shield are worn, but each detail is clearly defined. Neck and tail feathers are very lightly worn. Talons, arrows and olive branch show slight wear.

Traces of mint luster may still show.

VERY FINE *Light to moderate even wear. All major features are sharp.*

HALF DOLLARS—CAPPED BUST 1807–1836

VF-30 *Choice*

OBVERSE: Curls above eye, ear and clasp are worn almost smooth in spots. Balance of hair is well detailed. Ear and shoulder clasp show clearly. Drapery and eye are well defined. Star centers are weak.

REVERSE: Feathers are worn but most details are visible. Some details in neck, shield and talons are well worn. Eyelid is visible. Horizontal shield lines flat but separated.

VF-20 *Typical*

OBVERSE: Over half the details still show in hair. Drapery and lower curls worn but bold. Ear, clasp and curls are worn but all plainly visible. Star centers are very weak.

REVERSE: Head and leg are worn, but some feathers are visible. Most details in wings are clear but edges are flat. Motto is complete. Half of the horizontal shield lines are separated.

FINE *Moderate to considerable even wear. Entire design clear and bold.*

F-12 OBVERSE: Over half the details show in hair, drapery and cap. All letters and parts of ear and clasp are visible. Eyelid is flattened. Star centers are worn flat. LIBERTY is complete.

REVERSE: Nearly half the feathers are visible in wings. Letters in motto are weak but clear. Head is nearly smooth but eye and some feathers show. Parts of shield worn smooth at top.

VERY GOOD *Well worn. Design clear but flat and lacking details.*

VG-8 OBVERSE: Entire head outlined with half of hair details worn smooth. Eye, ear and clasp are barely visible. All letters in LIBERTY are readable. Stars are flat.

HALF DOLLARS—CAPPED BUST 1807–1836

REVERSE: Eagle is boldly outlined with only a few feathers showing in left wing. Some letters in motto are very weak or partially worn away. Head, top of shield, talons and olive branch are nearly smooth. Eye is visible.

GOOD *Heavily worn. Design and legend visible but faint in spots.*

G-4 OBVERSE: Entire design well worn with very little detail remaining. Some letters in LIBERTY are worn away. Stars and date are weak but visible and may merge with rim.

REVERSE: Eagle is worn nearly flat but is completely outlined. Tops of some letters are worn nearly smooth and may merge with rim. Eye and motto are only partially visible.

ABOUT GOOD *Outlined design. Parts of date and legend worn smooth.*

AG-3 OBVERSE: Head is outlined with nearly all details worn away. Date readable but very weak. Stars merging into rim.

REVERSE: Entire design partially worn away.

Note: Coins of this design are often weakly struck, particularly around the outer border, stars, in the clasp, hair, and on the motto above the eagle.

1807–1808 LIBERTY may be very weak.

REFERENCES

Overton, Al C. *Early Half Dollar Die Varieties 1794–1836.* Colorado Springs, 1970.

MINT STATE *Absolutely no trace of wear.*

MS-70 UNCIRCULATED
A flawless coin exactly as it was minted, with no trace of wear or injury. Must have full mint luster and brilliance or light toning. Any unusual die or striking traits must be described.

MS-67 UNCIRCULATED
Virtually flawless but with very minor imperfections.

MS-65 UNCIRCULATED
No trace of wear; nearly as perfect as MS-67 except for some small blemish. Has full mint luster but may be unevenly toned, or lightly fingermarked. A few barely noticeable nicks or marks may be present.

MS-63 UNCIRCULATED
A mint state coin with attractive mint luster, but noticeable detracting contact marks or minor blemishes.

MS-60 UNCIRCULATED
A strictly Uncirculated coin with no trace of wear, but with blemishes more obvious than for MS-63. May lack full mint luster, and surface may be dull, spotted or heavily toned.

ABOUT UNCIRCULATED *Small trace of wear visible on highest points.*

AU-58 *Very Choice*
Has some signs of abrasion: drapery at front of bust, shoulder clasp, cap, and hair above eye and at tips of curls; eagle's claws, arrowheads, and edges of wings.

AU-55 *Choice*
OBVERSE: Only a trace of wear shows on highest points of cap and hair above eye.
REVERSE: A trace of wear shows on arrowheads and talons.
Three-quarters of the mint luster is still present.

AU-50 *Typical*

OBVERSE: Traces of wear show on hair above eye and over the ear. Drapery clasp is clear and bold. Cap and drapery around bust show light signs of wear.

REVERSE: Traces of wear show on talons, arrowheads, and edges of wings.

Half of the mint luster is still present.

EXTREMELY FINE *Very light wear on only the highest points.*

EF-45 *Choice*

OBVERSE: Slight wear shows on high points of cap, and hair above eye and over the ear. Drapery is worn at shoulder and bustline. Trace of wear on lowest curl. Star details are full.

REVERSE: High points of wings, head, talons, shield and arrowheads are lightly worn. Lines in feathers are clearly defined.

Part of the mint luster is still present.

EF-40 *Typical*

OBVERSE: Wear shows on hair above eye and ear, and lightly on the cap and curls. Drapery lightly worn at neckline in spots. Ear and shoulder clasp are bold. Star details are complete.

REVERSE: High points of eagle and shield are worn, but each detail is clearly defined. Neck and tail feathers are very lightly worn at center. Talons, arrows and olive branch show slight wear.

Traces of mint luster may still show.

VERY FINE *Light to moderate even wear. All major features are sharp.*

HALF DOLLARS—CAPPED BUST, REEDED EDGE
1836–1839

VF-30   *Choice*

OBVERSE: Curls above eye, ear and clasp are worn almost smooth in spots. Balance of hair and drapery is well detailed. Ear and shoulder clasp show clearly. Star centers are visible.

REVERSE: Feathers are worn but most details are visible. Some details in neck, shield and talons are well worn. Eyelid is visible. Horizontal shield lines worn but separated.

VF-20   *Typical*

OBVERSE: Over half the details still show in hair. Drapery and lower curls worn but bold. Ear, clasp and curls are worn but all plainly visible. Star centers are weak.

REVERSE: Head and leg are worn but some feathers are visible. Most details in wings are clear but edges are flat. Horizontal shield lines are flat but separated.

FINE   *Moderate to considerable even wear. Entire design clear and bold.*

F-12   OBVERSE: Over half the details show in hair, drapery, and cap. All letters, and parts of ear and clasp are visible. Eyelid is flattened. Star centers are very weak. LIBERTY is complete.

REVERSE: Half the feathers are visible in the wings. Talons and arrowheads are flat but clear. Head is nearly smooth but eye and some feathers show. Parts of shield worn smooth at top.

VERY GOOD   *Well worn. Design clear but flat and lacking details.*

VG-8   OBVERSE: Entire head outlined with half of all details worn smooth. Eye, ear and clasp are barely visible. All letters in LIBERTY are readable. Stars are flat.

REVERSE: Eagle is boldly outlined with about half of feathers showing in wings. Head, top of shield, talons and olive branch are nearly smooth. Eye is visible.

HALF DOLLARS—CAPPED BUST, REEDED EDGE
1836–1839

GOOD   *Heavily worn. Design and legend visible but faint in spots.*

G-4   OBVERSE: Entire design well worn with very little detail remaining. At least three letters in LIBERTY are visible. Stars and date are visible but may merge with rim.

REVERSE: Eagle is worn nearly flat but is completely outlined. Tops of some letters are worn nearly smooth and may merge with rim. Eye and shield are only partially visible.

ABOUT GOOD   *Outlined design. Parts of date and legend worn smooth.*

AG-3   OBVERSE: Head is outlined with nearly all details worn away. Date readable but very weak. Stars merging into rim.

REVERSE: Entire design partially worn away.

REFERENCES

Beistle, M. L. *Register of United States Half Dollar Die Varieties and Sub-Varieties.* Shippensburg, Pa., 1929.

HALF DOLLARS—LIBERTY SEATED 1839–1891

MINT STATE   *Absolutely no trace of wear.*

MS-70   UNCIRCULATED
A flawless coin exactly as it was minted, with no trace of wear or injury. Must have full mint luster and brillance or light toning. Any unusual die or striking traits must be described.

MS-67   UNCIRCULATED
Virtually flawless but with very minor imperfections.

MS-65   UNCIRCULATED
No trace of wear; nearly as perfect as MS-67 except for some small blemish. Has full mint luster but may be unevenly toned or lightly fingermarked. A few barely noticeable nicks or marks may be present.

MS-63   UNCIRCULATED
A mint state coin with attractive mint luster, but noticeable detracting contact marks or minor blemishes.

MS-60   UNCIRCULATED
A strictly Uncirculated coin with no trace of wear, but with blemishes more obvious than for MS-63. May lack full mint luster, and surface may be dull, spotted or heavily toned.

ABOUT UNCIRCULATED   *Small trace of wear visible on highest points.*

AU-58   *Very Choice*
Has some signs of abrasion: high points of head, breast and knees; neck, head, beak and tops of wings. Weak spots in the design are usually caused by striking and not wear.

AU-55   *Choice*
OBVERSE: Only a trace of wear shows on highest points of hair above eye, breast and right leg.
REVERSE: A trace of wear shows on head, beak and above eye.
   Three-quarters of the mint luster is still present.

AU-50 *Typical*

OBVERSE: Traces of wear show on knees, breast and edge of hairline. Foot is separated from sandal.

REVERSE: Traces of wear show on talons, neck, head and tips of wings.

Half of the mint luster is still present.

EXTREMELY FINE *Very light wear on only the highest points.*

EF-45 *Choice*

OBVERSE: Slight wear shows on high points of knees, breast and hair at forehead. Drapery is worn at shoulder and bustline. LIBERTY is sharp and scroll edges are raised.

REVERSE: High points of eagle and arrows lightly worn. Talons are clearly defined. Neck feathers are fully separated.

Part of the mint luster is still present.

EF-40 *Typical*

OBVERSE: Wear shows on knees, breast, head and shoulder. Drapery lightly worn at neckline in spots. LIBERTY is complete and scroll edges are raised.

REVERSE: High points of eagle and arrows are worn, but each detail is clearly defined. Neck feathers and talons are distinct.

Traces of mint luster may still show.

VERY FINE *Light to moderate even wear. All major features are sharp.*

VF-30 *Choice*

OBVERSE: Wear spots show on shoulder, breast, knees and legs. Neckline is weak but has some visible details in center. LIBERTY and scroll are complete. Fingers at pole are flat but separated. All lines in shield are distinct.

REVERSE: Leaves are worn but three-quarters of the details are visible. Most details in feathers and talons are clear.

VF-20 *Typical*

OBVERSE: Over half the details show in the gown. Hair, shoulder and legs are worn but bold. Every letter in LIBERTY is visible. Horizontal shield lines are weak at center.

REVERSE: Three-quarters of the feathers are visible. Arrowheads and talons are worn, but some details are visible. Half the details in leaves are clear.

FINE *Moderate to considerable even wear. Entire design clear and bold.*

F-12 OBVERSE: Some details show in hair, cap, and at the shoulder and breast. All shield lines and letters in LIBERTY are weak but visible. Foot and sandal are separated.

REVERSE: Some details in feathers are visible. Shield border is partially visible on right side. Talons are flat but separated. Letters in legend are worn but clear. Letters IN and ST are weak in motto on coins from 1866 through 1891.

VERY GOOD *Well worn. Design clear but flat and lacking details.*

VG-8 OBVERSE: Entire shield is weak but three-quarters outlined. Most gown details are worn smooth. Four letters in LIBERTY are clear. Rim is complete.

REVERSE: Eagle and leaves show only bold outline. Some of shield is very weak. Legend and rim are clear.

HALF DOLLARS—LIBERTY SEATED 1839-1891

GOOD *Heavily worn. Design and legend visible but faint in spots.*

G-4 OBVERSE: Entire design well worn with very little detail remaining. Date is weak but visible. Shield is worn smooth. Three-quarters of rim is plain.

REVERSE: Eagle is worn flat but is completely outlined. Tops of some letters are worn nearly smooth. For coins after 1865, motto is partially visible.

ABOUT GOOD *Outlined design. Parts of date and legend worn smooth.*

AG-3 OBVERSE: Liberty is outlined with nearly all details worn away. Date readable but very weak. Stars merging into rim.

REVERSE: Entire design partially worn away. Legend merging into rim.

Note: Coins of this design are sometimes weakly struck, particularly in the lines of the clasp on Liberty's gown.

Prooflike specimens of pieces dated 1879 through 1890 are frequently seen.

1839 Eagle's left wing, left leg and claw are usually weakly struck.

1840 Weaknesses on both sides are characteristic.

1852 Obverse sometimes shows flatness in date and stars. New Orleans Mint coins are usually not fully struck.

1854-1855 Philadelphia Mint coins tend to be slightly weak on Liberty's head.

New Orleans Mint dies frequently show outlining of the stars and legends.

San Francisco Mint coins frequently are weakly struck in eagle's feathers and talons.

HALF DOLLARS—BARBER 1892–1915

MINT STATE   *Absolutely no trace of wear.*

MS-70   UNCIRCULATED
A flawless coin exactly as it was minted, with no trace of wear or injury. Must have full mint luster and brilliance or light toning. Any unusual die or striking traits must be described.

MS-67   UNCIRCULATED
Virtually flawless but with very minor imperfections.

MS-65   UNCIRCULATED
No trace of wear; nearly as perfect as MS-67 except for some small blemish. Has full mint luster but may be unevenly toned or lightly fingermarked. A few barely noticeable nicks or marks may be present.

MS-63   UNCIRCULATED
A mint state coin with attractive mint luster, but noticeable detracting contact marks or minor blemishes.

MS-60   UNCIRCULATED
A strictly Uncirculated coin with no trace of wear, but with blemishes more obvious than for MS-63. May lack full mint luster, and surface may be dull, spotted or heavily toned.

ABOUT UNCIRCULATED   *Small trace of wear visible on highest points.*

AU-58   *Very Choice*
Has some signs of abrasion: high points of cheek and hair below LIBERTY; eagle's head and tips of tail and wings.

AU-55   *Choice*
OBVERSE: Only a trace of wear shows on highest points of hair below BER in LIBERTY.
REVERSE: A trace of wear shows on head, tip of tail and tips of wings.
   Three-quarters of the mint luster is still present.

AU-50   *Typical*
OBVERSE: Traces of wear show on cheek, tips of leaves and hair below LIBERTY.

REVERSE: Traces of wear show on head, neck, tail and tips of wings. Half of the mint luster is still present.

EXTREMELY FINE *Very light wear on only the highest points.*

EF-45 *Choice*

OBVERSE: Slight wear shows on high points of upper leaves, cheek and hair above forehead. LIBERTY is sharp and band edges are bold.

REVERSE: High points of head, neck, wings and talons lightly worn. Lines in center tail feathers are clearly defined.

Part of the mint luster is still present.

EF-40 *Typical*

OBVERSE: Light wear shows on leaves, cheek, cap and hair above forehead. LIBERTY is sharp and band edges are clear.

REVERSE: High points of head, neck, wings, and tail are lightly worn, but all details are clearly defined. Leaves show trace of wear at edges.

Traces of mint luster may still show.

VERY FINE *Light to moderate even wear. All major features are sharp.*

VF-30 *Choice*

OBVERSE: Wear spots show on leaves, cap, hair and cheek. Bottom row of leaves is weak but has some visible details. LIBERTY and band are complete. Folds in cap are distinct.

REVERSE: Wear shows on shield but all details are visible. Most of the details in neck and tail are clear. Motto is complete.

VF-20 *Typical*

OBVERSE: Over half the details still show in leaves. Hair and ribbon worn but bold. Every letter in LIBERTY is visible. Bottom folds in cap are full.

REVERSE: Shield is worn but all details are visible. Half the details in feathers are clear. Wings, tail and legs show small wear spots. Motto is clear.

FINE *Moderate to considerable even wear. Entire design clear and bold.*

F-12 OBVERSE: Some details show in hair, cap and facial features. All letters in LIBERTY are weak but visible. Upper row of leaves is outlined, but bottom row is worn nearly smooth. Rim is full and bold.

REVERSE: Half the feathers are plainly visible. Wear spots show in center of neck, motto and arrows. Horizontal shield lines are merged; vertical lines are separated. Letters in legend are worn but clear.

VERY GOOD *Well worn. Design clear but flat and lacking details.*

VG-8 OBVERSE: Entire head weak, and most details in face are heavily worn. Three letters in LIBERTY are clear. Rim is complete.

REVERSE: Eagle shows only a small amount of detail. Arrows and leaves are flat. Most of shield is very weak. Parts of eye and motto visible.

GOOD *Heavily worn. Design and legend visible but faint in spots.*

G-4 OBVERSE: Entire design well worn with very little detail remaining. Legend and date weak but visible. LIBERTY is worn away.

REVERSE: Eagle worn flat but is completely outlined. Ribbon worn nearly smooth. Legend weak but visible. Rim worn to tops of letters.

ABOUT GOOD *Outlined design. Parts of date and legend worn smooth.*

AG-3 OBVERSE: Head is outlined with nearly all details worn away. Date readable but partially worn away. Legend merging into rim.

REVERSE: Entire design partially worn away and legend merges with rim.

Note: New Orleans issues are often softly struck.

1906-O and 1908-O exhibit a swelling appearance extending from the lower cheek area down through the jaw and neck of Liberty.

MINT STATE *Absolutely no trace of wear.*

MS-70 UNCIRCULATED
A flawless coin exactly as it was minted, with no trace of wear or injury. Must have full mint luster and brilliance or light toning. Unusual die or striking traits must be described.

MS-67 UNCIRCULATED
Virtually flawless but with very minor imperfections.

MS-65 UNCIRCULATED
No trace of wear; nearly as perfect as MS-67 except for some small blemish. Has full mint luster but may be unevenly toned or lightly fingermarked. May be weakly struck in one or two small spots. A few minute nicks or marks may be present.

MS-63 UNCIRCULATED
A mint state coin with attractive mint luster, but noticeable detracting contact marks or minor blemishes.

MS-60 UNCIRCULATED
A strictly Uncirculated coin with no trace of wear, but with blemishes more obvious than for MS-63. May lack full mint luster, and surface may be dull, spotted or heavily toned. A few small spots may be weakly struck.

Uncirculated coins for this type are frequently graded at intermediate levels from MS-60 to MS-70. For specific details refer to pages 16-17 of the introductions.

ABOUT UNCIRCULATED *Small trace of wear visible on highest points.*

AU-58 *Very Choice*
Has some signs of abrasion: hair above temple, right arm, left breast; high points of eagle's head, breast, legs and wings. Coins of this design frequently show weakly struck spots, and usually lack full head and hand details.

AU-55 *Choice*
OBVERSE: Only a trace of wear shows on highest points of head, breast, and right arm.
REVERSE: A trace of wear shows on left leg between breast and left wing.
Three-quarters of the mint luster is still present.

Prime Focal Areas

Obverse: Length of Liberty's body. Right field.
Reverse: Breast, leg, and forward wing of eagle.

Secondary Areas

Obverse: Left field, sun and date area.
Reverse: Head, rear wing, and field above eagle.
Rock on which eagle stands.

	CONTACT MARKS	HAIRLINES	LUSTER	EYE APPEAL
MS-70	None show under magnification	None show under magnification	Very attractive Fully original	Outstanding
MS-69	1 or 2 miniscule none in prime focal areas	None visible	Very attractive Fully original	Exceptional
MS-68	3 or 4 miniscule none in prime focal areas	None visible	Attractive Fully original	Exceptional
MS-67	3 or 4 miniscule 1 or 2 may be in prime focal areas	None visible without magnification	Above average Fully original	Exceptional
MS-66	Several small; a few may be in prime focal areas	None visible without magnification	Above average Fully original	Above average
MS-65	Light and scattered without major distracting marks in prime focal areas	May have a few scattered	Fully original	Very pleasing
MS-64	May have light scattered marks; a few may be in prime focal areas	May have a few scattered or small patch in secondary areas	Average Full original	Pleasing
MS-63	May have distracting marks in prime focal areas	May have a few scattered or small patch	May be original or slightly impaired	Rather attractive
MS-62	May have distracting marks in prime focal and/or secondary areas	May have a few scattered to noticeable patch	May be original or impaired	Generally acceptable
MS-61	May have a few heavy (or numerous light) marks in prime focal and/or secondary areas	May have noticeable patch or continuous hairlining over surfaces	May be original or impaired	Unattractive
MS-60	May have heavy marks in all areas	May have noticeable patch or continuous hairlining throughout	May be original or impaired	Poor

[255]

AU-50 *Typical*

OBVERSE: Traces of wear show on head, breast, arms and left leg.

REVERSE: Traces of wear show on high points of wings and at center of head. All leg feathers are visible.

Half of the mint luster is still present.

EXTREMELY FINE *Very light wear on only the highest points.*

EF-45 *Choice*

OBVERSE: Light wear spots show on head, breast, arms, left leg and foot. Nearly all gown lines are clearly visible. Sandal details are bold and complete. Knee is lightly worn but full and rounded.

REVERSE: Small flat spots show on high points of breast and legs. Wing feathers have nearly full details.

Part of the mint luster is still present.

EF-40 *Typical*

OBVERSE: Wear shows on head, breast, arms and left leg. Nearly all gown lines are visible. Sandal details are complete. Breast and knee are nearly flat.

REVERSE: High points of eagle are lightly worn. Half the breast and leg feathers are visible. Central part of feathers below neck is well worn.

Traces of mint luster may still show.

VERY FINE *Light to moderate even wear. All major features are sharp.*

VF-30 *Choice*

OBVERSE: Wear spots show on head, breast, arms and legs. Left leg is rounded but worn from above knee to ankle. Gown line crossing body is partially visible. Knee is flat. Outline of breast can be seen.

REVERSE: Breast and legs are moderately worn but clearly separated, with some feathers visible between them. Feather ends and folds are clearly visible in right wing. Pupil in eye is visible.

VF-20 *Typical*

OBVERSE: Left leg is worn nearly flat. Wear spots show on head, breast, arms and foot. Lines on skirt are visible but may be weak on coins before 1921. Breast is outlined.

REVERSE: Entire eagle is lightly worn but most major details are visible. Breast, central part of legs, and top edge of right wing are worn flat.

FINE *Moderate to heavy even wear. Entire design clear and bold.*

F-12 OBVERSE: Gown stripes worn but show clearly except for coins before 1921 where only half are visible. Right leg is lightly worn. Left leg nearly flat and sandal is worn but visible. Center of body worn but some of the gown is visible.

REVERSE: Breast is worn smooth. Half the wing feathers are visible although well worn in spots. Top two layers of feathers are visible in left wing. Rim is full.

VERY GOOD *Well worn. Design clear but flat and lacking details.*

VG-8 OBVERSE: Entire design is weak. Most details in gown are worn smooth except for coins after 1921, where half the stripes must show. All letters and date are clear but top of motto may be weak. Rim is complete. Drapery across body is partially visible.

REVERSE: About one-third of the feathers are visible, and large feathers at ends of wings are well separated. Eye is visible. Rim is full and all letters are clear.

HALF DOLLARS—LIBERTY WALKING 1916–1947

GOOD   *Heavily worn. Design and legend visible but faint in spots.*

G-4   OBVERSE: Entire design well worn with very little detail remaining. Legend and date are weak but visible. Top of date may be worn flat. Rim is flat but nearly complete.

REVERSE: Eagle worn nearly flat but is completely outlined. Lettering and motto worn but clearly visible.

ABOUT GOOD   *Outlined design. Parts of date and legend worn smooth.*

AG-3   OBVERSE: Figure is outlined with nearly all details worn away. Legend visible but half worn away. Date weak but readable. Rim merges with lettering.

REVERSE: Entire design partially worn away. Letters merge with rim.

Note: Coins of this design, especially San Francisco issues 1940–1946, are often weakly struck in spots, particularly at Liberty's head, hand holding branch, drapery lines of dress, and on the eagle's leg feathers. On many of these coins the breast may show light rub from contact with other coins in uncirculated rolls.

1917–S (OBV.)	1927–S	1943–S
1918–D, S	1928–S	1944–S*
1919–D, S	1935–D, S	1945–S
1920–D	1940–S*	
1921–S	1941–S*	
1923–S	1942–S	

* coins that seldom are found with a good strike.

MINT STATE *Absolutely no trace of wear.*

MS-70 UNCIRCULATED
A flawless coin exactly as it was minted, with no trace of wear or injury. Must have full mint luster and brilliance or light toning. Any unusual striking traits must be described.

MS-67 UNCIRCULATED
Virtually flawless but with very minor imperfections.

MS-65 UNCIRCULATED
No trace of wear; nearly as perfect as MS-67 except for some small blemish. Has full mint luster but may be unevenly toned or lightly fingermarked. A few barely noticeable nicks or marks may be present.

MS-63 UNCIRCULATED
A mint state coin with attractive mint luster, but noticeable detracting contact marks or minor blemishes.

MS-60 UNCIRCULATED
A strictly Uncirculated coin with no trace of wear, but with blemishes more obvious than for MS-63. May lack full mint luster, and surface may be dull, spotted or heavily toned.

ABOUT UNCIRCULATED *Small trace of wear visible on highest points.*

AU-58 *Very Choice*
Has some signs of abrasion: high points of cheek, shoulder, and hair left of ear; straps around beam, lines and lettering on bell.

AU-55 *Choice*
OBVERSE: Only a trace of wear shows on highest points of cheek and hair left of ear.
REVERSE: A trace of wear shows on highest spots of lettering on bell.
Nearly all of the mint luster is still present.

AU-50 *Typical*
OBVERSE: Traces of wear show on cheek, hair on shoulder and left of ear.

HALF DOLLARS—FRANKLIN 1948–1963

REVERSE: Traces of wear show on bell at lettering and along ridges at bottom.

Three-quarters of the mint luster is still present.

EXTREMELY FINE *Very light wear on only the highest points.*

EF-45 *Choice*

OBVERSE: Slight wear shows on cheek and high points of hair behind ear and along shoulder. Hair lines at back of head are sharp and detailed.

REVERSE: High points of straps on beam are lightly worn. Lines at bottom of bell are worn but clearly defined and separated. Lettering on bell is very weak at center.

Half of the mint luster is still present.

EF-40 *Typical*

OBVERSE: Wear shows on high points of cheek and hair behind ear and at shoulder.

REVERSE: High points of beam straps and lines along bottom of bell are lightly worn, but details are clearly defined and partially separated. Lettering on bell is worn away at center.

Part of the mint luster is still present.

VERY FINE *Light to moderate even wear. All major features are sharp.*

VF-30 *Choice*

OBVERSE: Wear spots show on hair at shoulder and behind ear, on cheek and jaw. Hair lines are weak but have nearly full visible details.

REVERSE: Wear shows on bell lettering but some of the details are visible. Straps on beam are plain. Half of line details at bottom of bell are worn smooth.

VF-20 *Typical*

OBVERSE: Three-quarters of the lines still show in hair. Cheek lightly worn but bold. Some hair details around the ear are visible.

REVERSE: Wear shows on beam but most details are visible. Bell is worn but bold. Lines across bottom of bell are flat near crack.

FINE *Moderate to heavy even wear. Entire design clear and bold.*

F-12 OBVERSE: Hair details show only at back and side of head. Designer's initials weak but clearly visible. Part of cheek is worn flat.

REVERSE: Most of lines at bottom of bell are worn smooth. Parts of straps on beam are nearly smooth. Rim is full.

VERY GOOD *Well worn. Design clear but flat and lacking details.*

VG-8 OBVERSE: Entire head is weak, and most details in hair from temple to ear are worn smooth. All letters and date are bold. Ear and designer's initials are visible. Rim is complete.

REVERSE: Bell is well worn with very little detail remaining. Straps on beam are weak but visible. Rim merges with letters.

Note: Bell lines on these pieces are usually not fully separated. The following are often found weakly struck: 1949-S, 1951-S, 1952-S, 1953-S and 1954-S.

MINT STATE *Absolutely no trace of wear.*

MS-70 UNCIRCULATED
A flawless coin exactly as it was minted, with no trace of wear or injury. Must have full mint luster and brilliance or light toning. Any unusual striking traits must be described.

MS-67 UNCIRCULATED
Virtually flawless but with very minor imperfections.

MS-65 UNCIRCULATED
No trace of wear; nearly as perfect as MS-67 except for some small blemish. Has full mint luster but may be unevenly toned or lightly fingermarked. A few barely noticeable nicks or marks may be present.

MS-63 UNCIRCULATED
A mint state coin with attractive mint luster, but noticeable detracting contact marks or minor blemishes.

MS-60 UNCIRCULATED
A strictly Uncirculated coin with no trace of wear, but with blemishes more obvious than for MS-63. Has full mint luster, but surface may be dull, spotted or heavily toned.

ABOUT UNCIRCULATED *Small trace of wear visible on highest points.*

AU-58 *Very Choice*
Has some signs of abrasion: high points of cheek and jawbone, center of neck, hair below part; bundle of arrows, center tail feather, right wing tip.

AU-55 *Choice*
OBVERSE: Only a trace of wear shows on highest points of cheek, jawbone and hair below part.
REVERSE: A trace of wear shows on central tail feather.
Nearly all of the mint luster is still present.

EXTREMELY FINE   *Very light wear on only the highest points.*

EF-40   *Typical*

OBVERSE: Slight wear shows on cheek, along jawbone and on high points of hair below part. Hair lines are sharp and detailed.

REVERSE: High points of arrows and right wing tip are lightly worn. Central tail feathers are worn but clearly defined and fully separated.

   Three-quarters of the mint luster is still present.

VERY FINE   *Light to moderate even wear. All major features are sharp.*

VF-30   *Choice*

OBVERSE: Wear spots show on hair below part, and along cheek and jaw. Hair lines are weak but have nearly full visible details.

REVERSE: Wear shows on arrow points but some details are visible. All central tail feathers are plain. Wing tips are lightly worn.

Note: Clad pieces are sometimes weakly struck in spots.
   Bicentennial coins can be graded by the obverse.

DOLLARS—FLOWING HAIR 1794–1795

MINT STATE *Absolutely no trace of wear.*

MS-70 UNCIRCULATED
A flawless coin exactly as it was minted, with no trace of wear or injury. Must have full mint luster and brilliance or light toning. Any unusual die, planchet or striking traits must be described.

MS-67 UNCIRCULATED
Virtually flawless but with very minor imperfections.

MS-65 UNCIRCULATED
No trace of wear; nearly as perfect as MS-67 except for some small blemish. Has full mint luster but may be unevenly toned or lightly fingermarked. A few small nicks or adjustment file marks may be present.

MS-63 UNCIRCULATED
A mint state coin with attractive mint luster, but noticeable detracting contact marks or minor blemishes.

MS-60 UNCIRCULATED
A strictly Uncirculated coin with no trace of wear, but with blemishes more obvious than for MS-63. May lack full mint luster, and surface may be dull, spotted or heavily toned.

ABOUT UNCIRCULATED *Small trace of wear visible on highest points.*

AU-58 *Very Choice*
Has some signs of abrasion: high points of bust, shoulder, and hair above forehead; eagle's breast, head, and top edges of wings. Shallow or weak spots in the relief are usually caused by improper striking and not wear.

AU-55 *Choice*
OBVERSE: Only a trace of wear shows on highest points of hair above forehead.
REVERSE: A trace of wear shows on breast.
    Three-quarters of the mint luster is still present.

AU-50   *Typical*

OBVERSE: Traces of wear show on hair above and beside forehead.
REVERSE: Traces of wear show on breast and head.
Half of the mint luster is still present.

EXTREMELY FINE   *Very light wear on only the highest points.*

EF-45   *Choice*

OBVERSE: Slight wear shows on high points of hair from forehead to neck.
Very light wear at eyebrow, shoulder and bustline. Stars fully detailed.
REVERSE: High points of wings, breast and head are lightly worn. Lines in
feathers are clearly defined.
Part of the mint luster is still present.

EF-40   *Typical*

OBVERSE: Wear shows on hair from forehead to neck, and lightly on the
cheek and bust. Lightly worn at neckline in spots. Stars fully detailed.
REVERSE: High points of eagle are worn, but each detail is clearly defined.
Head, wings and breast are lightly worn.
Traces of mint luster can be seen.

VERY FINE   *Light to moderate even wear. All major features are sharp.*

VF-30   *Choice*

OBVERSE: Three-quarters of flowing hair details show. Hair above forehead
is worn but has some bold features. Parts of star centers, eyebrow and ear
are very weak.
REVERSE: Feathers are worn but more than half of the wing details are
visible. Some of the details in head and breast are clear unless weakly struck.

VF-20   *Typical*

OBVERSE: Half of the details still show in hair. Eyebrow, ear and bust are
worn but bold. Parts of shoulder are smooth. Every letter and star is plainly
visible. Star centers are nearly flat.

REVERSE: Head and breast are worn, but some feathers are visible. Half of details in wings and tail are clear.

FINE   *Moderate to heavy even wear. Entire design clear and bold.*

F-12   OBVERSE: Some details show in hair ends and below ear. All letters, date and stars are visible. The ear and eye are clear. Hair at top of forehead is outlined.

REVERSE: Some feathers are visible in body, wings and tail. Breast and head are smooth. Eye is visible. Letters in legend are worn but clear.

VERY GOOD   *Well worn. Design clear but flat and lacking details.*

VG-8   OBVERSE: Entire head is weak, and most hair details are worn smooth. Date and LIBERTY are weak but clear. Parts of the eye and ear are visible. Stars are outlined.

REVERSE: Eagle is boldly outlined with only a few details showing in wings and tail. Breast is smooth. Some letters are very weak.

GOOD   *Heavily worn. Design and legend visible but faint in spots.*

G-4   OBVERSE: Entire design worn smooth with very little detail remaining. Legend, stars and date are well worn but all visible.

REVERSE: Eagle worn flat but is completely outlined. Tops of some letters are worn nearly smooth.

ABOUT GOOD *Outlined design. Parts of date and legend worn smooth.*

AG-3   OBVERSE: Head is outlined with nearly all details worn away. Date readable but very weak. Stars merging into rim.

REVERSE: Entire design flat and partially worn away.

Note: Examples of this design are often weakly struck, particularly on the eagle's breast and feathers. File adjustment marks are frequently seen, and are a normal part of the manufacturing process.

1794 is usually weakly struck at date, UNITED, and stars on left side of obverse.

MINT STATE *Absolutely no trace of wear.*

MS-70 UNCIRCULATED
A flawless coin exactly as it was minted, with no trace of wear or injury. Must have full mint luster and brilliance or light toning. Any unusual die or striking traits must be described.

MS-67 UNCIRCULATED
Virtually flawless but with very minor imperfections.

MS-65 UNCIRCULATED
No trace of wear; nearly as perfect as MS-67 except for some small blemish. Has full mint luster but may be unevenly toned or lightly fingermarked. A few small nicks or adjustment file marks may be present.

MS-63 UNCIRCULATED
A mint state coin with attractive mint luster, but noticeable detracting contact marks or minor blemishes.

MS-60 UNCIRCULATED
A strictly Uncirculated coin with no trace of wear, but with blemishes more obvious than for MS-63. May lack full mint luster, and surface may be dull, spotted or heavily toned.

ABOUT UNCIRCULATED *Small trace of wear visible on highest points.*

AU-58 *Very Choice*
Has some signs of abrasion: high points of bust, shoulder, and hair above forehead; eagle's breast and top edges of wings. Shallow or weak spots in the relief are usually caused by improper striking and not wear.

AU-55 *Choice*
OBVERSE: Only a trace of wear shows on highest points of hair above forehead.
REVERSE: A trace of wear shows on breast.
Three-quarters of the mint luster is still present.

DOLLARS—DRAPED BUST, SMALL EAGLE 1795-1798

AU-50 *Typical*

OBVERSE: Trace of wear shows on hair above and beside forehead. Drapery has trace of wear at shoulder and bustline.

REVERSE: Traces of wear show on breast and left leg.

Half of the mint luster is still present.

EXTREMELY FINE   *Very light wear on only the highest points.*

EF-45 *Choice*

OBVERSE: Slight wear shows on high points of hair from forehead to the ear. Drapery is worn at shoulder and bustline.

REVERSE: High points of wing tips, breast and left leg are lightly worn. Lines in feathers are clearly defined.

Part of the mint luster is still present.

EF-40 *Typical*

OBVERSE: Wear shows on hair from forehead to ear, and lightly on the cheek and bust. Drapery lightly worn at neckline in spots.

REVERSE: High points of wings are worn but each detail is clearly defined. Left leg and breast are slightly worn.

Traces of mint luster can be seen.

VERY FINE   *Light to moderate even wear. All major features are sharp.*

VF-30 *Choice*

OBVERSE: Three-quarters of hair details show. Hair above forehead is worn but has some bold features. Parts of drapery are worn smooth.

REVERSE: Wing edges are worn but most central details are visible. Some of the details in left leg and breast are clear unless weakly struck.

VF-20 *Typical*

OBVERSE: Over half of the details still show in hair. Forehead and bust are worn but bold. Parts of drapery are smooth. Letters and star centers are plainly visible.

REVERSE: Left leg and breast are worn but some feathers are visible. About three-quarters of details in wings are clear.

FINE *Moderate to heavy even wear. Entire design clear and bold.*

F-12 OBVERSE: Some details show in hair ends, curls and at left of ear. All letters, date and stars are visible. The eye and ear are clear. Bust is worn with few drapery lines remaining.

REVERSE: Half the feathers are visible in wings. Breast and left leg are smooth. Letters in legend are worn but clear.

VERY GOOD *Well worn. Design clear but flat and lacking details.*

VG-8 OBVERSE: Entire head is weak, and most hair details and drapery are worn smooth. Date and LIBERTY are weak but clear. Parts of the eye and ear are visible. Stars are outlined.

REVERSE: Eagle is boldly outlined with only a few details showing in wings. Breast and left leg are smooth. Some letters are very weak. Rim is full.

GOOD *Heavily worn. Design and legend visible but faint in spots.*

G-4 OBVERSE: Entire design worn smooth with very little detail remaining. Legend, stars and date are well worn but visible.

DOLLARS—DRAPED BUST, SMALL EAGLE 1795–1798

REVERSE: Eagle is worn flat and only outlined. Tops of some letters are worn nearly smooth. Rim is full.

ABOUT GOOD *Outlined design. Parts of date and legend worn smooth.*

AG-3 OBVERSE: Head is outlined with nearly all details worn away. Date readable but very weak. Stars merging into rim.
REVERSE: Entire design flat and partially worn away. Legend merges with rim.

Note: Examples of this design are often weakly struck, particularly on the eagle's breast and feathers. File adjustment marks are occasionally seen, and are a normal part of the manufacturing process.

1796, small date and letters. The reverse is usually weak. One variety of the 1796 (B-5) shows a die lump on the reverse at right top of I in AMERICA.

1797, 7 stars right, small letters. The reverse is always weak.

1798, 15 stars. The reverse is usually weak.

DOLLARS—DRAPED BUST, HERALDIC EAGLE 1798–1803

MINT STATE *Absolutely no trace of wear.*

MS-70 UNCIRCULATED
A flawless coin exactly as it was minted, with no trace of wear or injury. Must have full mint luster and brilliance or light toning. Any unusual die or striking traits must be described.

MS-67 UNCIRCULATED
Virtually flawless but with very minor imperfections.

MS-65 UNCIRCULATED
No trace of wear; nearly as perfect as MS-67 except for some small blemish. Has full mint luster but may be unevenly toned or lightly fingermarked. A few small nicks or adjustment file marks may be present.

MS-63 UNCIRCULATED
A mint state coin with attractive mint luster, but noticeable detracting contact marks or minor blemishes.

MS-60 UNCIRCULATED
A strictly Uncirculated coin with no trace of wear, but with blemishes more obvious than for MS-63. May lack full mint luster, and surface may be dull, spotted or heavily toned.

ABOUT UNCIRCULATED *Small trace of wear visible on highest points.*

AU-58 *Very Choice*
Has some signs of abrasion: high points of bust, shoulder and hair above forehead; eagle's head, breast, edges of wings and clouds. Shallow or weak spots in the motto are usually caused by improper striking and not wear.

AU-55 *Choice*
OBVERSE: Only a trace of wear shows on highest points of hair above forehead.
REVERSE: A trace of wear shows on the clouds.
Three-quarters of the mint luster is still present.

DOLLARS—DRAPED BUST, HERALDIC EAGLE 1798–1803

AU-50 *Typical*

OBVERSE: Trace of wear shows on hair above and behind forehead. Drapery has trace of wear at shoulder and bustline.

REVERSE: Traces of wear show on breast feathers and clouds.

Half of the mint luster is still present.

EXTREMELY FINE *Very light wear on only the highest points.*

EF-45 *Choice*

OBVERSE: Slight wear shows on high points of hair from forehead to the ear. Drapery is worn at shoulder and bustline.

REVERSE: High points of wing edges, breast feathers and clouds are lightly worn. Lines in shield are clearly defined.

Part of the mint luster is still present.

EF-40 *Typical*

OBVERSE: Wear shows on hair from forehead to ear, and lightly on the cheek and bust. Drapery lightly worn at neckline in spots.

REVERSE: High points of clouds and wings are worn, but each detail is clearly defined. Head and breast are slightly worn. Lines in shield are separated.

Traces of mint luster can be seen.

VERY FINE *Light to moderate even wear. All major features are sharp.*

VF-30 *Choice*

OBVERSE: Three-quarters of hair details show. Hair at back of head is worn but has some bold features. Parts of drapery are worn smooth.

REVERSE: Wing edges are worn but three-quarters of central details are visible. Clouds, head and motto show wear.

Horizontal shield lines worn but separated.

VF-20 *Typical*

OBVERSE: Over half of the details still show in hair. Forehead and bust are

[273]

worn but bold. Parts of drapery are smooth. Letters and star centers are plainly visible.

REVERSE: Head and breast are worn, but some feathers are visible. Some lines in shield are merged together. About three-quarters of details in wings are clear. Motto is complete.

FINE *Moderate to heavy even wear. Entire design clear and bold.*

F-12 OBVERSE: Some details show in hair ends, curls and at left of ear. All letters, date and stars are visible. The eye and ear are clear. Bust is worn with few drapery lines remaining.

REVERSE: Half the feathers are visible in wings. Breast and head are smooth. Letters in legend are worn but clear. Clouds and top of shield show considerable wear.

VERY GOOD *Well worn. Design clear but flat and lacking details.*

VG-8 OBVERSE: Entire head is weak, and most hair details and drapery are worn smooth. Date and LIBERTY are weak but clear. Parts of the eye and ear are visible. Stars are outlined with some tips worn flat.

REVERSE: Eagle is boldly outlined with only a few details showing in wings. Clouds, head and top of shield are smooth. Some letters in legend are very weak; parts of motto are missing. Rim is full.

GOOD *Heavily worn. Design and legend visible but faint in spots.*

DOLLARS—DRAPED BUST, HERALDIC EAGLE 1798–1803

G-4   OBVERSE: Entire design worn smooth with very little detail remaining. Legend, stars and date are well worn but visible.

REVERSE: Eagle is worn flat and only outlined. Tops of some letters are worn nearly smooth. Only half of the stars are completely outlined. Rim is full.

ABOUT GOOD   *Outlined design. Parts of date and legend worn smooth.*

AG-3   OBVERSE: Head is outlined with nearly all details worn away. Date readable but very weak. Stars merging into rim.

REVERSE: Entire design flat and partially worn away. Legend merges with rim.

Note: Examples of this design are often weakly struck, particularly on the motto, shield, clouds and wing feathers. File adjustment marks are occasionally seen, and are a normal part of the manufacturing process.

REFERENCES

Bolender, M. H. *The United States Early Silver Dollars from 1794-1803.* Freeport, Ill., 1950.

DOLLARS—GOBRECHT DESIGN 1836–1839

MINT STATE   *Absolutely no trace of wear.*

MS-70   UNCIRCULATED
A flawless coin exactly as it was minted, with no trace of wear or injury. Must have full mint luster or light toning. Any unusual striking traits must be described.

MS-67   UNCIRCULATED
Virtually flawless but with very minor imperfections.

MS-65   UNCIRCULATED
No trace of wear; nearly as perfect as MS-67 except for a few minute bag marks or surface mars. Has full mint luster but may be unevenly toned.

MS-63   UNCIRCULATED
A mint state coin with attractive mint luster, but noticeable detracting contact marks or minor blemishes.

MS-60   UNCIRCULATED
A strictly Uncirculated coin with no trace of wear, but with bag marks and other abrasions more obvious than for MS-63. May have a few small rim mars and weakly struck spots. Has full mint luster but may lack brilliance, and surface may be spotted or heavily toned.

ABOUT UNCIRCULATED   *Small trace of wear visible on highest points.*

AU-58   *Very Choice*

Has some signs of wear: high points of right leg, breast and hair above eye; eagle's head, beak and breast. Weak spots in the design are usually caused by striking and not wear.

AU-55   *Choice*

OBVERSE: Only a trace of wear shows on highest points of hair above eye, breast and right leg.
REVERSE: A trace of wear shows on head, beak and above eye. Most of the mint luster is still present, although sometimes marred by light surface abrasions.

DOLLARS—GOBRECHT DESIGN 1836-1839

AU-50 *Typical*

OBVERSE: Traces of wear show on knees, breast and edge of hairline. Foot is separated from sandal.

REVERSE: Traces of wear show on talons, neck, head and tips of wings.

Three-quarters of the mint luster is still present.

EXTREMELY FINE *Very light wear on only the highest points.*

EF-45 *Choice*

OBVERSE: Slight wear shows on high points of knees, breast and hair at forehead. Drapery is worn at shoulder and bustline. LIBERTY is sharp and scroll edges are raised.

REVERSE: High points of eagle are lightly worn. Head is clearly defined. Neck feathers are fully separated.

Half of the mint luster is still present.

EF-40 *Typical*

OBVERSE: Wear shows on knees, head and shoulder. Drapery lightly worn at neck in spots. LIBERTY is complete and scroll edges are raised.

REVERSE: High points of eagle are worn, but each detail is clearly defined.

Partial mint luster is visible.

VERY FINE *Light to moderate even wear. All major features are sharp.*

VF-30 *Choice*

OBVERSE: Wear spots show on shoulder, breast, knees and legs. Neckline is weak but has some visible details in center. LIBERTY and scroll are bold. Fingers at pole are flat but separated. All lines in shield are distinct.

REVERSE: Breast is worn but three-quarters of details are visible. Most details in feathers and head are clear. Wing tips show a trace of wear.

VF-20 *Typical*

OBVERSE: Over half the details show in the gown. Hair, shoulder and legs are worn but bold. LIBERTY and shield lines visible but possibly weak at center.

REVERSE: Three-quarters of the feathers are visible. Breast and talons are worn, but some details are visible.

DOLLARS—LIBERTY SEATED 1840–1873

MINT STATE *Absolutely no trace of wear.*

MS-70 UNCIRCULATED
A flawless coin exactly as it was minted, with no trace of wear or injury. Must have full mint luster or light toning. Any unusual striking traits must be described.

MS-67 UNCIRCULATED
Virtually flawless but with very minor imperfections.

MS-65 UNCIRCULATED
No trace of wear; nearly as perfect as MS-67 except for a few minute bag marks or surface mars. Has full mint luster but may be unevenly toned.

MS-63 UNCIRCULATED
A mint state coin with attractive mint luster, but noticeable detracting contact marks or minor blemishes.

MS-60 UNCIRCULATED
A strictly Uncirculated coin with no trace of wear, but with bag marks and other abrasions more obvious than for MS-63. May have a few small rim mars and weakly struck spots. Has full mint luster but may lack brilliance, and surface may be spotted or heavily toned.

For these coins, bag abrasions and scuff marks are considered different from circulation wear. Full mint luster and lack of any wear are necessary to distinguish MS-60 from AU-58.

ABOUT UNCIRCULATED *Small trace of wear visible on highest points.*

AU-58 *Very Choice*
Has some signs of wear: high points of right leg, breast and hair above eye; eagle's head, beak and above eye. Weak spots in the design are usually caused by striking and not wear.

AU-55 *Choice*
OBVERSE: Only a trace of wear shows on highest points of hair above eye, breast and right leg.

[278]

REVERSE: A trace of wear shows on head, beak and above eye. Most of the mint luster is still present, although sometimes marred by light bag marks and surface abrasions.

AU-50 *Typical*

OBVERSE: Traces of wear show on knees, breast, and edge of hairline. Foot is separated from sandal.

REVERSE: Traces of wear show on talons, neck, head and tips of wings.

Three-quarters of the mint luster is still present. Surface abrasions and bag marks are more noticeable than for AU-55.

EXTREMELY FINE *Very light wear on only the highest points.*

EF-45 *Choice*

OBVERSE: Slight wear shows on high points of knees, breast and hair at forehead. Drapery is worn at shoulder and bustline. LIBERTY is sharp and scroll edges are raised.

REVERSE: High points of eagle and arrows lightly worn. Talons are clearly defined. Neck feathers are fully separated.

Half of the mint luster is still present.

EF-40 *Typical*

OBVERSE: Wear shows on knees, head and shoulder. Drapery lightly worn at neck in spots. LIBERTY is complete and scroll edges are raised.

REVERSE: High points of eagle and arrows are worn, but each detail is clearly defined. Neck feathers and talons are distinct.

Partial mint luster is visible.

VERY FINE *Light to moderate even wear. All major features are sharp.*

VF-30 *Choice*

OBVERSE: Wear spots show on shoulder, breast, knees and legs. Neckline is weak but has some visible details in center. LIBERTY and scroll are bold. Fingers at pole are flat but separated. All lines in shield are distinct.

REVERSE: Leaves are worn but three-quarters of details are visible. Most details in feathers and talons are clear. Center of horizontal lines in shield shows a trace of wear.

VF-20   *Typical*

OBVERSE: Over half the details show in the gown. Hair, shoulder and legs are worn but bold. LIBERTY and shield lines visible but possibly weak at center.

REVERSE: Three-quarters of the feathers are visible. Arrowheads and talons are worn, but some details are visible. Half the details in leaves are clear. Horizontal lines in shield show wear.

FINE   *Moderate to considerable even wear. Entire design clear and bold.*

F-12   OBVERSE: Some details show in bottom folds of gown, hair, cap, and at shoulder and breast. Shield lines weak at center. Four letters in LIBERTY are clear. Foot and sandal are separated.

REVERSE: Some details in feathers are visible. Most of shield border is visible on right side. Talons are flat but separated. Letters in legend are worn but clear. Horizontal lines in shield heavily worn. For 1866–1873 pieces, IN and ST of motto are weak.

VERY GOOD   *Well worn. Design clear but flat and lacking details.*

VG-8   OBVERSE: Entire shield is weak, and most gown details are worn smooth. Some letters in LIBERTY are clear. Rim is complete.

REVERSE: Eagle shows only bold outline. Most horizontal lines in shield are gone. Legend and rim are clear.

DOLLARS—LIBERTY SEATED 1840-1873

GOOD *Heavily worn. Design and legend visible but faint in spots.*

G-4 OBVERSE: Entire design well worn with very little detail remaining. Date is weak but visible. Shield is worn smooth. Most of rim is visible.

REVERSE: Eagle is worn flat but completely outlined. Tops of some letters are worn nearly smooth. For 1866–1873 pieces, the motto is partially visible.

ABOUT GOOD *Outlined design. Parts of date and legend worn smooth.*

AG-3 OBVERSE: Liberty is outlined with nearly all details worn away. Date readable but very weak. Stars merging into rim.

REVERSE: Entire design partially worn away. Legend merging into rim.

Note: Pieces dated 1840 to 1859 are often found with weakness on upper left wing. 1857 sometimes has a weakly struck head on the obverse. Pieces dated 1870 to 1873 are from a distorted obverse hub with the word LIBERTY too exposed, resulting in part of the word being worn off of Fine grade coins.

This type is often found in prooflike condition; the 1870-CC generally looks this way when Uncirculated.

TRADE DOLLARS—1873–1885

MINT STATE *Absolutely no trace of wear.*

MS-70 UNCIRCULATED
A flawless coin exactly as it was minted, with no trace of wear or injury. Must have full mint luster and brilliance or light toning. Any unusual striking traits must be described.

MS-67 UNCIRCULATED
Virtually flawless but with very minor imperfections.

MS-65 UNCIRCULATED
No trace of wear; nearly as perfect as MS-67 except for a few minute bag marks or surface mars. Has full mint luster but may be unevenly toned.

MS-63 UNCIRCULATED
A mint state coin with attractive mint luster, but noticeable detracting contact marks or minor blemishes.

MS-60 UNCIRCULATED
A strictly Uncirculated coin with no trace of wear, but with bag marks and other abrasions more obvious than for MS-63. May have a few small rim mars and weakly struck spots. Has full mint luster but surface may lack brilliance and may be spotted or heavily toned.

For these coins, bag abrasions and scuff marks are considered different from circulation wear. Full mint luster and lack of any wear are necessary to distinguish MS-60 from AU-58.

ABOUT UNCIRCULATED *Small trace of wear visible on highest points.*

AU-58 *Very Choice*
Has some signs of wear: high points of head above ear, left knee and breast; eagle's head and left wing.

AU-55 *Choice*
OBVERSE: Trace of wear shows on head above ear, left breast and knee cap.
REVERSE: High points of left wing and head show a trace of wear.

Most of the mint luster is still present, although sometimes marred by light bag marks and surface abrasions.

AU-50 *Typical*

OBVERSE: Traces of wear visible on head above ear, left breast and knee cap. Shoulder and wheat show a trace of wear.

REVERSE: Traces of wear show on head and both wings.

Three-quarters of the mint luster is still present. Surface abrasions and bag marks are more noticeable than for AU-55.

EXTREMELY FINE   *Very light wear on only the highest points.*

EF-45 *Choice*

OBVERSE: Wear visible on head above ear, left breast and leg. Traces of wear show on wheat and shoulder.

REVERSE: Wear shows on head and both wings.

Half of the mint luster is still present.

EF-40 *Typical*

OBVERSE: Wear shows on head, left leg, foot and breast. Slight wear visible on shoulder and wheat.

REVERSE: Head shows wear but eye is visible and beak clear. Trace of wear visible on leaves at right.

Partial mint luster is visible.

VERY FINE   *Light to moderate even wear. All major features are sharp.*

VF-30 *Choice*

OBVERSE: Head is worn but coronet outlined with some hair details above and below. Knee and leg show wear; both knee points are sharp. Left breast visible. Wear shows on shoulder and wheat.

REVERSE: Most details show on head. Three-quarters of details visible in wings. Left talon has some separation. Trace of wear shows on ribbon under E of motto.

VF-20 *Typical*

OBVERSE: Very little hair detail visible around coronet. Wear shows on knee and leg but knee points are clear. Breasts, shoulder and wheat are worn.

REVERSE: Half of head details and almost three-quarters of wing details are visible. Lettering shows wear, and there are wear spots under E and M of motto.

FINE *Moderate to considerable even wear. Entire design clear and bold.*

F-12 OBVERSE: Coronet and surrounding detail partially visible. Hair knot shows details. Most stems in wheat are separated. LIBERTY is worn but readable.

REVERSE: Eye, ear and nostril visible on head. Half of wing feathers are visible. Talons show little or no detail. Motto readable but very weak.

VERY GOOD *Well worn. Design clear but flat and lacking details.*

VG-8 OBVERSE: Hair at back of lower neck and over left shoulder is visible. Shoulder has a garment line at top. Some wheat stems are separated. Motto is partially visible.

REVERSE: Slight spot visible for eye. One-third of wing feathers shows. Motto is partially readable. Rim is complete.

TRADE DOLLARS—1873–1885

GOOD *Heavily worn. Design and legend visible but faint in spots.*

G-4 OBVERSE: Eye is visible as a spot. Nose and mouth are visible. Shoulder is smooth. Very little detail remains in wheat. Motto is gone, and rim merges with stars in spots.

REVERSE: Eagle worn nearly flat but is completely outlined. Motto is gone, and rim merges with letters in spots.

ABOUT GOOD *Outlined design. Parts of date and legend worn smooth.*

AG-3 OBVERSE: Design outlined with nearly all details worn away. Date readable but worn. Rim merging with stars.

REVERSE: Entire design partially worn away. Rim merges into legend.

Note: Pieces from all issues are sometimes found unevenly struck; details of the wheat sheaf and parts of the wing may be weak.

On Proofs dated 1879–1883, flat spots are often seen on heads and stars.

Oriental chop marks (small Chinese characters) are found punched into many of these coins. Such chop marks do not alter the grade (but do alter the value), and must be mentioned whenever present.

MINT STATE   *Absolutely no trace of wear.*

MS-70   UNCIRCULATED
A flawless coin exactly as it was minted, with no trace of wear or injury. Must have full mint luster and brilliance or light toning. Any unusual striking traits must be described.

MS-67   UNCIRCULATED
Virtually flawless but with very minor imperfections.

MS-65   UNCIRCULATED
No trace of wear; nearly as perfect as MS-67 except for a few additional minute bag marks or surface mars. Has full mint luster but may be unevenly toned. Any unusual striking traits must be described.

MS-63   UNCIRCULATED
A mint state coin with attractive mint luster, but noticeable detracting contact marks or minor blemishes.

MS-60   UNCIRCULATED
A strictly Uncirculated coin with no trace of wear, but with bag marks and other abrasions more obvious than for MS-63. May have a few small rim mars and weakly struck spots. Has full mint luster but may lack brilliance, and surface may be spotted or heavily toned.
Business strike silver dollars were all placed in mint bags of 1,000 coins. Subsequent handling of bags caused bag marks and abrasions on virtually all coins, which should not be confused with circulation wear. Full mint luster and lack of any wear are necessary to distinguish MS-60 from AU-58.

Uncirculated coins of this type are frequently graded at intermediate levels from MS-60 to MS-70. For specific details refer to pages 21- 22 of the introduction.

ABOUT UNCIRCULATED   *Small trace of wear visible on highest points.*

AU-58   *Very Choice*
Has some signs of wear: hair above eye and ear, edges of cotton leaves and bolls, high upper fold of cap; high points of eagle's breast and tops of legs. Weakly struck spots are common and should not be confused with actual wear.

Prime Focal Areas

Obverse: Face, neck, and field in front of Liberty.
Reverse: Eagle's body and wings. Fields to either side, and above eagle.

Secondary Areas

Obverse: Cap and field behind Liberty's head. Date and field to right.
Reverse: Legend and denomination. Outer periphery.

	CONTACT MARKS	HAIRLINES	LUSTER	EYE APPEAL
MS-70	None show under magnification	None show under magnification	Very attractive Fully original	Outstanding
MS-69	1 or 2 miniscule none in prime focal areas	None visible	Very attractive Fully original	Exceptional
MS-68	3 or 4 miniscule none in prime focal areas	None visible	Attractive Fully original	Exceptional
MS-67	3 or 4 miniscule 1 or 2 may be in prime focal areas	None visible without magnification	Above average Fully original	Exceptional
MS-66	Several small; a few may be in prime focal areas	None visible without magnification	Above average Fully original	Above average
MS-65	Light and scattered without major distracting marks in prime focal areas	May have a few scattered	Fully original	Very pleasing
MS-64	May have light scattered marks; a few may be in prime focal areas	May have a few scattered or small patch in secondary areas	Average Full original	Pleasing
MS-63	May have distracting marks in prime focal areas	May have a few scattered or small patch	May be original or slightly impaired	Rather attractive
MS-62	May have distracting marks in prime focal and/or secondary areas	May have a few scattered to noticeable patch	May be original or impaired	Generally acceptable
MS-61	May have a few heavy (or numerous light) marks in prime focal and/or secondary areas	May have noticeable patch or continuous hairlining over surfaces	May be original or impaired	Unattractive
MS-60	May have heavy marks in all areas	May have noticeable patch or continuous hairlining throughout	May be original or impaired	Poor

[287]

AU-55 *Choice*

OBVERSE: Slight trace of wear shows on hair above ear, eye, edges of cotton leaves, and high upper fold of cap. Luster fading from cheek.

REVERSE: Slight trace of wear shows on breast, tops of legs and talons.

Most of the mint luster is still present, although marred by light bag marks and surface abrasions.

AU-50 *Typical*

OBVERSE: Traces of wear show on hair above eye, ear, edges of cotton leaves, and high upper fold of cap. Partial detail visible on tops of cotton bolls. Luster gone from cheek.

REVERSE: There are traces of wear on breast, tops of legs, wing tips and talons.

Three-quarters of the mint luster is still present. Surface abrasions and bag marks are more noticeable than for AU-55.

EXTREMELY FINE   *Very light wear on only the highest points.*

EF-45 *Choice*

OBVERSE: Slight wear on hair above date, forehead and ear. Lines in hair well detailed and sharp. Slight flat spots on edges of cotton leaves. Minute signs of wear on cheek.

REVERSE: High points of breast are lightly worn. Tops of legs and right wing tip show wear. Talons are slightly flat.

Half of the mint luster is still present.

EF-40 *Typical*

OBVERSE: Wear shows on hair above date, forehead and ear. Lines in hair well detailed. Flat spots visible on edges of cotton leaves. Cheek lightly worn.

REVERSE: Almost all feathers gone from breast. Tops of legs, wing tips and feathers on head show wear. Talons are flat.

Partial mint luster is visible.

VERY FINE   *Light to moderate even wear. All major features are sharp.*

DOLLARS—MORGAN 1878-1921

VF-30 *Choice*

OBVERSE: Wear shows on high points of hair from forehead to ear. Some strands visible in hair above ear. There are smooth areas on cotton leaves and at top of cotton bolls.

REVERSE: Wear shows on leaves of wreath and tips of wings. Only a few feathers visible on breast and head.

VF-20 *Typical*

OBVERSE: Smooth spots visible on hair from forehead to ear. Cotton leaves heavily worn but separated. Wheat grains show wear.

REVERSE: Some leaves on wreath are well worn. Breast is smooth, and only a few feathers show on head. Tips of wings are weak but lines are complete.

FINE *Moderate to heavy even wear. Entire design clear and bold.*

F-12 OBVERSE: Hairline along face is clearly defined. Lower two cotton leaves smooth but distinct from cap. Some wheat grains merging. Cotton bolls flat but the two lines in each show clearly.

REVERSE: One-quarter of eagle's right wing and edge of left wing are smooth. Head, neck and breast are flat and merging. Tail feathers slightly worn. Top leaves in wreath show heavy wear.

VERY GOOD *Well worn. Design clear but flat and lacking details.*

VG-8 OBVERSE: Most details in hair are worn smooth. All letters and date are clear. Cotton bolls flat and leaves merging in spots.

REVERSE: One half of eagle's right wing and one-third of left wing are smooth. All leaves in wreath are worn. Rim is complete.

GOOD *Heavily worn. Design and legend visible but faint in spots.*

G-4 OBVERSE: Hair is well worn with very little detail remaining. Date, letters and design clearly outlined. Rim is full.

REVERSE: Eagle is worn nearly flat but is completely outlined. Design elements smooth but visible. Legend is all visible; rim is full.

ABOUT GOOD *Outlined design. Parts of date and legend worn smooth.*

AG-3 OBVERSE: Head is outlined with nearly all details worn away. Date readable but worn. Legend merging into rim.

REVERSE: Entire design partially worn away. Rim merges into legend.

Note: Portions of the design are often weakly struck, especially on the hair above the ear and on the eagle's breast for dollars from 1878 to 1904.

A flat breast eagle reverse design was used for 1878-S, CC and some 1878, 1879-S and 1880-CC issues. These tend to show more breast feathers in each grade than the round breast eagle design.

New Orleans issues are often found weakly struck, particularly above the ear on the obverse and the eagle's breast on the reverse. Dates most prone to such weakness are 1887 to 1897.

The three 1921 issues, particularly the 1921-S, are often softly struck on the eagle's breast feathers and lower wreath on the reverse.

Some of these dollars have a prooflike surface. This should be mentioned in any description of such pieces, but the coins should be graded independently of their prooflike quality.

The following test is commonly accepted to determine the prooflike quality of such pieces: Place the coin upright at the end of a clearly printed ruler. If the printed lines are observably reflected at a distance of 1″ to 2″, it is called Semi-Prooflike. At 2″ to 4″ it is termed Prooflike. Beyond 4″ is Deep Mirror Prooflike.

DOLLARS—PEACE 1921–1935

MINT STATE *Absolutely no trace of wear.*

MS-70 UNCIRCULATED
A flawless coin exactly as it was minted, with no trace of wear or injury. Must have full mint luster or light toning. Any unusual striking traits must be described.

MS-67 UNCIRCULATED
Virtually flawless but with very minor imperfections.

MS-65 UNCIRCULATED
No trace of wear; nearly as perfect as MS-67 except for a few additional minute bag marks or surface mars. Has full mint luster but may be unevenly toned.

MS-63 UNCIRCULATED
A mint state coin with attractive mint luster, but noticeable detracting contact marks or minor blemishes.

MS-60 UNCIRCULATED
A strictly Uncirculated coin with no trace of wear, but with bag marks and other abrasions more obvious than for MS-63. May have a few small rim mars and may be weakly struck. Has full mint luster but may lack brilliance, and surface may be spotted or heavily toned.

Business strike silver dollars were all placed in mint bags of 1,000 coins. Subsequent handling of bags caused bag marks and abrasions on virtually all coins, which should not be confused with circulation wear. Full mint luster and lack of any wear are necessary to distinguish MS-60 from AU-58.

Uncirculated coins of this type are frequently graded at intermediate levels from MS-60 to MS-70. For specific details refer to pages 21-22 of the introduction.

ABOUT UNCIRCULATED *Small trace of wear visible on highest points.*

AU-58 *Very Choice*
Has some signs of wear: high points of cheek and hair; high points of feathers on right wing and leg. Weakly struck spots are common and should not be confused with actual wear.

Prime Focal Areas
  Obverse: Liberty's face and neck. Fields in front of face and below head.
  Reverse: Eagle's body and neck. Fields to either side of eagle.

Secondary Areas
  Obverse: Liberty's hair and fields behind head.
  Reverse: Legend above eagle. Lower eagle, rock, and lower field behind eagle.

	CONTACT MARKS	HAIRLINES	LUSTER	EYE APPEAL
MS-70	None show under magnification	None show under magnification	Very attractive Fully original	Outstanding
MS-69	1 or 2 miniscule none in prime focal areas	None visible	Very attractive Fully original	Exceptional
MS-68	3 or 4 miniscule none in prime focal areas	None visible	Attractive Fully original	Exceptional
MS-67	3 or 4 miniscule 1 or 2 may be in prime focal areas	None visible without magnification	Above average Fully original	Exceptional
MS-66	Several small; a few may be in prime focal areas	None visible without magnification	Above average Fully original	Above average
MS-65	Light and scattered without major distracting marks in prime focal areas	May have a few scattered	Fully original	Very pleasing
MS-64	May have light scattered marks; a few may be in prime focal areas	May have a few scattered or small patch in secondary areas	Average Full original	Pleasing
MS-63	May have distracting marks in prime focal areas	May have a few scattered or small patch	May be original or slightly impaired	Rather attractive
MS-62	May have distracting marks in prime focal and/or secondary areas	May have a few scattered to noticeable patch	May be original or impaired	Generally acceptable
MS-61	May have a few heavy (or numerous light) marks in prime focal and/or secondary areas	May have noticeable patch or continuous hairlining over surfaces	May be original or impaired	Unattractive
MS-60	May have heavy marks in all areas	May have noticeable patch or continuous hairlining throughout	May be original or impaired	Poor

[292]

DOLLARS—PEACE 1921–1935

AU-55   *Choice*

OBVERSE: Trace of wear shows on hair over ear and above forehead. Slight wear visible on cheek.

REVERSE: High points of feathers on right wing show a trace of wear. Most of the mint luster is still present, although marred by light bag marks and surface abrasions.

AU-50   *Typical*

OBVERSE: Traces of wear visible on neck, hair over ear and above forehead. Cheek shows slight wear.

REVERSE: Traces of wear show on head and high points of feathers on right wing.

Three-quarters of the mint luster is still present. Surface abrasions and bag marks are more noticeable than for AU-55.

EXTREMELY FINE   *Very light wear on only the highest points.*

EF-45   *Choice*

OBVERSE: Hair around face shows slight wear, but most hair strands are visible. Lower edge of neck lightly worn.

REVERSE: Top of neck and head behind eye show slight wear. Central wing and leg feathers lightly worn.

Half of the mint luster is still present.

EF-40   *Typical*

OBVERSE: Slight flattening visible on high points of hair; most hair strands clearly separated. Entire face and lower edge of neck lightly worn.

REVERSE: Wear shows on head behind eye and top of neck. Some flat spots visible on central wing and leg feathers.

Partial mint luster is visible.

VERY FINE   *Light to moderate even wear. All major features are sharp.*

VF-30 *Choice*

OBVERSE: Hair details weak around face. Upper wave of hair shows light wear. Hair above ear worn but single strands well defined.

REVERSE: Feather detail on right wing very weak. There is wear on leg feathers and neck. Motto shows a trace of wear.

VF-20 *Typical*

OBVERSE: Very little hair detail visible around face. Wear shows on upper wave of hair. Hair above ear worn but some single strands are clear.

REVERSE: Detail on right wing worn but the three horizontal lines of feather layers show. Flattening visible on leg feathers and neck. Motto and talons lightly worn.

FINE *Moderate to heavy even wear. Entire design clear and bold.*

F-12 OBVERSE: All hair around face is smooth. Slight wear shows on hair at back of neck and on bun. Rays show a trace of wear.

REVERSE: All feathers on right leg are worn away. Lower third of neck feathers visible. Only the lowest horizontal line of feather layers will show. Parts of PEACE and E PLURIBUS weak but readable.

VERY GOOD *Well worn. Design clear but flat and lacking details.*

VG-8 OBVERSE: Hair is flattened and rays have weak spots. Part of motto is weak. Rim is complete.

REVERSE: Most feather details worn away, with flattening on right leg, wing, and upper neck and head. Portions of rays, PEACE, and E PLURIBUS missing. Rim is complete.

DOLLARS—PEACE 1921–1935

GOOD   *Heavily worn. Design and legend visible but faint in spots.*

G-4   OBVERSE: Date, letters and design clearly outlined. Well worn with very little detail remaining. Rim merges with letters in spots.

       REVERSE: Eagle worn nearly flat but is completely outlined. PEACE barely readable. Rim merges with letters in spots.

ABOUT GOOD   *Outlined design. Parts of date and legend worn smooth.*

AG-3   OBVERSE: Head is outlined with nearly all details worn away. Date readable but worn. Legend merging into rim.

       REVERSE: Entire design partially worn away. Rim merges into legend.

Note: A lower relief and rounded design, plus worn dies from extended use, resulted in most Peace dollars lacking sharp detail and smooth fields. In grading this type of dollar, consideration must be given to the following characteristics:

    1921   Struck in higher relief, and usually seen with hair weak over ear on the obverse. Wing feathers on reverse are often weak by eagle's legs.

    1922–1928   Struck in low relief and lack sharpness of details and lettering. 1923-S and 1925-S are usually very weakly struck.

    1934–1935   Generally low relief but obverse design shows sharper details.

REFERENCES

Van Allen, Leroy C. and Mallis, A. George, *Comprehensive Catalogue and Encyclopedia of U.S. Morgan and Peace Silver Dollars.* New York, 1976.

Miller, W. *The Morgan and Peace Dollar Textbook.* Metaire, Louisiana, 1983.

DOLLARS—EISENHOWER 1971–1978

MINT STATE   *Absolutely no trace of wear.*

MS-70   UNCIRCULATED
A flawless coin exactly as it was minted, with no trace of wear or injury. Must have full mint luster and brilliance or light toning. Any unusual striking traits must be described.

MS-67   UNCIRCULATED
Virtually flawless but with very minor imperfections.

MS-65   UNCIRCULATED
No trace of wear; nearly as perfect as MS-67 except for some small blemish. Has full mint luster but may be unevenly toned or lightly fingermarked. A few minute nicks or marks may be present.

MS-63   UNCIRCULATED
A mint state coin with attractive mint luster, but noticeable detracting contact marks or minor blemishes.

MS-60   UNCIRCULATED
A strictly Uncirculated coin with no trace of wear, but with blemishes more obvious than for MS-63. Has full mint luster, but surface may be dull, spotted or heavily toned.

ABOUT UNCIRCULATED   *Small trace of wear visible on highest points.*

AU-58   *Very Choice*

Has some signs of abrasion: high points of cheek and jawbone, center of neck, edge of bust; head, high points of ridges and feathers in wings and legs.

AU-55   *Choice*
OBVERSE: Only a trace of wear shows on highest points of jawbone and at center of neck.
REVERSE: A trace of wear shows on high points of feathers in wings and legs.
   Nearly all of the mint luster is still present.

DOLLARS—EISENHOWER 1971–1978

EXTREMELY FINE   *Very light wear on only the highest points.*

EF-45   *Choice*

OBVERSE: Slight wear shows on cheek, along jawbone and on high points at edge of bust. Hair lines are sharp and detailed.

REVERSE: High points of head, legs and wing ridges are lightly worn. Central feathers are all clearly defined.

Three-quarters of the mint luster is still present.

VERY FINE   *Light to moderate even wear. All major features are sharp.*

VF-30   *Choice*

OBVERSE: Wear spots show on hair below part, and along cheek and jaw. Hair lines are weak but have nearly full visible details. Slight wear shows at center of neck and along edge of bust.

REVERSE: Wear shows on head and feathers in wings and legs, but all details are visible. All central tail feathers are plain. Wing and leg ridges are lightly worn.

Note: The Bicentennial issue can be graded by the obverse.

MINT STATE *Absolutely no trace of wear.*

MS-70 UNCIRCULATED
A flawless coin exactly as it was minted, with no trace of wear or injury. Must have full mint luster and brilliance or light toning. Any unusual striking traits must be described.

MS-67 UNCIRCULATED
Virtually flawless but with very minor imperfections.

MS-65 UNCIRCULATED
No trace of wear; nearly as perfect as MS-67 except for some small blemish. Has full mint luster but may be unevenly toned or lightly fingermarked. A few minute nicks or marks may be present.

MS-63 UNCIRCULATED
A mint state coin with attractive mint luster, but noticeable detracting contact marks or minor blemishes.

MS-60 UNCIRCULATED
A strictly Uncirculated coin with no trace of wear, but with blemishes more obvious than for MS-63. Has full mint luster, but surface may be dull, spotted or heavily toned.

ABOUT UNCIRCULATED *Small trace of wear visible on highest points.*

AU-58 *Very Choice*
Has some signs of abrasion: high points of cheekbone, hair in center of head, and collar button; head, high points of ridges and feathers in wings and legs.

AU-55 *Choice*
OBVERSE: Only a trace of wear shows on highest points of cheekbone, hair and collar button.

REVERSE: A trace of wear shows on head, and high points of feathers in wings and legs.

Nearly all of the mint luster is still present.

MINT STATE *Absolutely no trace of wear.*

MS-70 UNCIRCULATED
A flawless coin exactly as it was minted, with no trace of wear or injury. Must have full mint luster and brilliance. Any unusual die or planchet traits must be described.

MS-67 UNCIRCULATED
Virtually flawless but with very minor imperfections.

MS-65 UNCIRCULATED
No trace of wear; nearly as perfect as MS-67 except for some small blemish. Has full mint luster and brilliance but may show slight discoloration. A few barely noticeable nicks or marks may be present.

MS-63 UNCIRCULATED
A mint state coin with attractive mint luster, but noticeable detracting contact marks or minor blemishes.

MS-60 UNCIRCULATED
A strictly Uncirculated coin with no trace of wear, but with blemishes more obvious than for MS-63. May lack full mint luster and brilliance.

ABOUT UNCIRCULATED *Small trace of wear visible on highest points.*

AU-58 *Very Choice*

Has some signs of abrasion: hair near coronet; tips of leaves.

AU-55 *Choice*

OBVERSE: There is a trace of wear at upper hair line below coronet.
REVERSE: Trace of wear visible on tips of leaves.
  Three-quarters of the mint luster is still present.

AU-50 *Typical*

OBVERSE: There is a trace of wear on hair lines near coronet, and below the ear.

GOLD DOLLARS—TYPE I 1849–1854

REVERSE: Trace of wear visible on tips of leaves.
Half of the mint luster is still present.

EXTREMELY FINE   *Very light wear on only the highest points.*

EF-45   *Choice*

OBVERSE: Slight wear shows on highest wave of hair, hairline and below ear. All major details are sharp. Beads at top of coronet are well defined.

REVERSE: Leaves show visible wear at tips but central details are clearly defined.

Part of the mint luster is still present.

EF-40   *Typical*

OBVERSE: Slight wear shows on highest wave of hair, hairline and below ear. All major details are sharp. Beads at top of coronet are well defined.

REVERSE: Leaves show visible wear at tips but central details are clearly defined.

Traces of mint luster will show.

VERY FINE   *Light to moderate even wear. All major features are sharp.*

VF-30   *Choice*

OBVERSE: Beads on top of coronet are well defined. LIBERTY is complete. Hair around face and neck slightly worn but strands fully separated. Star centers show some details.

REVERSE: There is light even wear on legend and date. Some details show in center of leaves.

VF-20   *Typical*

OBVERSE: Beads at top of coronet are partially separated. LIBERTY is complete. Hair around face and neck noticeably worn but well outlined. Some star centers show details.

REVERSE: There is light even wear on legend and date. Only traces of leaf ribs are visible. Bow knot is flat on high point.

GOLD DOLLARS—TYPE I 1849–1854

FINE *Moderate to heavy even wear. Entire design clear and bold.*

F-12   OBVERSE: LIBERTY is complete but weak. Ear lobe is visible. Hairlines and beads on coronet are worn smooth. Stars are clearly outlined, but centers are flat.

REVERSE: Legend within wreath is worn and weak in spots. Leaves and wreath are well outlined. Rim is full and edge beveled.

VERY GOOD *Well worn. Design clear but flat and lacking details.*

VG-8   OBVERSE: Only the outline of hair is visible. Four letters in LIBERTY are clear.

REVERSE: Only the outline of leaves is visible. Legend and numeral are worn and very weak.

GOOD *Heavily worn. Design and legend visible but faint in spots.*

G-4   OBVERSE: Head is outlined with nearly all details worn away. Stars are weak. Full rim shows.

REVERSE: Date and legend well worn but readable. Leaves are outlined. Full rim shows.

Note: The gold dollars struck at Charlotte and Dahlonega are crude compared to those of the Philadelphia Mint. Frequently they have rough edges, and the die work appears to be generally inferior. In grading coins from these branch mints, consideration must be made for these factors.

1849-D is usually weakly struck.

GOLD DOLLARS—TYPE II 1854–1856

MINT STATE   *Absolutely no trace of wear.*

MS-70   UNCIRCULATED
A flawless coin exactly as it was minted, with no trace of wear or injury. Must have full mint luster and brilliance. Any unusual die or planchet traits must be described.

MS-67   UNCIRCULATED
Virtually flawless but with very minor imperfections.

MS-65   UNCIRCULATED
No trace of wear; nearly as perfect as MS-67 except for some small blemish. Has full mint luster and brilliance but may show slight discoloration. A few barely noticeable nicks or marks may be present.

MS-63   UNCIRCULATED
A mint state coin with attractive mint luster, but noticeable detracting contact marks or minor blemishes.

MS-60   UNCIRCULATED
A strictly Uncirculated coin with no trace of wear, but with blemishes more obvious than for MS-63. May lack full mint luster and brilliance.

ABOUT UNCIRCULATED *Small trace of wear visible on highest points.*

AU-58   *Very Choice*

Has some signs of abrasion: hair over Liberty's eye; bow knot.

AU-55   *Choice*
OBVERSE: There is a trace of wear on hair over eye.
REVERSE: Trace of wear visible on bow knot.
   Three-quarters of mint luster is still present.

AU-50   *Typical*
OBVERSE: There is a trace of wear on hair over eye, at curl below ear and at top of feathers.

GOLD DOLLARS—TYPE II 1854–1856

REVERSE: Trace of wear visible on tips of leaves and bow knot. Half of the mint luster is still present.

EXTREMELY FINE   *Very light wear on only the highest points.*

EF-45   *Choice*

OBVERSE: There is slight wear on hair at forehead, below ear, on tops of feathers and on cheek. All major details are sharp.

REVERSE: Slight wear shows on tips of leaves, bow knot, wreath and 1 DOLLAR.

Part of the mint luster is still present.

EF-40   *Typical*

OBVERSE: There is slight wear on highest wave of hair, on hairline, below ear, on top of feathers and on cheek. All major details are sharp.

REVERSE: Slight wear shows on tips of leaves, bow knot, wreath, legend and date.

Traces of mint luster will show.

VERY FINE   *Light to moderate even wear. All major features are sharp.*

VF-30   *Choice*

OBVERSE: Hair above forehead and around neck worn, but some details are visible. LIBERTY is complete. Legend is strong.

REVERSE: Wear shows on legend. Leaves and bow knot show some detail.

VF-20   *Typical*

OBVERSE: Hair, feathers and curl tips are outlined with only slight detail. LIBERTY worn but visible.

REVERSE: Bow knot well worn. Slight detail visible in leaves. Some indentation remains on cotton bolls.

GOLD DOLLARS—TYPE II 1854–1856

FINE   *Moderate to heavy even wear. Entire design clear and bold.*

F-12   OBVERSE: Hair and some feathers smooth. Earlobe visible. TY in LIBERTY almost smooth.

REVERSE: Bow knot, leaves and cotton bolls outlined only, with no details visible.

VERY GOOD   *Well worn. Design clear but flat and lacking details.*

VG-8   OBVERSE: The headdress is outlined only. Earlobe partially visible. Three or four letters in LIBERTY will be clear.

REVERSE: Wreath is outlined and lacks any detail. Legend and date very weak but visible.

GOOD   *Heavily worn. Design and legend visible but faint in spots.*

G-4   OBVERSE: Headdress is outlined only. Legend worn but visible. LIBERTY smooth.

REVERSE: Wreath outlined. Date and legend well worn but visible.

Note: Clash marks are frequently seen and should be described. They do not alter the condition of the coin.

Nearly all of these coins have weakly struck spots on the reverse, especially at LL in DOLLAR and in the date.

GOLD DOLLARS—TYPE III 1856–1889

MINT STATE *Absolutely no trace of wear.*

MS-70 UNCIRCULATED
A flawless coin exactly as it was minted, with no trace of wear or injury. Must have full mint luster and brilliance. Any unusual die or planchet traits must be described.

MS-67 UNCIRCULATED
Virtually flawless but with very minor imperfections.

MS-65 UNCIRCULATED
No trace of wear; nearly as perfect as MS-67 except for some small blemish. Has full mint luster and brilliance but may show slight discoloration. A few barely noticeable nicks or marks may be present.

MS-63 UNCIRCULATED
A mint state coin with attractive mint luster, but noticeable detracting contact marks or minor blemishes.

MS-60 UNCIRCULATED
A strictly Uncirculated coin with no trace of wear, but with blemishes more obvious than for MS-63. May lack full mint luster and brilliance.

ABOUT UNCIRCULATED *Small trace of wear visible on highest points.*

AU-58 *Very Choice*

Has some signs of abrasion: hairline over Liberty's eye; bow knot.

AU-55 *Choice*
OBVERSE: There is a trace of wear at hairline over eye.
REVERSE: Trace of wear visible on ribbon bow knot.
   Three-quarters of the mint luster is still present.

AU-50 *Typical*
OBVERSE: There is a trace of wear at hairline and at top of feathers.
REVERSE: Trace of wear visible on tips of leaves and bow knot.
   Half of the mint luster is still present.

EXTREMELY FINE   *Very light wear on only the highest points.*

EF-45   *Choice*
> OBVERSE: There is slight wear at hairline, hair near ear, tops of feathers and on cheek.
> REVERSE: Slight wear visible on tips of leaves, bow knot, wreath and legend.
> Part of the mint luster is still present.

EF-40   *Typical*
> OBVERSE: Slight wear shows at hairline, on hair near ear, tops of feathers and on cheek. All major details are sharp.
> REVERSE: Slight wear shows on tips of leaves, bow knot, wreath, legend and date.
> Traces of mint luster will show.

VERY FINE   *Light to moderate even wear. All major features are sharp.*

VF-30   *Choice*
> OBVERSE: Hair above forehead and around neck worn. Feather curls are outlined but show some detail. LIBERTY complete. Legend strong.
> REVERSE: Wear shows on legend. Leaves and bow knot show some detail.

VF-20   *Typical*
> OBVERSE: Hair, feathers and curl tips are outlined with only slight detail. LIBERTY worn but visible.
> REVERSE: Bow knot well worn. Slight detail visible in leaves. Some indentation remains on cotton bolls.

GOLD DOLLARS—TYPE III 1856–1889

FINE   *Moderate to heavy even wear. Entire design clear and bold.*

F-12   OBVERSE: Hair and some feathers smooth. Earlobe visible. Part of LIBER-TY worn almost smooth.
REVERSE: Bow knot, leaves and cotton bolls outlined only, with no details visible.

Note: This type is seldom found in grades below Fine. LIBERTY is sometimes weakly struck; occasionally it is missing even on Uncirculated specimens.

$1 Gold, Type 1:   Many dates come weakly struck in the hair below "LIBERTY" and behind the ear. Most Charlotte and Dahlonega pieces of *all* denominations come weakly struck to *very* weakly struck 98% of the time. The 1849–D is a date that is unusually weakly struck.

$1 Gold, Type 2:   The rule on both 1854 and 1855 (esp. the '55) is that the "LL" and "85" are weakly struck on the reverse. On some specimens the middle digits are virtually non-existant.

$1 Gold, Type 3:   The 1856 and 1857 are occasionally seen with very weak strikes on the upper half of the coin, and can come weakly struck in general. The same also applies to the 1874. After this date, the Type 3's are generally well struck and sometimes proof-like in appearance.

REFERENCES

Akers, David W., *Gold Dollars.* Englewood, Ohio, 1975. (and other gold denominations)

Breen, Walter, *Major Varieties of U.S. Gold Dollars.* Chicago, 1964. (and other gold denominations)

Bowers, Q. David, *United States Gold Coins, An Illustrated History.* Wolfeboro, NH, 1982.

MINT STATE *Absolutely no trace of wear.*

MS-70 UNCIRCULATED
A flawless coin exactly as it was minted, with no trace of wear or injury. Must have full mint luster and brilliance. Any unusual die or planchet traits must be described.

MS-67 UNCIRCULATED
Virtually flawless but with very minor imperfections.

MS-65 UNCIRCULATED
No trace of wear; nearly as perfect as MS-67 except for some small blemish. Has full mint luster and brilliance but may show slight discoloration. A few barely noticeable nicks or adjustment file marks may be present.

MS-63 UNCIRCULATED
A mint state coin with attractive mint luster, but noticeable detracting contact marks or minor blemishes.

MS-60 UNCIRCULATED
A strictly Uncirculated coin with no trace of wear, but with blemishes more obvious than for MS-63. May lack full mint luster and brilliance.

ABOUT UNCIRCULATED—*Small trace of wear visible on highest points.*

AU-58 *Very Choice*

Has some signs of abrasion: cap, highest point of hair; wings, clouds.

AU-55 *Choice*

OBVERSE: There is a trace of wear on cap and highest point of hair.
REVERSE: Trace of wear visible on wing tips and clouds.
    Three-quarters of the mint luster is still present.

AU-50 *Typical*

OBVERSE: There is a trace of wear on cap, high point of hair, cheeks and drapery.
REVERSE: Trace of wear visible on wing tips, clouds and feathers.
    Half of the mint luster is still present.

EXTREMELY FINE *Very light wear on only the highest points.*

EF-45 *Choice*

OBVERSE: Most details of cap and hair visible. Light wear shows on cheek and drapery.

REVERSE: Very light wear shows on edges of wings, clouds and feathers.

Part of the mint luster is still present.

EF-40 *Typical*

OBVERSE: Some detail on cap visible. Wear shows on hair near ear and on cheek. Drapery worn, with some details visible.

REVERSE: Very light wear visible on wing edges, centers of clouds and feathers. Arrows are complete; feathers well defined.

Traces of mint luster will show.

VERY FINE *Light to moderate even wear. All major features are sharp.*

VF-30 *Choice*

OBVERSE: Top of cap shows slight detail. Wear shows on hair near ear and cheek. Drapery worn, with slight detail visible.

REVERSE: Wear visible on wing feathers, arrowheads and shield. Leaves and tail show some details.

VF-20 *Typical*

OBVERSE: Cap and drapery show hardly any detail. Hair worn but completely outlined. Cheek almost smooth.

REVERSE: Wings, clouds, lines of shield and feathers worn. Motto worn but complete. Berries visible. Leaves and tail show little detail.

FINE   *Moderate to heavy even wear. Entire design clear and bold.*

F-12   OBVERSE: Cap almost smooth; drapery outlined only. Hair detail faintly visible; cheek smooth. Eye, nose and mouth show some detail.

REVERSE: Wings well worn, with few lines in shield visible. Clouds, leaves and tail smooth. Motto complete although some letters weak.

VERY GOOD   *Well worn. Design clear but flat and lacking details.*

VG-8   OBVERSE: Cap partially outlined; hair outlined; cheek completely smooth. Lettering and date visible. Some detail of eye, nose and mouth show.

REVERSE: Only eagle's outline shows. Most of lettering worn away.

Note: Adjustment file marks frequently occur on this type. Weak spots are common. The 1796 issue without stars is graded the same as later coins.

QUARTER EAGLES—CAPPED HEAD 1808–1834

MINT STATE *Absolutely no trace of wear.*

MS-70 UNCIRCULATED
A flawless coin exactly as it was minted, with no trace of wear or injury. Must have full mint luster and brilliance. Any unusual die or planchet traits must be described.

MS-67 UNCIRCULATED
Virtually flawless but with very minor imperfections.

MS-65 UNCIRCULATED
No trace of wear; nearly as perfect as MS-67 except for some small blemish. Has full mint luster and brilliance but may show slight discoloration. A few barely noticeable nicks or marks may be present.

MS-63 UNCIRCULATED
A mint state coin with attractive mint luster, but noticeable detracting contact marks or minor blemishes.

MS-60 UNCIRCULATED
A strictly Uncirculated coin with no trace of wear, but with blemishes more obvious than for MS-63. May lack full mint luster and brilliance.

ABOUT UNCIRCULATED *Small trace of wear visible on highest points.*

AU-58 *Very Choice*

Has some signs of abrasion: hair above eye, top of cap, cheek; wing tips, claws.

AU-55 *Choice*
OBVERSE: There is a trace of wear above eye and on top of cap.
REVERSE: Trace of wear visible on wing tips and claws.
　　Three-quarters of the mint luster is still present.

AU-50 *Typical*
OBVERSE: There is a trace of wear above eye, on top of cap, on cheek and hair above ear.

REVERSE: Trace of wear visible on top edge of right wing, feathers, claw and shield.

Half of the mint luster is still present.

EXTREMELY FINE *Very light wear on only the highest points.*

EF-45 *Choice*

OBVERSE: There is light wear above eye, top of cap and on cheek. Wear shows on high points of hair. Trace of wear visible on bust.

REVERSE: Light wear shows on top edges of wings, feathers, claws, neck and shield.

Part of the mint luster is still present.

EF-40 *Typical*

OBVERSE: There is light wear above eye, top of cap, on cheek and bust. Wear shows on high points of hair. Stars sharp with all details visible.

REVERSE: Light wear shows on both edges of wings. Trace of wear visible on feathers, neck, leaves and arrows. Wear shows on claws and center of shield.

Traces of mint luster will show.

VERY FINE *Light to moderate even wear. All major features are sharp.*

VF-30 *Choice*

OBVERSE: Most details in cap visible. High points of hair flat but details visible. LIBERTY bold.

REVERSE: Wings evenly worn but most feathers visible. Wear shows in centers of claws and shield. Motto is complete.

VF-20 *Typical*

OBVERSE: Only a little detail shows in cap. Hair flat with very little detail. Cheek worn, stars flat, LIBERTY worn but complete.

REVERSE: Half of wing details are visible. Some details show on neck and shield. Motto is complete.

QUARTER EAGLES—CAPPED HEAD 1808–1834

FINE   *Moderate to heavy even wear. Entire design clear and bold.*

F-12   OBVERSE: Cap and hair show very little detail. Eye complete and ear half visible. Stars show some detail. LIBERTY weak but readable.

REVERSE: Wings and feathers show very little detail. Neck smooth. Eye visible. Arrows worn but visible, and there is no detail in feathers. Motto very weak but readable.

VERY GOOD   *Well worn. Design clear but flat and lacking details.*

VG-8   OBVERSE: Cap and hair smooth and outlined. Stars smooth. Date clear but only parts of LIBERTY visible.

REVERSE: Wings, feathers and neck smooth and show no details. Eye partially visible. Shield shows no detail. Part of motto visible.

Note: 1808 is usually softly struck, but can be graded by the same standards as the 1821-1834 coins.

1821–1827 have lower detail and flatter denticles, while 1829–1834 have rounded details and sharp denticles.

MINT STATE *Absolutely no trace of wear.*

MS-70 UNCIRCULATED
A flawless coin exactly as it was minted, with no trace of wear or injury. Must have full mint luster and brilliance. Any unusual die or planchet traits must be described.

MS-67 UNCIRCULATED
Virtually flawless but with very minor imperfections.

MS-65 UNCIRCULATED
No trace of wear; nearly as perfect as MS-67 except for some small blemish. Has full mint luster and brilliance but may show slight discoloration. A few barely noticeable nicks or marks may be present.

MS-63 UNCIRCULATED
A mint state coin with attractive mint luster, but noticeable detracting contact marks or minor blemishes.

MS-60 UNCIRCULATED
A strictly Uncirculated coin with no trace of wear, but with blemishes more obvious than for MS-63. May lack full mint luster and brilliance.

ABOUT UNCIRCULATED *Small trace of wear visible on highest points.*

AU-58 *Very Choice*

Has some signs of abrasion: hair and cheek; wings.

AU-55 *Choice*

OBVERSE: There is a trace of wear on hair above eye and ear.
REVERSE: Trace of wear visible on upper edges of wings.
    Three-quarters of the mint luster is still present.

AU-50 *Typical*

OBVERSE: There is a trace of wear on hair above forehead, at top of head, above eye and ear.
REVERSE: Trace of wear visible on head and top edges of wings.
    Half of the mint luster is still present.

EXTREMELY FINE *Very light wear on only the highest points.*

EF-45 *Choice*
OBVERSE: There is light wear on high points of hair and a trace of wear on cheek.
REVERSE: Light wear shows on upper edges of wings, head and on feathers.
Part of the mint luster is still present.

EF-40 *Typical*
OBVERSE: Light wear shows on high points of hair. Slight wear visible on cheek. Stars sharp with details visible.
REVERSE: Slight wear shows on top edges of wings, feathers, neck and head. Shield well defined.
Traces of mint luster will show.

VERY FINE *Light to moderate even wear. All major features are sharp.*

VF-30 *Choice*
OBVERSE: Top of hair shows some detail. Details visible on most of stars. LIBERTY bold and clear.
REVERSE: Three-quarters of wing and neck feathers visible. Shield has one-half of details.

VF-20 *Typical*
OBVERSE: Hair outlined with very little detail. Only a few stars show any details. LIBERTY worn but clear.
REVERSE: Half of wing and neck feathers are visible. Some details show in shield.

FINE   *Moderate to heavy even wear. Entire design clear and bold.*

F-12   OBVERSE: Hair and cheek smooth. Stars outlined with no details visible. LIBERTY worn but visible.

REVERSE: Some of wing and neck feathers visible. Eagle's head is smooth. Shield shows little detail.

Note: Coins of this type seldom appear in grades lower than Fine.

Pieces dated 1836 and 1837 are softly struck at the center, and except for 1838 and 1839, the earlier dates are almost never well struck up in the hair curls.

QUARTER EAGLES—CORONET HEAD 1840–1907

MINT STATE *Absolutely no trace of wear.*

MS-70 UNCIRCULATED
A flawless coin exactly as it was minted, with no trace of wear or injury. Must have full mint luster and brilliance. Any unusual die or planchet traits must be described.

MS-67 UNCIRCULATED
Virtually flawless but with very minor imperfections.

MS-65 UNCIRCULATED
No trace of wear; nearly as perfect as MS-67 except for some small blemish. Has full mint luster and brilliance but may show slight discoloration. A few barely noticeable nicks or marks may be present.

MS-63 UNCIRCULATED
A mint state coin with attractive mint luster, but noticeable detracting contact marks or minor blemishes.

MS-60 UNCIRCULATED
A strictly Uncirculated coin with no trace of wear, but with blemishes more obvious than for MS-63. May lack full mint luster and brilliance.

ABOUT UNCIRCULATED *Small trace of wear visible on highest points.*

AU-58 *Very Choice*

Has some signs of abrasion: tip of coronet, hair; wings, claws.

AU-55 *Choice*
OBVERSE: There is a trace of wear on tip of coronet and above eye.
REVERSE: Trace of wear visible on wing tips.
   Three-quarters of the mint luster is still present.

AU-50 *Typical*
OBVERSE: There is a trace of wear on coronet, hair above ear, eye and forehead.
REVERSE: Trace of wear visible on wing tips, below eye and on claw.
   Half of the mint luster is still present.

EXTREMELY FINE   *Very light wear on only the highest points.*

EF-45   *Choice*

OBVERSE: There is light wear on coronet, hair above ear, eye, forelocks and top of head.

REVERSE: Light wear shows on edges and tips of wings, neck, below eye and on claws.

Part of the mint luster is still present.

EF-40   *Typical*

OBVERSE: Light wear shows on coronet, hair above ear and eye, forelocks, and cheek. All major details sharp.

REVERSE: Light wear shows on edges and tips of wings, neck, below eye, on feathers and claws. Shield well defined.

Traces of mint luster will show.

VERY FINE   *Light to moderate even wear. All major features are sharp.*

VF-30   *Choice*

OBVERSE: Light wear visible on coronet; hair is worn but shows considerable detail. Most stars show details. LIBERTY bold and clear.

REVERSE: Light wear shows on edges and tips of wings. Some detail shows on head and neck feathers. Vertical shield lines complete but some not separated; horizontal lines worn in center.

VF-20   *Typical*

OBVERSE: Hair outlined with very little detail. Only a few stars show any details. LIBERTY clear but not bold.

REVERSE: Half of wing feathers visible. Half of lines in shield are clear.

FINE *Moderate to heavy even wear. Entire design clear and bold.*

F-12 OBVERSE: Hair and cheek smooth. Stars outlined with no visible details. LIBERTY worn but visible.

REVERSE: Wings show very little detail. Head and one claw outlined only, with no details visible. Neck almost smooth. Most of shield lines merge.

Note: Coins of this type seldom appear in grades lower than Fine. Pieces made at Charlotte, Dahlonega, and New Orleans are frequently found weakly struck. Those from San Francisco often lack feather details.

Weakly struck pieces are most common for 1853, 1856, 1857-S, 1859-S, 1867-S, 1869-S and 1876-S.

Most coins after 1880 are well struck with sharp details.

MINT STATE *Absolutely no trace of wear.*

MS-70 UNCIRCULATED
A flawless coin exactly as it was minted, with no trace of wear or injury. Must have full mint luster and brilliance. Any unusual die or planchet traits must be described.

MS-67 UNCIRCULATED
Virtually flawless but with very minor imperfections.

MS-65 UNCIRCULATED
No trace of wear; nearly as perfect as MS-67 except for some small blemish. Has full mint luster and brilliance but may show slight discoloration. A few barely noticeable nicks or marks may be present.

MS-63 UNCIRCULATED
A mint state coin with attractive mint luster, but noticeable detracting contact marks or minor blemishes.

MS-60 UNCIRCULATED
A strictly Uncirculated coin with no trace of wear, but with blemishes more obvious than for MS-63. May lack full mint luster and brilliance.

ABOUT UNCIRCULATED *Small trace of wear visible on highest points.*

AU-58 *Very Choice*

Has some signs of abrasion: cheekbone, headdress, headband feathers; shoulder of eagle's left wing.

AU-55 *Choice*
OBVERSE: There is a trace of wear on cheekbone.
REVERSE: Trace of wear visible on shoulder of eagle's left wing.
 Three-quarters of the mint luster is still present.

AU-50 *Typical*
OBVERSE: There is a trace of wear on cheekbone and headdress.
REVERSE: Trace of wear visible on shoulder of wing, head and breast.
 Half of the mint luster is still present.

EXTREMELY FINE *Very light wear on only the highest points.*

EF-45 *Choice*
OBVERSE: There is light wear on cheekbone, headdress and headband.
REVERSE: Light wear shows on upper portion of wing, head, neck and breast.
Part of the mint luster is still present.

EF-40 *Typical*
OBVERSE: Light wear shows on cheekbone, jaw and headband. Slight wear
visible on feathers of headdress. Stars sharp.
REVERSE: Light wear shows on wing, head, neck and breast. Leg has full
feather detail.
Traces of mint luster will show.

VERY FINE *Light to moderate even wear. All major features are sharp.*

VF-30 *Choice*
OBVERSE: Cheekbone shows flat spot. Small feathers clear; large feathers
show some detail. Most of headband detail visible.
REVERSE: Wear shows on wing and neck. Some breast feathers show details.
Most of leg feathers visible.

VF-20 *Typical*
OBVERSE: Cheekbone worn about halfway. Small feathers clear, but large
feathers show a little detail. Hair cord knot is distinct. Headband shows some
detail.
REVERSE: Little detail shows on breast and leg feathers. Top of wing and
neck worn. Second layer of wing feathers shows.

QUARTER EAGLES—INDIAN HEAD 1908–1929

FINE *Moderate to heavy even wear. Entire design clear and bold.*

F-12   OBVERSE: Cheekbone worn; all feathers worn with very little detail visible. Stars outlined, with no details visible. Hair cord knot is worn but visible.

REVERSE: Wing worn, with only partial feathers at bottom visible. All lettering worn but visible.

Note: Coins of this type are seldom collected in grades lower than Fine.

Mint marks are often weakly struck, and wear down quickly because they are higher than other parts of the design.

The 1910, 1914-D and 1925-D almost always come with a weak strike. Although most people think that the 1908 comes weakly struck, the fact is that the reverse die was never prepared with full feathers, and by contrast to later dates appears very soft.

THREE-DOLLAR GOLD PIECES—1854–1889

MINT STATE   *Absolutely no trace of wear.*

MS-70   UNCIRCULATED
A flawless coin exactly as it was minted, with no trace of wear or injury. Must have full mint luster and brilliance. Any unusual die or planchet traits must be described.

MS-67   UNCIRCULATED
Virtually flawless but with very minor imperfections.

MS-65   UNCIRCULATED
No trace of wear; nearly as perfect as MS-67 except for some small blemish. Has full mint luster and brilliance but may show slight discoloration. A few barely noticeable nicks or marks may be present.

MS-63   UNCIRCULATED
A mint state coin with attractive mint luster, but noticeable detracting contact marks or minor blemishes.

MS-60   UNCIRCULATED
A strictly Uncirculated coin with no trace of wear, but with blemishes more obvious than for MS-63. May lack full mint luster and brilliance.

ABOUT UNCIRCULATED   *Small trace of wear visible on highest points.*

AU-58   *Very Choice*
Has some signs of abrasion: above eye, tops of feathers; bow knot, leaves.

AU-55   *Choice*
OBVERSE: There is a trace of wear on top curves of feathers.
REVERSE: Trace of wear visible on bow knot.
   Three-quarters of the mint luster is still present.

AU-50   *Typical*
OBVERSE: There is a trace of wear on top curves of feathers and on high parts of hair.
REVERSE: Trace of wear visible on bow knot and tips of leaves.
   Half of the mint luster is still present.

EXTREMELY FINE *Very light wear on only the highest points.*

EF-45 *Choice*

OBVERSE: There is light wear on tops of feathers, on hair at high points, and above eye.

REVERSE: Light wear shows on bow knot, leaves and cotton bolls.

Part of the mint luster is still present.

EF-40 *Typical*

OBVERSE: Light wear shows on tops of feathers. Hair shows wear but all details visible.

REVERSE: Light wear visible on bow knot, leaves and wreath.

Traces of mint luster will show.

VERY FINE *Light to moderate even wear. All major features are sharp.*

VF-30 *Choice*

OBVERSE: Curled feathers show very little detail. Hair above eye worn, with no details visible.

REVERSE: There is moderate wear on bow knot. Leaves and cotton bolls show a little detail.

VF-20 TYPICAL

OBVERSE: Curled feathers and hair near curls show slight details. Beads and LIBERTY clear.

REVERSE: Bow knot well worn. Slight detail visible in leaves. Some indentation remains on cotton bolls.

FINE *Moderate to heavy even wear. Entire design clear and bold.*

F-12 OBVERSE: Curled feathers smooth. Hair smooth with very little detail showing. Beads partially visible. LIBERTY weak but readable.

REVERSE: Bow knot, leaves and cotton bolls outlined only, with no details visible.

Note: Coins of this series are seldom found in less than Fine condition.

The 1854-D and 1854-O are usually weakly struck below LIBERTY, even on Mint State specimens. Also, the bow and ribbon on the reverse are very often weakly struck. Almost all "S" mint $3's are weakly struck.

MINT STATE *Absolutely no trace of wear.*

MS-70 UNCIRCULATED
A flawless coin exactly as it was minted, with no trace of wear or injury. Must have full mint luster and brilliance. Any unusual die or planchet traits must be described.

MS-67 UNCIRCULATED
Virtually flawless but with very minor imperfections.

MS-65 UNCIRCULATED
No trace of wear; nearly as perfect as MS-67 except for some small blemish. Has full mint luster and brilliance but may show slight discoloration. A few barely noticeable nicks or adjustment file marks may be present.

MS-63 UNCIRCULATED
A mint state coin with attractive mint luster, but noticeable detracting contact marks or minor blemishes.

MS-60 UNCIRCULATED
A strictly Uncirculated coin with no trace of wear, but with blemishes more obvious than for MS-63. May lack full mint luster and brilliance.

ABOUT UNCIRCULATED *Small trace of wear visible on highest points.*

AU-58 *Very Choice*

Has some signs of abrasion: cap, drapery, hair near ear, cheek; eagle's wings, leg, breast.

AU-55 *Choice*
OBVERSE: There is a trace of wear on cap.
REVERSE: Trace of wear visible on top edges of wings.
Three-quarters of the mint luster is still present.

AU-50 *Typical*
OBVERSE: There is a trace of wear on cap and on drapery.
REVERSE: Trace of wear visible on edges of wings, breast and on left leg.
Half of the mint luster is still present.

EXTREMELY FINE *Light wear on only the highest points.*

EF-45 *Choice*
OBVERSE: There is light wear on cap, drapery and high points of hair.
REVERSE: Light wear shows on wings, breast and left leg.
Part of the mint luster is still present.

EF-40 *Typical*
OBVERSE: Light wear shows on cap, drapery, high points of hair and on cheek.
REVERSE: Light wear visible on wings, head, breast and legs.
Traces of mint luster will show.

VERY FINE *Light to moderate even wear. All major features are sharp.*

VF-30 *Choice*
OBVERSE: Top of cap, hair and drapery show some detail. Wear visible on cheekbone.
REVERSE: Light wear shows on wings and head. There is moderate wear on breast and legs with a little detail visible.

VF-20 *Typical*
OBVERSE: There is moderate wear on cap, drapery and hair with some details visible. Cheek almost smooth. LIBERTY clear.
REVERSE: Moderate wear shows on wings, head, breast and legs; a little detail is visible.

HALF EAGLES—SMALL EAGLE REVERSE 1795–1798

FINE *Moderate to heavy even wear. Entire design clear and bold.*

F-12 OBVERSE: Cap almost smooth; drapery and hair outlined with only a little detail visible. Cheekbone smooth. LIBERTY worn but complete.
REVERSE: Lower wing features visible. Head and left leg worn. Breast almost smooth.

VERY GOOD *Well worn. Design clear but flat and lacking details.*

VG-8 OBVERSE: Cap, drapery, hair and cheekbone are smooth. LIBERTY and stars visible. Date is complete.
REVERSE: Eagle outlined only. Legend weak but visible.

Note: File adjustment marks on these coins are common and a normal part of the manufacturing process.

MINT STATE   *Absolutely no trace of wear.*

MS-70   UNCIRCULATED
A flawless coin exactly as it was minted, with no trace of wear or injury. Must have full mint luster and brilliance. Any unusual die or planchet traits must be described.

MS-67   UNCIRCULATED
Virtually flawless but with very minor imperfections.

MS-65   UNCIRCULATED
No trace of wear; nearly as perfect as MS-67 except for some small blemish. Has full mint luster and brilliance but may show slight discoloration. A few barely noticeable nicks or adjustment file marks may be present.

MS-63   UNCIRCULATED
A mint state coin with attractive mint luster, but noticeable detracting contact marks or minor blemishes.

MS-60   UNCIRCULATED
A strictly Uncirculated coin with no trace of wear, but with blemishes more obvious than for MS-63. May lack full mint luster and brilliance.

ABOUT UNCIRCULATED   *Small trace of wear visible on highest points.*

AU-58   *Very Choice*

Has some signs of abrasion: cap, drapery, hair, cheek; wings, clouds.

AU-55   *Choice*

OBVERSE: There is a trace of wear on cap.
REVERSE: Trace of wear visible on wings and clouds.
   Three-quarters of the mint luster is still present.

AU-50   *Typical*

OBVERSE: There is a trace of wear on cap and on drapery.
REVERSE: Trace of wear visible on wings, clouds and feathers.
   Half of the mint luster is still present.

EXTREMELY FINE *Light wear on only the highest points.*

EF-45 *Choice*

OBVERSE: There is light wear on cap, drapery and high points of hair.

REVERSE: Light wear shows on wings, clouds, feathers and tail.

Part of the mint luster is still present.

EF-40 *Typical*

OBVERSE: Light wear shows on cap, drapery, high points of hair and on cheek.

REVERSE: Light wear visible on wings, clouds, feathers, top of shield and tail. Arrows are complete and feathers well defined.

Traces of mint luster will show.

VERY FINE *Light to moderate even wear. All major features are sharp.*

VF-30 *Choice*

OBVERSE: Top of cap, hair and drapery show some detail. There is wear on cheekbone.

REVERSE: Wear visible on wings, clouds, head and tail. Shield shows wear but lines are clearly visible.

VF-20 *Typical*

OBVERSE: There is moderate wear on cap, drapery and hair with little detail visible. Cheekbone almost smooth. LIBERTY bold.

REVERSE: Wings, clouds, lines of shield and feathers are moderately worn with little detail visible. Motto shows wear but is complete.

HALF EAGLES—LARGE EAGLE REVERSE 1795–1807

FINE   *Moderate to heavy even wear. Entire design clear and bold.*

F-12   OBVERSE: Cap almost smooth; drapery and hair outlined with only a little detail visible. Cheekbone is smooth. LIBERTY worn but complete.

REVERSE: Wings worn; a few lines in shield are visible. Clouds, leaves and tail are smooth. Motto complete, although some letters are weak.

VERY GOOD   *Well worn. Design clear but flat and lacking details.*

VG-8   OBVERSE: Cap, drapery, hair and cheekbone are smooth. LIBERTY and stars visible. Date complete.

REVERSE: Eagle outlined only. Part of motto visible.

Note: File adjustment marks are occasionally seen on these coins and are a normal part of the manufacturing process.

MINT STATE *Absolutely no trace of wear.*

MS-70   UNCIRCULATED
A flawless coin exactly as it was minted, with no trace of wear or injury. Must have full mint luster and brilliance. Any unusual die or planchet traits must be described.

MS-67   UNCIRCULATED
Virtually flawless but with very minor imperfections.

MS-65   UNCIRCULATED
No trace of wear; nearly as perfect as MS-67 except for some small blemish. Has full mint luster and brilliance but may show slight discoloration. A few barely noticeable nicks or marks may be present.

MS-63   UNCIRCULATED
A mint state coin with attractive mint luster, but noticeable detracting contact marks or minor blemishes.

MS-60   UNCIRCULATED
A strictly Uncirculated coin with no trace of wear, but with blemishes more obvious than for MS-63. May lack full mint luster and brilliance.

ABOUT UNCIRCULATED *Small trace of wear visible on highest points.*

AU-58   *Very Choice*

Has some signs of abrasion: cap, hair; wings and claws.

AU-55   *Choice*
OBVERSE: There is a trace of wear on cap.
REVERSE: Trace of wear visible on wings.
   Three-quarters of the mint luster is still present.

AU-50   *Typical*
OBVERSE: There is a trace of wear on cap and hair curls above ear.
REVERSE: Trace of wear visible on wings and claws.
   Half of the mint luster is still present.

EXTREMELY FINE   *Light wear on only the highest points.*

EF-45   *Choice*

OBVERSE: There is light wear on cap, cheek and highest points of hair.

REVERSE: Light wear shows on wings and claws. Shield shows all line details.

Part of the mint luster is still present.

EF-40   *Typical*

OBVERSE: Light wear visible on cap, cheek, high points of hair and above eye. Three-quarters of the large curls are detailed.

REVERSE: Light wear shows on wings, neck, leaves, arrows and claws. All lines in shield are clear.

Traces of mint luster will show.

VERY FINE   *Light to moderate even wear. All major features are sharp.*

VF-30   *Choice*

OBVERSE: Most of details in cap are visible. There is light wear along back of hair but details are visible. LIBERTY bold.

REVERSE: Wings show wear but most details are visible. There is moderate wear on claws, shield, neck and head. Motto complete.

VF-20   *Typical*

OBVERSE: Cap and hair show moderate wear with only a little detail showing. Ear lobe worn. Stars flat but well defined. LIBERTY shows wear but is complete.

REVERSE: Half of wing details visible. Some details on neck and shield visible. Motto weak but readable.

FINE *Moderate to heavy even wear. Entire design clear and bold.*

F-12   OBVERSE: Cap and hair show very little detail. Eye is complete; ear is partially visible. Stars show some detail. LIBERTY is weak but visible.

REVERSE: Wings, claws and shield are worn with very little detail visible. Neck is smooth. Motto very weak but visible.

VERY GOOD   *Well worn. Design clear but flat and lacking details.*

VG-8   OBVERSE: Cap and hair outlined only. Cheek smooth. LIBERTY only partially visible. Stars outlined with no center details.

REVERSE: Wings, claws and neck smooth. No shield details visible. Part of motto visible.

Note: Coins dated 1807 through 1812 must show fine details in the clasp on the left shoulder to be graded About Uncirculated.

HALF EAGLES—CLASSIC HEAD 1834-1838

MINT STATE *Absolutely no trace of wear.*

MS-70 UNCIRCULATED
A flawless coin exactly as it was minted, with no trace of wear or injury. Must have full mint luster and brilliance. Any unusual die or planchet traits must be described.

MS-67 UNCIRCULATED
Virtually flawless but with very minor imperfections.

MS-65 UNCIRCULATED
No trace of wear; nearly as perfect as MS-67 except for some small blemish. Has full mint luster and brilliance but may show slight discoloration. A few barely noticeable bag marks and surface abrasions may be present.

MS-63 UNCIRCULATED
A mint state coin with attractive mint luster, but noticeable detracting contact marks or minor blemishes.

MS-60 UNCIRCULATED
A strictly Uncirculated coin with no trace of wear, but with blemishes more obvious than for MS-63. Has full mint luster but may lack brilliance. Surface may be lightly marred by minor bag marks and abrasions.

ABOUT UNCIRCULATED *Small trace of wear visible on highest points.*

AU-58 *Very Choice*

Has some signs of wear: hair; wings.

AU-55 *Choice*
OBVERSE: There is a trace of wear on highest point of hair and above eye.
REVERSE: Trace of wear visible on wings.
    Three-quarters of the mint luster is still present.

AU-50 *Typical*
OBVERSE: There is a trace of wear on high point of hair, above eye and ear.
REVERSE: Trace of wear on wings and head.
    Half of the mint luster is still present.

[335]

EXTREMELY FINE   *Light wear on only the highest points.*

EF-45   *Choice*
OBVERSE: There is light wear on high points of hair. Trace of wear shows on cheek.
REVERSE: Light wear visible on wings, head and feathers.
Part of the mint luster is still present.

EF-40   *Typical*
OBVERSE: Hair well defined with light wear on high points. Slight wear shows on cheek. Stars sharp with all details visible.
REVERSE: Light wear visible on wings, feathers, neck and head. Shield shows very light wear but is well defined.
Traces of mint luster will show.

VERY FINE   *Light to moderate even wear. All major features are sharp.*

VF-30   *Choice*
OBVERSE: Light wear shows on edges of headband. There is light wear on hair from LIBERTY to date, but most details show. Earlobe shows wear. LIBERTY bold.
REVERSE: Three-quarters of wing and neck feathers visible. One-half of shield details visible.

VF-20   *Typical*
OBVERSE: Hair outlined with some detail showing. Most detail in stars visible. Earlobe worn. LIBERTY shows wear but is complete.
REVERSE: Half of wing and neck feathers visible.

HALF EAGLES—CLASSIC HEAD 1834–1838

FINE *Moderate to heavy even wear. Entire design clear and bold.*

F-12 OBVERSE: Headband edges worn. Hair outlined with very little detail. Half the detail in stars visible. Ear outlined only. LIBERTY complete but some letters weak.

REVERSE: Some of wing and neck feathers are visible. Head almost smooth but shows slight detail. Some details in shield visible.

VERY GOOD *Well worn. Design clear but flat and lacking details.*

VG-8 OBVERSE: Cap outlined at top; hair and cheek smooth. Most of LIBERTY visible. Hardly any detail shows in stars.

REVERSE: Eagle shows very little detail.

Note: Pieces dated 1836 and 1837 are softly struck at the center. All dates before 1838 are almost never well struck up in the hair curls.

HALF EAGLES—CORONET HEAD 1839–1908

MINT STATE *Absolutely no trace of wear.*

MS-70 UNCIRCULATED
A flawless coin exactly as it was minted, with no trace of wear or injury. Must have full mint luster and brilliance. Any unusual die or planchet traits must be described.

MS-67 UNCIRCULATED
Virtually flawless but with very minor imperfections.

MS-65 UNCIRCULATED
No trace of wear; nearly as perfect as MS-67 except for some small blemish. Has full mint luster and brilliance but may show slight discoloration. A few barely noticeable bag marks and surface abrasions may be present.

MS-63 UNCIRCULATED
A mint state coin with attractive mint luster, but noticeable detracting contact marks or minor blemishes.

MS-60 UNCIRCULATED
A strictly Uncirculated coin with no trace of wear, but with blemishes more obvious than for MS-63. Has full mint luster but may lack brilliance. Surface may be lightly marred by minor bag marks and abrasions.

ABOUT UNCIRCULATED *Small trace of wear visible on highest points.*

AU-58 *Very Choice*

Has some signs of wear: hair, coronet; wings.

AU-55 *Choice*
OBVERSE: There is a trace of wear on tip of coronet and hair above eye.
REVERSE: Trace of wear visible on wing tips.
　　Three-quarters of the mint luster is still present.

AU-50 *Typical*
OBVERSE: There is a trace of wear on coronet, above ear and eye.
REVERSE: Trace of wear visible on wing tips, below eye and on claw.
　　Half of the mint luster is still present.

EXTREMELY FINE *Light wear on only the highest points.*

EF-45   *Choice*
OBVERSE: There is light wear on coronet, hair above ear, eye, forelocks and top of head.
REVERSE: Light wear shows on edges and tips of wings, neck, below eye and on claws.
   Part of the mint luster is still present.

EF-40   *Typical*
OBVERSE: Light wear shows on coronet, hair above ear and eye, on forelocks, top of head and on cheek. All major details are sharp.
REVERSE: Light wear visible on edges and tips of wings, neck, below eye, feathers and claws. Shield is well defined.
   Traces of mint luster will show.

VERY FINE *Light to moderate even wear. All major features are sharp.*

VF-30   *Choice*
OBVERSE: Light wear shows on coronet, hair and stars but most details are visible. LIBERTY bold.
REVERSE: Light wear visible on edges and tips of wings. Head and neck feathers show some detail. Vertical lines in shield complete but some not separated; horizontal lines worn in center.

VF-20   *Typical*
OBVERSE: Hair worn but major details visible. Top line of coronet broken. Some stars show partial detail. LIBERTY clear but not bold.
REVERSE: Half of wing feathers are visible. Half of lines in shield are clear.

FINE *Moderate to heavy even wear. Entire design clear and bold.*

F-12 OBVERSE: Hair and cheekbone smooth. Top line of coronet worn. LIBERTY worn but visible.

REVERSE: Wings show very little detail. Head and one claw outlined only, with no details visible. Neck almost smooth. Most of shield lines merge. (For the 1866 through 1908 group, the motto is worn but readable.)

Note: Coins of this type are seldom collected in grades lower than Fine.

The Charlotte and Dahlonega minted coins are almost always weakly struck.

1854-O, 1855-O, 1867-S, 1869-S, 1873-CC, 1875-CC and 1884-CC are dates that are generally seen weakly struck.

Most 1859-C and all 1860-C half eagles were struck from an improperly hardened reverse die that quickly lost its detail, so that circulated specimens appear to be in lower grade than they are.

MINT STATE *Absolutely no trace of wear.*

MS-70 UNCIRCULATED
A flawless coin exactly as it was minted, with no trace of wear or injury. Must have full mint luster and brilliance. Any unusual die or planchet traits must be described.

MS-67 UNCIRCULATED
Virtually flawless but with very minor imperfections.

MS-65 UNCIRCULATED
No trace of wear; nearly as perfect as MS-67 except for some small blemish. Has full mint luster and brilliance but may show slight discoloration. A few barely noticeable bag marks and surface abrasions may be present.

MS-63 UNCIRCULATED
A mint state coin with attractive mint luster, but noticeable detracting contact marks or minor blemishes.

MS-60 UNCIRCULATED
A strictly Uncirculated coin with no trace of wear, but with blemishes more obvious than for MS-63. Has full mint luster but may lack brilliance. Surface may be lightly marred by minor bag marks and abrasions.

ABOUT UNCIRCULATED *Small trace of wear visible on highest points.*

AU-58 *Very Choice*

Has some signs of wear: cheekbone, headdress, headband feathers; shoulder of eagle's left wing.

AU-55 *Choice*
OBVERSE: There is a trace of wear on cheekbone.
REVERSE: Trace of wear visible on shoulder of eagle's left wing.
Three-quarters of the mint luster is still present.

AU-50 *Typical*
OBVERSE: There is a trace of wear on cheekbone and headdress.
REVERSE: Trace of wear visible on shoulder of wing, head and breast.
Half of the mint luster is still present.

EXTREMELY FINE *Light wear on only the highest points.*

EF-45 *Choice*
OBVERSE: There is light wear on cheekbone, headdress and headband.
REVERSE: Light wear shows on upper portion of wing, head, neck and breast.
Part of the mint luster is still present.

EF-40 *Typical*
OBVERSE: Light wear shows on cheekbone, jaw and headband. Slight wear visible on feathers of headdress. Stars are sharp.
REVERSE: Light wear shows on wing, head, neck and breast. Leg has full feather detail.
Traces of mint luster will show.

VERY FINE *Light to moderate even wear. All major features are sharp.*

VF-30 *Choice*
OBVERSE: Cheekbone shows flat spot. Small feathers clear; large feathers show some details. Most of headband detail visible.
REVERSE: Wear shows on wing and neck. Some breast feathers show details. Most of leg feathers visible.

VF-20 *Typical*
OBVERSE: Cheekbone worn about half-way. Headdress feathers show some details. Hair cord knot is distinct. Headband shows only a little detail.
REVERSE: Little detail shows on breast and leg feathers. Top of wing and neck worn. Second layer of wing feathers shows.

FINE *Moderate to heavy even wear. Entire design clear and bold.*

F-12 OBVERSE: Cheekbone worn; all feathers worn with very little detail visible. Stars outlined, with no details visible. Hair cord knot is worn but visible.

REVERSE: Wing worn, with only partial feathers at bottom visible. All lettering worn but visible.

Note: Coins of this type are seldom collected in grades lower than Fine.

Mint marks are often very weakly struck.

The 1909-O, 1910-S, 1912-S and 1915-S are usually encountered with weak strikes.

MINT STATE *Absolutely no trace of wear.*

MS-70 UNCIRCULATED
A flawless coin exactly as it was minted, with no trace of wear or injury. Must have full mint luster and brilliance. Any unusual die or planchet traits must be described.

MS-67 UNCIRCULATED
Virtually flawless but with very minor imperfections.

MS-65 UNCIRCULATED
No trace of wear; nearly as perfect as MS-67 except for some small blemish. Has full mint luster and brilliance but may show slight discoloration. A few barely noticeable nicks or adjustment file marks may be present.

MS-63 UNCIRCULATED
A mint state coin with attractive mint luster, but noticeable detracting contact marks or minor blemishes.

MS-60 UNCIRCULATED
A strictly Uncirculated coin with no trace of wear, but with blemishes more obvious than for MS-63. May lack full mint luster and brilliance.

ABOUT UNCIRCULATED *Small trace of wear visible on highest points.*

AU-58 *Very Choice*
Has some signs of abrasion: cap, drapery, hair, cheek; eagle's wings, leg, breast.

AU-55 *Choice*
OBVERSE: There is a trace of wear on cap and on hair above forehead.
REVERSE: Trace of wear visible on wings.
    Three-quarters of the mint luster is still present.

AU-50 *Typical*
OBVERSE: There is a trace of wear on cap, hair above forehead and behind ear, and on drapery.
REVERSE: Trace of wear shows on wings, head and breast.
    Half of the mint luster is still present.

EXTREMELY FINE *Light wear on only the highest points.*

EF-45 *Choice*
OBVERSE: There is light wear on cap, drapery and high points of hair.
REVERSE: Light wear shows on wings and head. Wear visible on central feathers of breast.
Part of the mint luster is still present.

EF-40 *Typical*
OBVERSE: Light wear shows on cap, cheek and drapery. Almost all points of hair show some wear.
REVERSE: Light wear visible on wings. There is wear on head and breast.
Traces of mint luster will show.

VERY FINE *Light to moderate even wear. All major features are sharp.*

VF-30 *Choice*
OBVERSE: Top of cap, hair and drapery show some details. Light wear shows on cheekbone.
REVERSE: There is light wear on wings. Moderate wear shows on head, breast and legs with a little detail visible.

VF-20 *Typical*
OBVERSE: Cap shows some detail; drapery shows very little detail. Hair behind head worn with very little detail visible. Cheekbone almost smooth. LIBERTY clear.
REVERSE: There is moderate wear on wings, head, breast and legs, with a little detail visible.

EAGLES—SMALL EAGLE REVERSE 1795–1797

FINE *Moderate to heavy even wear. Entire design clear and bold.*

F-12 OBVERSE: Cap is almost smooth; drapery and hair outlined with little detail visible. Cheekbone is smooth. LIBERTY worn but complete.

REVERSE: Wings have only lower feathers visible. Head, leg and breast considerably worn. Legend worn but complete.

VERY GOOD *Well worn. Design clear but flat and lacking details.*

VG-8 OBVERSE: Cap, drapery, hair and cheekbone are smooth. LIBERTY and stars visible. Date complete.

REVERSE: Eagle outlined only. Legend weak but visible.

Note: File adjustment marks on these coins are common and a normal part of the manufacturing process.

MINT STATE *Absolutely no trace of wear.*

MS-70 UNCIRCULATED
A flawless coin exactly as it was minted, with no trace of wear or injury. Must have full mint luster and brilliance. Any unusual die or planchet traits must be described.

MS-67 UNCIRCULATED
Virtually flawless but with very minor imperfections.

MS-65 UNCIRCULATED
No trace of wear; nearly as perfect as MS-67 except for some small blemish. Has full mint luster and brilliance but may show slight discoloration. A few barely noticeable nicks or adjustment file marks may be present.

MS-63 UNCIRCULATED
A mint state coin with attractive mint luster, but noticeable detracting contact marks or minor blemishes.

MS-60 UNCIRCULATED
A strictly Uncirculated coin with no trace of wear, but with blemishes more obvious than for MS-63. May lack full mint luster and brilliance.

ABOUT UNCIRCULATED *Small trace of wear visible on highest points.*
AU-58 *Very Choice*

Has some signs of abrasion: cap, drapery, hair, cheek; wings, clouds.

AU-55 *Choice*
OBVERSE: There is a trace of wear on cap and hair above forehead.
REVERSE: Trace of wear visible on wings and clouds.
Three-quarters of the mint luster is still present.

AU-50 *Typical*
OBVERSE: There is a trace of wear on cap, hair above forehead and behind ear, and on drapery.
REVERSE: Trace of wear visible on wings, clouds and feathers.
Half of the mint luster is still present.

EXTREMELY FINE *Light wear on only the highest points.*

EF-45 *Choice*

OBVERSE: There is light wear on cap, drapery and high points of hair.

REVERSE: Light wear shows on wings, clouds, feathers and tail.

Part of the mint luster is still present.

EF-40 *Typical*

OBVERSE: Light wear shows on cap, cheek and drapery. Almost all points of hair show some wear.

REVERSE: Light wear visible on wings, clouds, feathers, top of shield and tail.

Traces of mint luster will show.

VERY FINE *Light to moderate even wear. All major features are sharp.*

VF-30 *Choice*

OBVERSE: Top of cap, hair and drapery show some details. Light wear shows on cheekbone.

REVERSE: There is light wear on wings, clouds, head and tail. Shield shows wear but lines are clearly visible.

VF-20 *Typical*

OBVERSE: Cap shows some detail, but drapery almost smooth. Hair behind head worn with very little detail visible. Cheekbone almost smooth. LIBERTY clear.

REVERSE: Wings, clouds, lines of shield and feathers are moderately worn with little detail visible. Motto shows wear but is complete. Berries visible. Leaves and tail show some detail.

FINE *Moderate to heavy even wear. Entire design clear and bold.*

F-12 OBVERSE: Cap almost smooth; drapery and hair outlined with little detail visible. Cheekbone smooth. LIBERTY worn but complete.

REVERSE: Wings worn. A few lines in shield visible. Clouds, leaves and tail smooth. Motto complete although some letters weak.

VERY GOOD *Well worn. Design clear but flat and lacking details.*

VG-8 OBVERSE: Cap, drapery, hair and cheekbone smooth. LIBERTY and stars visible. Date is complete.

REVERSE: Eagle outlined only. Part of legend visible.

Note: File adjustment marks on these coins are common and a normal part of the manufacturing process. Pieces dated 1804 are sometimes weakly struck.

EAGLES—CORONET HEAD 1838–1907

MINT STATE *Absolutely no trace of wear.*

MS-70 UNCIRCULATED
A flawless coin exactly as it was minted, with no trace of wear or injury. Must have full mint luster and brilliance. Any unusual die or planchet traits must be described.

MS-67 UNCIRCULATED
Virtually flawless but with very minor imperfections.

MS-65 UNCIRCULATED
No trace of wear; nearly as perfect as MS-67 except for some small blemish. Has full mint luster and brilliance but may show slight discoloration. A few barely noticeable bag marks and surface abrasions may be present.

MS-63 UNCIRCULATED
A mint state coin with attractive mint luster, but noticeable detracting contact marks or minor blemishes.

MS-60 UNCIRCULATED
A strictly Uncirculated coin with no trace of wear, but with blemishes more obvious than for MS-63. Has full mint luster but may lack brilliance. Surface may be lightly marred by minor bag marks and abrasions.

ABOUT UNCIRCULATED *Small trace of wear visible on highest points.*

AU-58 *Very Choice*

Has some signs of wear: hair, coronet; wings.

AU-55 *Choice*
OBVERSE: There is a trace of wear on hair above eye and on coronet.
REVERSE: Trace of wear visible on wing tips.
Three-quarters of the mint luster is still present.

AU-50 *Typical*
OBVERSE: There is a trace of wear on hair at ear and above eye, and on coronet.
REVERSE: Trace of wear visible on wing tips, below eye and on claw.
Half of the mint luster is still present.

EAGLES—CORONET HEAD 1838–1907

EXTREMELY FINE *Light wear on only the highest points.*

EF-45 *Choice*

OBVERSE: There is light wear on coronet, hair above ear, eye, forelocks and top of head.

REVERSE: Light wear shows on edges and tips of wings, neck, below eye and on claws.

Part of the mint luster is still present.

EF-40 *Typical*

OBVERSE: Light wear shows on coronet, hair, cheek and stars. All major details sharp.

REVERSE: Light wear visible on wings, head, neck and claws. Shield is well defined.

Traces of mint luster will show.

VERY FINE *Light to moderate even wear. All major features are sharp.*

VF-30 *Choice*

OBVERSE: There is light wear on coronet, hair and stars but most details are visible. There is a break on top line of coronet over two letters in LIBERTY. Cheek worn. LIBERTY bold.

REVERSE: Light wear visible on wings and head but some details show. Vertical lines in shield complete but some are not separated; horizontal lines worn in center.

VF-20 *Typical*

OBVERSE: Hair worn but major details visible. Break on top line of coronet extends over at least three letters in LIBERTY. Cheek well worn. Stars worn but show most details. LIBERTY clear but shows wear.

REVERSE: Over half of wing feathers are visible. Very little detail shows in head.

FINE   *Moderate to heavy even wear. Entire design clear and bold.*

F-12   OBVERSE: Hair and cheekbone smooth. Top line of coronet worn. Some details show in stars. LIBERTY worn but visible.

REVERSE: Wings show little detail. Head and one claw outlined only, with no details visible. Neck is almost smooth. Most of shield lines merge. (In the 1866 through 1907 group, the motto is worn but readable.)

Note: Coins of this type are seldom collected in grades lower than Fine.

The following dates are frequently seen weakly struck: 1841-O, 1844-O, 1847-O, 1848-O, 1851-O, 1852-O, 1854-O, 1861-S, 1862-S, 1864-S, 1868-S, 1873-S, 1874-S, 1880-S, 1883-S, 1888-S, 1893-S, 1896-S, 1906-S and most of the Carson City issues.

EAGLES—INDIAN HEAD 1907–1933

MINT STATE   *Absolutely no trace of wear.*

MS-70   UNCIRCULATED
A flawless coin exactly as it was minted, with no trace of wear or injury. Must have full mint luster and brilliance. Any unusual die or planchet traits must be described.

MS-67   UNCIRCULATED
Virtually flawless but with very minor imperfections.

MS-65   UNCIRCULATED
No trace of wear; nearly as perfect as MS-67 except for some small blemish. Has full mint luster and brilliance but may show slight discoloration. A few minute bag marks and surface abrasions may be present.

MS-63   UNCIRCULATED
A mint state coin with attractive mint luster, but noticeable detracting contact marks or minor blemishes.

MS-60   UNCIRCULATED
A strictly Uncirculated coin with no trace of wear, but with blemishes more obvious than for MS-63. Has full mint luster but may lack brilliance. Surface may be lightly marred by minor bag marks and abrasions.

ABOUT UNCIRCULATED   *Small trace of wear visible on highest points.*

AU-58   *Very Choice*
Has some signs of wear: above eye, cheek; wing.

AU-55   *Choice*
OBVERSE: There is a trace of wear above eye.
REVERSE: Trace of wear visible on wing.
   Three-quarters of the mint luster is still present.

AU-50   *Typical*
OBVERSE: There is a trace of wear on hair above eye and on forehead.
REVERSE: Trace of wear visible on wing.
   Half of the mint luster is still present.

EAGLES—INDIAN HEAD 1907–1933

EXTREMELY FINE *Light wear on only the highest points.*

EF-45 *Choice*
OBVERSE: There is light wear on hair above eye, forehead, and on cheekbone.
REVERSE: Light wear shows on wing and head.
  Part of the mint luster is still present.

EF-40 *Typical*
OBVERSE: Light wear shows on hair, cheekbone and feathers.
REVERSE: Light wear visible on wing and head.
  Traces of mint luster will show.

VERY FINE *Light to moderate even wear. All major features are sharp.*

VF-30 *Choice*
OBVERSE: There is light wear along forehead but most detail shows. Moderate wear visible on cheekbone. Light wear shows where feathers meet headband.
REVERSE: Left wing shows more than half the details. Some details in head are visible.

VF-20 *Typical*
OBVERSE: Over half the hair detail is visible. Moderate wear shows on cheekbone. Some feathers do not touch headband.
REVERSE: There is moderate wear on left wing which shows at least one-quarter of the detail. Head almost smooth. All lettering bold.

FINE *Moderate to heavy even wear. Entire design clear and bold.*

F-12 OBVERSE: Hair smooth with almost no details; cheekbone almost smooth. No feathers touch headband but most feather details visible.

REVERSE: Left wing top and head are worn nearly smooth. Lettering worn but visible.

Note: Coins of this type are seldom collected in grades lower than Fine.

Some issues in this series are softly struck. Those from the San Francisco Mint are prone to be weakly struck, particularly on the eagle's wing and neck areas. This is especially true of 1910-S and 1920-S.

The eagle's breast feathers are usually weak on all coins of this design. Hair detail of 1907 and 1908 no motto issues is noticeably weaker than on most later dates.

DOUBLE EAGLES—LIBERTY HEAD 1850–1907

MINT STATE   *Absolutely no trace of wear.*

MS-70   UNCIRCULATED
A flawless coin exactly as it was minted, with no trace of wear or injury. Must have full mint luster and brilliance. Any unusual die or planchet traits must be described.

MS-67   UNCIRCULATED
Virtually flawless but with very minor imperfections.

MS-65   UNCIRCULATED
No trace of wear; nearly as perfect as MS-67 except for some additional small blemish. Has full mint luster and brilliance but may show slight discoloration. A few minute bag marks and surface abrasions are usually present.

MS-63   UNCIRCULATED
A mint state coin with attractive mint luster, but noticeable detracting contact marks or minor blemishes.

MS-60   UNCIRCULATED
A strictly Uncirculated coin with no trace of wear, but with blemishes more obvious than for MS-63. Has full mint luster but may lack brilliance. Surface is usually lightly marred by minor bag marks and abrasions.
Uncirculated coins of this type are frequently graded at intermediate levels from MS-60 to MS-70. For specific details refer to pages 21-22 of the introduction.

ABOUT UNCIRCULATED   *Small trace of wear visible on highest points.*

AU-58   *Very Choice*
Has some signs of wear: hair, coronet; eagle's neck and wing, top of shield.

AU-55   *Choice*
OBVERSE: There is a trace of wear on hair.
REVERSE: Trace of wear visible on wing tips and neck.
Three-quarters of the mint luster is still present.

AU-50   *Typical*
OBVERSE: There is a trace of wear on hair at top and over eye, and on coronet.   [355]

Prime Focal Areas
  Obverse: Liberty's face, neck, and field in front of face.
  Reverse: Field areas to either side of eagle.

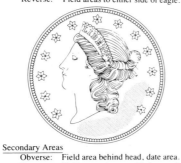

Secondary Areas
  Obverse: Field area behind head, date area.
  Reverse: Field areas above and below eagle.

	CONTACT MARKS	HAIRLINES	LUSTER	EYE APPEAL
MS-70	None show under magnification	None show under magnification	Very attractive , Fully original	Outstanding
MS-69	1 or 2 miniscule none in prime focal areas	None visible	Very attractive Fully original	Exceptional
MS-68	3 or 4 miniscule none in prime focal areas	None visible	Attractive Fully original	Exceptional
MS-67	3 or 4 miniscule 1 or 2 may be in prime focal areas	None visible without magnification	Above average Fully original	Exceptional
MS-66	Several small; a few may be in prime focal areas	None visible without magnification	Above average Fully original	Above average
MS-65	Light and scattered without major distracting marks in prime focal areas	May have a few scattered	Fully original	Very pleasing
MS-64	May have light scattered marks; a few may be in prime focal areas	May have a few scattered or small patch in secondary areas	Average Full original	Pleasing
MS-63	May have distracting marks in prime focal areas	May have a few scattered or small patch	May be original or slightly impaired	Rather attractive
MS-62	May have distracting marks in prime focal and/or secondary areas	May have a few scattered to noticeable patch	May be original or impaired	Generally acceptable
MS-61	May have a few heavy (or numerous light) marks in prime focal and/or secondary areas	May have noticeable patch or continuous hairlining over surfaces	May be original or impaired	Unattractive
MS-60	May have heavy marks in all areas	May have noticeable patch or continuous hairlining throughout	May be original or impaired	Poor

[356]

DOUBLE EAGLES—LIBERTY HEAD 1850–1907

REVERSE: Trace of wear visible on wing tips, neck and at top of shield. Half of the mint luster is still present.

EXTREMELY FINE   *Light wear on only the highest points.*

EF-45   *Choice*

OBVERSE: There is light wear on hair and coronet prongs.

REVERSE: Light wear shows on edges and tips of wings, head and neck, and on horizontal shield lines.

Part of the mint luster is still present.

EF-40   *Typical*

OBVERSE: Light wear shows on hair, coronet prongs and cheek.

REVERSE: Light wear visible on wings, head, neck, horizontal shield lines and tail.

Traces of mint luster will show.

VERY FINE   *Light to moderate even wear. All major features are sharp.*

VF-30   *Choice*

OBVERSE: About one-quarter of hair detail below coronet visible; half the detail shows above coronet. Cheek and some coronet prongs worn. Stars show wear but all details visible.

REVERSE: Most of wing details visible. Top part of shield shows moderate wear. About half the detail in tail visible.

VF-20   *Typical*

OBVERSE: Less than half detail above coronet visible. About half the coronet prongs are considerably worn. Stars are flat but show most details. LIBERTY shows wear but is very clear.

REVERSE: Some wing details visible. Shield shows very little detail at top. Tail is worn with very little detail.

DOUBLE EAGLES—LIBERTY HEAD 1850–1907

FINE *Moderate to heavy even wear. Entire design clear and bold.*

F-12 OBVERSE: All hair lines well worn with very little detail visible. About one-quarter of details within coronet visible. Stars show little detail. LIBERTY readable.

REVERSE: Wings show very little detail. Head and neck smooth. Eye visible. Tail and top of shield smooth.

Note: Coins of this type are seldom collected in grades lower than Fine.

The hair curl under the ear is sometimes weakly struck.

In the group between 1866 and 1876, the reverse motto is sometimes weakly struck.

Pieces made at the Carson City mint are usually found weakly struck and heavily bag marked.

Most of the New Orleans pieces are not fully struck up.

Philadelphia coins that are rarely seen fully struck include 1878, 1888, 1902, 1905 and 1906.

Double Eagles dated before 1866 lack detail or relief because of the design rather than striking inadequacies.

DOUBLE EAGLES—SAINT-GAUDENS 1907–1932

MINT STATE *Absolutely no trace of wear.*

MS-70 UNCIRCULATED
A flawless coin exactly as it was minted, with no trace of wear or injury. Must have full mint luster and brilliance. Any unusual die or planchet traits must be described.

MS-67 UNCIRCULATED
Virtually flawless but with very minor imperfections.

MS-65 UNCIRCULATED
No trace of wear; nearly as perfect as MS-67 except for some additional small blemish. Has full mint luster and brilliance but may show slight discoloration. A few minute bag marks and surface abrasions are usually present.

MS-63 UNCIRCULATED
A mint state coin with attractive mint luster, but noticeable detracting contact marks or minor blemishes.

MS-60 UNCIRCULATED
A strictly Uncirculated coin with no trace of wear, but with blemishes more obvious than for MS-63. Has full mint luster but may lack brilliance. Surface is usually lightly marred by minor bag marks and abrasions.
Uncirculated coins of this type are frequently graded at intermediate levels from MS-60 to MS-70. For specific details refer to pages 16-17 of the introduction.

ABOUT UNCIRCULATED *Small trace of wear visible on highest points.*

AU-58 *Very Choice*
Has some signs of wear: forehead, breast, knee, nose; eagle's wings and breast.

AU-55 *Choice*
OBVERSE: There is a trace of wear on left breast and left knee.
REVERSE: Trace of wear visible on wing.

Three-quarters of the mint luster is still present.

Prime Focal Areas

Obverse: Breast and knee of Liberty. Fields above rays.
Reverse: Eagle's wing and field above eagle.

Secondary Areas

Obverse: Left side of gown. Sun rays to either side of Liberty.
Reverse: Head and breast of eagle. Field areas around eagle's head, sun and motto above.

	CONTACT MARKS	HAIRLINES	LUSTER	EYE APPEAL
MS-70	None show under magnification	None show under magnification	Very attractive Fully original	Outstanding
MS-69	1 or 2 miniscule none in prime focal areas	None visible	Very attractive Fully original	Exceptional
MS-68	3 or 4 miniscule none in prime focal areas	None visible	Attractive Fully original	Exceptional
MS-67	3 or 4 miniscule 1 or 2 may be in prime focal areas	None visible without magnification	Above average Fully original	Exceptional
MS-66	Several small; a few may be in prime focal areas	None visible without magnification	Above average Fully original	Above average
MS-65	Light and scattered without major distracting marks in prime focal areas	May have a few scattered	Fully original	Very pleasing
MS-64	May have light scattered marks; a few may be in prime focal areas	May have a few scattered or small patch in secondary areas	Average Full original	Pleasing
MS-63	May have distracting marks in prime focal areas	May have a few scattered or small patch	May be original or slightly impaired	Rather attractive
MS-62	May have distracting marks in prime focal and/or secondary areas	May have a few scattered to noticeable patch	May be original or impaired	Generally acceptable
MS-61	May have a few heavy (or numerous light) marks in prime focal and/or secondary areas	May have noticeable patch or continuous hairlining over surfaces	May be original or impaired	Unattractive
MS-60	May have heavy marks in all areas	May have noticeable patch or continuous hairlining throughout	May be original or impaired	Poor

[360]

DOUBLE EAGLES—SAINT-GAUDENS 1907–1932

AU-50 *Typical*
OBVERSE: There is a trace of wear on nose, breast and knee.
REVERSE: Trace of wear visible on wings.
Half of the mint luster is still present.

EXTREMELY FINE *Light wear on only the highest points.*

EF-45 *Choice*
OBVERSE: There is light wear on forehead, nose, breast and knee.
REVERSE: Light wear shows on wings and breast but all feathers are bold.
Part of the mint luster is still present.

EF-40 *Typical*
OBVERSE: Light wear shows on forehead, nose, breast, knee and just below left knee. Drapery lines on chest visible.
REVERSE: Light wear visible on wings and breast but all feathers bold.
Traces of mint luster will show.

VERY FINE *Light to moderate even wear. All major features are sharp.*

VF-30 *Choice*
OBVERSE: There is light wear on all features, extending above and below left knee and along part of right leg. Some of garment lines on chest are visible.
REVERSE: Light wear visible on left wing and breast; feathers show but some are weak.

VF-20 *Typical*
OBVERSE: Forehead moderately worn. Contours of breast worn. Only a few garment lines on chest are visible. Entire right leg shows moderate wear.
REVERSE: Half of feathers are visible in wings and breast.

FINE *Moderate to heavy even wear. Entire design clear and bold.*

F-12 OBVERSE: Forehead and garment smooth; breasts flat. Both legs worn with right bottom missing.

REVERSE: Less than half the wing details are visible. Only a little breast detail is visible.

Note: Coins of this type are seldom found in grades lower than Fine.

Some issues in this series are softly struck. The 1907 and 1920 are routinely found flatly struck, and the 1912, 1913, 1920-S, 1924-D and 1927-S are often found not fully struck up. The detailing of the 1907 and 1908 no motto issues is noticeably weaker than on most later dates.

COMMEMORATIVE COINS

United States commemorative coins were not made for general circulation, and the majority of them have been preserved in Uncirculated condition. In order to distinguish between strictly Uncirculated and About Uncirculated coins, Anthony Swiatek has made a study of the first points of wear for each commemorative coin type. All listings are half dollars unless otherwise designated. Uncirculated coins are frequently graded at intermediate levels from MS-60 to MS-70. For specific details refer to pages 21-22 of the introduction.

MS-70   UNCIRCULATED
A flawless coin exactly as it was minted, with no trace of wear or injury. Must have full mint luster and brilliance or light toning. Any unusual striking traits must be described.

MS-67   UNCIRCULATED
Virtually flawless but with very minor imperfections.

MS-65   UNCIRCULATED
A coin possessing full mint luster with no major detracting features such as slide marks on the high points, deep contact marks, visible or excessive hairlines, or evidence of cleaning.

MS-63   UNCIRCULATED
A coin with half or more of its original luster, but with noticeable detracting marks or minor blemishes.

MS-60   UNCIRCULATED
A mint state coin with no trace of wear but numerous contact marks or blemishes may be present. Surface may be fully lustrous or exhibit little or no luster (caused naturally or from chemical cleaning).

FIRST POINTS OF WEAR

ALABAMA*
OBVERSE: Gov. Kilby's forehead and area left of earlobe.
REVERSE: Eagle's lower neck and top of wings.

ALBANY
OBVERSE: Hip of beaver.
REVERSE: Sleeve of Gov. Dongan (figure at left).

ANTIETAM
OBVERSE: Gen. Lee's cheekbone.
REVERSE: Leaves of tree; rim of coin.

ARKANSAS
OBVERSE: Eagle's head and top of left wing.
REVERSE: Band of Liberty's cap behind eye.
Note: An occasional poor strike may be found.

ARKANSAS-ROBINSON
OBVERSE: Eagle's head and top of left wing.
REVERSE: Sen. Robinson's cheekbone.

BAY BRIDGE
OBVERSE: Bear's left shoulder.
REVERSE: Clouds.

DANIEL BOONE
OBVERSE: Hair behind Boone's ear.
REVERSE: Shoulder of Indian.

BRIDGEPORT
OBVERSE: Barnum's cheekbone.
REVERSE: Eagle's wing.

General Note: Issues marked with an asterisk should be carefully examined as they are often found with signs of handling or abrasion.

COMMEMORATIVE COINS

CALIFORNIA DIAMOND JUBILEE
OBVERSE: Folds of shirt sleeve.
REVERSE: Bear's shoulder.

CARVER-WASHINGTON*
OBVERSE: Carver's cheekbone. Some pieces were poorly struck in this area. Check the reverse for wear.
REVERSE: Lettering U.S.A. on map.

CINCINNATI MUSIC CENTER
OBVERSE: Hair at Foster's temple.
REVERSE: Left breast.

CLEVELAND
OBVERSE: Hair behind Cleaveland's ear.
REVERSE: Top of compass.

COLUMBIA, S.C.
OBVERSE: Right breast of Justice.
REVERSE: Top of palmetto tree.

COLUMBIAN EXPOSITION*
OBVERSE: Eyebrow, cheek, and hair at back of forehead. Hair area sometimes comes flatly struck.
REVERSE: Top of rear sail; right side of Eastern Hemisphere.

CONNECTICUT
OBVERSE: Top of wing.
REVERSE: Tree above ON and above TI.

DELAWARE
OBVERSE: Roof above entrance. The triangular section at top of entrance is weakly struck, giving an appearance of wear.
REVERSE: Center of lower middle sail.

ELGIN
OBVERSE: Pioneer's cheekbone.
REVERSE: Rifleman's left shoulder.
Note: Lack of detailed facial features is the result of striking, not wear. The infant is always weakly struck.

GETTYSBURG
OBVERSE: Both cheekbones.
REVERSE: Three ribbons on fasces.

GRANT—Gold Dollar and Half Dollar*
OBVERSE: Grant's cheekbone. Worn dies caused flatness in hair above ear.
REVERSE: Leaves of trees under U. Often weakly struck in branches above cabin.

HAWAII*
OBVERSE: Cook's cheekbone.
REVERSE: Fingers and hand holding spear.

HUDSON
OBVERSE: Center of lower middle sail.
REVERSE: Motto on ribbon (may also be weakly struck).

HUGUENOT-WALLOON*
OBVERSE: Coligny's cheekbone.
REVERSE: Rim near F and over RY; lower part of highest sail; center of stern.

IOWA
OBVERSE: Shafts of building near upper left and upper right windows.
REVERSE: Back of head and neck. The head sometimes comes flatly struck.

General Note: Issues marked with an asterisk should be carefully examined as they are often found with signs of handling or abrasion.

COMMEMORATIVE COINS

ISABELLA—Quarter*
OBVERSE: Isabella's cheekbone, and center of lower part of crown.
REVERSE: Strand of wool at lower left thigh.

LAFAYETTE—Silver Dollar*
OBVERSE: Washington's cheekbone; Lafayette's lower curl.
REVERSE: Fringe of epaulet; horse's blinder and left rear leg bone.

LEWIS AND CLARK—Gold Dollar*
OBVERSE: Lewis' temple.
REVERSE: Clark's temple.

LEXINGTON-CONCORD*
OBVERSE: Thighs of Minute Man.
REVERSE: Top edge of belfry.

LINCOLN-ILLINOIS*
OBVERSE: Hair above Lincoln's ear.
REVERSE: Eagle's breast. The breast was sometimes flatly struck. Look for differences in texture or color of the metal.

LONG ISLAND
OBVERSE: Dutch settler's cheekbone.
REVERSE: Center of lower middle sail.

LOUISIANA PURCHASE—Gold Dollar*
OBVERSE: Jefferson's or McKinley's cheekbone and sideburn.
REVERSE: Date and denomination.

LYNCHBURG
OBVERSE: Hair above Sen. Glass' ear.
REVERSE: Hair, folds of gown.

MAINE*
OBVERSE: Left hand of scythe holder; right hand of anchor holder. The moose and pine tree are weakly struck.
REVERSE: Bow knot.

MARYLAND*
OBVERSE: Calvert's nose. The nose usually appears flatly struck; check the reverse for wear.
REVERSE: Top of small crown; tops of draperies.

McKINLEY—Gold Dollar*
OBVERSE: McKinley's temple area; hair above ear.
REVERSE: Pillar above second 1 in date; bottom of flagpole.

MISSOURI*
OBVERSE: Hair in back of ear.
REVERSE: Frontiersman's arm and shoulder.

MONROE*
OBVERSE: Adams' cheekbone.
REVERSE: Below CT on upper figure.

NEW ROCHELLE
OBVERSE: Hip of calf.
REVERSE: Bulbous part of fleur-de-lis. On the center petal the midrib is flatly struck.

NORFOLK
OBVERSE: Lower rear sail.
REVERSE: Below crown on royal mace.

*General Note: Issues marked with an asterisk should be carefully examined as they are often found with signs of handling or abrasion.

COMMEMORATIVE COINS

OREGON TRAIL
OBVERSE: Hip of ox. Top rear of wagon was flatly struck in some years.
REVERSE: Indian's left thumb and fingers. Some pieces show flatness on thumb and first finger because of striking.

PANAMA PACIFIC*
OBVERSE: Columbia's left shoulder.
REVERSE: Eagle's breast.

PANAMA PACIFIC—Gold Dollar*
OBVERSE: Peak of cap.
REVERSE: Heads of dolphins; denomination.

PANAMA PACIFIC—Quarter Eagle*
OBVERSE: Columbia's head, breast, and knee.
REVERSE: Torch band; eagle's leg.

PANAMA PACIFIC—$50.00 Gold*
OBVERSE: Minerva's cheek.
REVERSE: Owl's upper breast.

PILGRIM*
OBVERSE: Cheekbone; hair over ear.
REVERSE: Crow's nest, stern, rim.

RHODE ISLAND
OBVERSE: Indian's right shoulder.
REVERSE: Center of anchor.

ROANOKE
OBVERSE: Brim of hat.
REVERSE: Head of standing figure.

SAN DIEGO
OBVERSE: Minerva's knees.
REVERSE: Top right edge of tower. The 1936-D was flatly struck in this area. Examine texture of surface to determine if wear exists.

SESQUICENTENNIAL*
OBVERSE: Washington's cheekbone.
REVERSE: Below the lower inscription on bell.
Note: This coin was struck from shallow dies.

SESQUICENTENNIAL—Quarter Eagle*
OBVERSE: Bottom of scroll held by Liberty.
REVERSE: Below top of tower; central portion above roof.

SPANISH TRAIL
OBVERSE: Top of cow's head.
REVERSE: Lettering at top.

STONE MOUNTAIN*
OBVERSE: Lee's elbow.
REVERSE: Eagle's breast.

TEXAS
OBVERSE: Eagle's upper leg and upper breast.
REVERSE: Forehead of Victory in center.

VANCOUVER
OBVERSE: McLaughlin's temple area.
REVERSE: Right knee.

VERMONT*
OBVERSE: Hair above Allen's ear and in temple area.
REVERSE: Upper shoulder.

General Note: Issues marked with an asterisk should be carefully examined as they are often found with signs of handling or abrasion.